MORGENTHAU
THE NEW DEAL
AND SILVER

Morgenthau the New Deal and Silver

A STORY OF PRESSURE POLITICS

Allan Seymour Everest

KING'S CROWN PRESS

Columbia University, New York

1950

332.42
E 93 m

PUBLISHED IN GREAT BRITAIN, CANADA, AND INDIA
BY GEOFFREY CUMBERLEGE, OXFORD UNIVERSITY PRESS
LONDON, TORONTO, AND BOMBAY

MANUFACTURED IN THE UNITED STATES OF AMERICA

To E. L. E.

PREFACE

The great movements and breath-taking events of the depression and war years in the United States leave most people baffled and bewildered by their diversity and complexity. The social, economic, political, and diplomatic aspects all vie for attention. Yet even after the most persistent and comprehensive study we can only imperfectly understand the period in its entirety. The era is still too close for a proper objectivity; furthermore, the official records and memoirs on which full knowledge will be based are only now becoming available.

Therefore, it seemed to me that the illumination of one small segment of the vast panorama would be worthwhile. I selected the subject of silver not only because it has a continuing significance for the nation, but because it throws light on one of the great dangers to democratic governments -- the existence of pressure groups in the country at large and of special-interest blocs in the national legislature.

I have attempted to do three things in this book. In the first place, the Roosevelt monetary ideas need clarification as a basis for understanding the silver program, which must be viewed in part as a result of his actions. Secondly, the objectives and tactics of the Congressional Silver Bloc are the underlying theme of the narrative. The Bloc was politically so strong that it was able to exact a series of compromises from the President, by which it achieved most of its goals. Significantly, the Bloc continues to function, and executed its latest coup in 1946.

Finally, the execution of the silver acts and their results both at home and abroad receive detailed attention. The Treasury, under the guidance of Secretary Morgenthau, early became disillusioned with the program it was required to execute. The Secretary modified it wherever possible on the domestic scene. Among foreign nations it created confusion and financial turmoil. The Treasury tried to heal the wounds abroad by monetary co-operation with the victims and by large purchases of their useless silver. The program was thus converted into an important weapon of diplomacy which bore fruit with the outbreak of war.

Among the many people who have assisted in this work, two deserve particular thanks. Out of his rich experience, Professor Allan Nevins, of Columbia University, has continuously given aid, counsel, and encouragement. Mr. Henry Morgenthau, Jr., has not only opened to me his great collection of diary notes, documents, press conferences, and news clippings, but has very kindly made suggestions for improving the text.

Allan S. Everest

Plattsburg, New York
December, 1949

CONTENTS

CONTENTS

I. THE GOOD OLD DAYS

FROM THE BEGINNING

The coinage of money from time immemorial has been a prerogative of kings and emperors. They have used it to unify their lands, extend their economic dominions, raise money for themselves and their programs, and in general consolidate their power.

But the gradual growth of democratic institutions brought a dawning realization that the power of coinage was a wonderful instrument in popular hands as well. People began to see all kinds of possibilities for manipulating the currency to the advantage of one group or another in the nation.

To the same extent that the United States has been a leader in the development of democracy, it has also been a pioneer in the discovery of new forms and functions for money. Popularly elected officials have been responsible to sections and classes for their policies in this respect. Today the full flowering of a democracy's tampering with the currency has been reached under the agitation for silver money, more money, and cheaper money.

As the first Secretary of the Treasury, it became Alexander Hamilton's duty to initiate a system of currency for the new republic. At that time, most of the civilized world had a bimetallic standard; knowing no other system, he instituted a double standard whereby fifteen parts of silver equaled one of gold.

The Hamiltonian currency did not function well. Silver dollars were never in popular use, partly because of their size. Further, his ratio overvalued silver so that gold was sold more profitably elsewhere than to the government. Quantities of gold consequently went to England in exact proof of Gresham's theory that the cheaper of two monetary metals drives the dearer from circulation.

In recognition of the faulty ratio, Congress in the 1830's adopted a new proportion of 16 to 1. This balance overvalued gold and occasioned the disappearance of silver

coins, creating great difficulty in the country's retail trade.
Congress took steps to remedy the situation in regard to
small coins. But the silver dollar still failed to gain general
circulation and was unknown at the time of the Civil War.
Therefore, in 1873, when the coinage laws were revised, it
was dropped from the list of coins to be issued. The move
was deliberately made after the bill had been before Congress
nearly three years, but it is doubtful if that body realized
what it had done. Unwittingly Congress had decreed that the
country was henceforth to operate on the gold standard.

Meanwhile Europe was also having monetary difficulties.
For centuries the leading nations had maintained a bimetallic
standard. As long as communications remained slow and arbitrage difficult, the standard was satisfactory. However, by
the end of the eighteenth century England and France were
in trouble because of their different ratios: London could not
keep her gold and France lost silver. Great Britain abandoned
free coinage of silver and presently adopted the single gold
standard. This example was followed by Western Europe
during the 1870's, when one nation after another adopted
some kind of a gold standard and hastened the modern flight
from silver. Yet these nations were able to make a relatively
peaceful transition from one currency to the other.

But the United States, a great silver-producing country,
was allowed no such blessing. Almost as soon as the new
coinage law appeared in 1873, agitation was started for remonetization of silver and a return to the "good old days."
The opening of rich new silver mines in the West greatly increased the output of the metal at the same time that large
parts of the world were reducing the market by turning to
gold. The price of silver began to fall, and the silver interests became alarmed at the prospects for their product.

The silver agitation gathered momentum in proportion to
the number of new mines, and to the increased representation in Washington of new Western states. The Senate, which
added two members for every new star in the flag, early became the stronghold of silver sentiment and the self-appointed
guardian of a group of states that could command an important block of votes.

Economically, the silver agitation was insignificant. Like
the agents of many another forward-looking industry, Western Congressmen embarked on a campaign to market the
wares of their home states. Since the government seemed to
be the most natural purchaser, or at least guarantor of its
price, they concentrated all their considerable talents on

making a sale of silver. In their sales talks they relied heavily on the American tradition of bimetallism, upon the evils of the gold standard that had failed to coin for the common man, and upon the degrading days that had now befallen one of the basic metals of national coinage.

Left politically to themselves, these agents of an old product in new quantities could never have made a sale. The so-called "Silver Bloc" represented at various times seven or eight states, with fourteen or sixteen Senators committed to a specific program. They were only a minority. Therefore, early in their collective career in Washington, they thoroughly learned the art of politics. The lesson they assimilated and applied was the mathematics of combination: if eight mining states want to sell their silver at a good price, and twenty agricultural states want more and cheaper money, the combination of twenty-eight states would command a majority of the Senate. Such a combination became feasible with the realization that silver money, cheaper money, and more money were mutually complementary demands, and that they represented a true community of interests.

The agriculturalists were receptive to the overtures of the silverites. Since the Civil War, when the business interests captured the government, the mid-West and the South had felt discrimination and distress. These sections had fathered granges, alliances, and political parties aimed at forcing national recognition of their needs and wants. Consequently, they were glad to join silverites and inflationists in a similar program.

Armed with a realization of this fact, the silver forces started a movement to condemn the "Crime of 1873" by proving it responsible for the subsequent depression and agricultural distress. The timing and the argument were well planned, since agricultural areas in a time of depression and low prices traditionally seek some kind of cheaper money with which to meet their perpetual indebtedness, and since the Greenback movement had been effectively checked.

The combined political forces produced two silver acts within a space of twelve years. The Treasury was required to embark on a large silver-purchasing program and the issuance of new currency. Under a provision of the Bland-Allison Act of 1878, President Hayes invited the Western nations to an international bimetallic conference in Paris. Already committed to a buying program, the United States was in a weak bargaining position with the other ten powers that participated. The debates were fruitless and the conference ended without result. Conferences were attempted again in 1880 and 1881, because of the growing conviction in the United States that bimetallism could be achieved only through international co-operation. The gatherings, together with subsequent American proposals for international action, accomplished nothing. Most of the European powers had just departed from silver, and they were not interested in its restoration, especially while American purchases were supporting the world silver market.

The second of the two laws, the Sherman Act of 1890, provided money in inflationary quantities, caused gold exportation, and contributed in some degree to the panic of 1893 before President Cleveland obtained its repeal in that year.

Nourished by a new depression and frustrated by the repeal of the Sherman Act, inflationists and silver interests gathered strength for the next election. Economically the silver campaign had a somewhat stronger basis than formerly. Because of the artificially high silver production promoted by the silver acts, repeal plus depression hit the silver-mining areas with greater impact than had the hard times of 1873. Whether unemployment and hard times were worse than in other states is debatable, but the suffering in the mining districts was concentrated where it was more easily discernible.

The discontent produced in 1896 a hard campaign, the last for many years in which silver, inflation, and agriculture effectively collaborated. At best it was an unstable coalition. The inflationists and farmers were most vocal during and after depressions, when credit and money were scarce while their debts continued. On the other hand, the silver interests waged a perpetual campaign for remonetization. Silver was one of several minerals upon which their prosperity depended, and they viewed its revival as an end in itself. They foreswore any attempt scientifically to find industrial uses for silver -- it was one of the two sacred metals that the Federal government was obligated to foster. They adopted many of the depression slogans, much of the lingo of the crusading farmer, but at heart they were dominated by the one concern of completely rehabilitating silver in the national and world currency systems.

Bryan in 1896 obtained 48 percent of the popular vote for the presidency in this "battle of the standards." Almost half of the nation spoke for free coinage of silver, with its concomitants of easier money and credit. But the crusaders saw the victory of the Eastern capitalistic forces, who in 1900 established an unqualified gold standard.

As a result of the campaign of 1896, silver became associated with the Democratic party, and the Republicans be-

came the "sound money" group. Yet it should be remembered
that Republican administrations passed the Bland-Allison
and Sherman Acts, and that the latter was repealed under
Cleveland, a Democrat. Before 1896 the Republicans had
never felt the need of developing a "sound money" position.
So it came about that until the advent of Woodrow Wilson, the
"traditional" silverites were out of office.

Moreover, with a better banking system and an increased
output of gold after 1890 the swelling of the nation's stocks
and their mildly inflationary effect helped maintain prosperity and lessen the demand for free coinage of silver -- in
many respects the gold standard alone provided what had been
sought in bimetallism.

THE FIRST WORLD WAR

Even under a Democratic president after 1914 no immediate action was sought. Between 1914 and 1918 the average
price of silver increased from about fifty-five cents an ounce
to nearly ninety-seven cents, and by January, 1920, to $1.33.[1]
The rule of supply and demand furnishes the chief reason
for this increase. Between 1913 and 1920 world silver production declined 24 percent, a result partly of revolution in
Mexico and partly of wartime dislocation of silver and the
related baser metals with which much of the world's silver
is found. But at the same time demand increased both through
new monetary uses in the Orient and Europe, and through
American requirements in films and jewelry.

Yet the price advance was traceable at least in part to a
general advance in the price of all commodities. The rise
before 1918 is, therefore, not phenomenal when viewed as a
part of wartime inflation. Indeed, there is evidence that the
inflationary cost of silver production, though probably not
60 percent above normal, as claimed by the silver interests,
together with the dislocation of the industry, forced the clos-
ing of some silver mines and threatened others with the same
ate.

At any rate, by 1918 a situation arose that gave the silver
advocates their first opportunity to ally themselves with
other interests in doing something about silver. Their field
of endeavor lay with India. During the war years that country built up a large excess of exports over imports. The
settlement of the American commercial obligations, it was
claimed, might seriously drain the country's gold reserves.
Furthermore, the British Ambassador reported a German

attempt to instill in the people of India a distrust of their new paper money, and this move was blamed for the current run on Indian redemption agencies. The Indian government did not have the silver reserves for a complete redemption and, if forced to admit the fact, would be faced with grave internal disturbances. India required rapid acquisitions of silver. Thus her need to prevent "revolution," as the Silver Senators described it, dovetailed with the American concern over an unfavorable trade balance with India, and with the inclinations of both silver and gold adherents in the United States.

Consequently, in 1918 the Pittman Act was placed on the statutes. It authorized the Secretary of the Treasury to reduce 350,000,000 silver dollars to bullion for sale to the exporters to India at a minimum of one dollar a fine ounce. The Treasury was at the same time to purchase new silver at one dollar to replace the melted coins. Actually, 271,000,-000 silver dollars were melted, and most of the bullion was sold for exportation.

The one-dollar price under the Act illustrated the difficulty of fixing a permanent quotation for such a commodity involved in world trade. The price was a compromise between the existing world market of approximately eighty cents and the legal American price of $1.29 demanded by the silver advocates. No one was happy with the result. The silver interests resented the government's holding down the price and preventing a free market from soaring to higher levels; but others during the period of government purchases coined the phrase "Crime of 1921," when the Treasury was paying one dollar while the silver market ranged no higher than seventy-one cents.

The Act had much greater significance than was generally recognized. By paying the producers of silver about thirty cents above the market, the government granted a bonus of some $58,000,000.[2] As the opening gun in the century's silver campaign, it encouraged silver adherents in the belief that the government could and would help reverse the world trend in silver prices, and that the likelihood of such action would be increased if the policy were linked to corollary measures for aiding another nation, incidentally promoting American commerical or diplomatic relations. Furthermore, it was a first and portentous step in the direction of the government's artificial fixing of the price of silver at a high level. Finally, the building up of a great silver reserve in India proved a boomerang to the American silver interests later in the same decade.

II. HARD TIMES FOR SILVER

In America it generally happens that a representative becomes somebody only from his position in the assembly. He is therefore perpetually haunted by a craving to acquire importance there, and he feels a petulant desire to be constantly obtruding his opinions upon his fellow members.

Tocqueville, II, 89 f.

THE POSTWAR DECLINE

Despite the promising outlook for silver during the war, the retreat of the metal did not stop, until by 1930 China was the only major country left on a silver standard. A steady decline in its purchasing value took place. A study in 1933 showed that "on a relative scale of purchasing power an ounce of silver bought $1.90 worth of goods in 1890, ninety cents' worth in 1915, and about thirty-five cents' worth today."[1] A decline occurred also in the market price of silver from a high of $1.30 in 1920 to a low of twenty-seven cents in 1931.

The sharpness of the decline may be explained by a number of factors. During the 1920's a considerable though uneven advance in the world's silver production took place until the peak output of 1929 was reached. Silver output does not readily respond to the supply and demand of the market. Nearly three-fourths of the world's silver and about four-fifths of that of the United States is a by-product of the mining of copper, lead, zinc, and gold.[2] Consequently, silver production is inflexible, a tendency that is increased by the heavy cost of extracting and refining the metal. Furthermore, unlike most metals, silver is not usually consumed in use, but continues to exist, if only as a part of the tremendous hoarded supply in the Orient.

During the postwar period there was a widespread lowering of the fineness of silver coins and large sales of demonetized metal by many countries. The profit to those governments that demonetized was a tempting source of income. Then, too, in view of the high market price of silver, coins were in danger of being melted for their overvalued bullion. Some nations also attempted to make silver currency more popular by such measures as producing smaller coins for general use. As early as 1920 Great Britain reduced the fineness of her silver coins by almost one-half. It was estimated that from 1919 to 1932 inclusive 541,000,000 ounces of demonetized and private hoards were sold on the world market, of which the principal source after 1927 was British India. The United Kingdom, French Indo-China, France, Siam, Belgium, Russia, Mexico, and other countries to a total of thirty-three engaged in the practice.[3] Sales were at their heaviest by 1930, at a time when silver as a commodity had suffered from the depression.

Few new uses developed to absorb the increased silver supply. Indeed, the depression decreased the purchasing power of the leading silver-using countries, thus reducing the absorption of the metal into their monetary systems. A number of the leading nations, after a wartime honeymoon with silver coinage, returned to gold during the decade, and their reduced silver requirements helped to depress the price of the metal.

India had long been silver's best customer; her population hoarded it in the form of silver bars and jewelry. She bought heavily when her crops were good and she had a favorable balance of trade. But for several years her farmers received depression prices for their crops. China had been the next best customer for years, but she was usually handicapped by her unfavorable balance of trade. Troubles at home always increased this adverse balance and thereby reduced her silver purchases. In the later years of the decade she had experienced war, flood, and famine. Consequently, by 1932 India and China were buying only about one-third of their former quota of silver.

Not only was the world market greatly oversupplied, but the rapidly changing price stimulated the activity of speculators, who caused even further fluctuations in price. As will presently become evident, the commercial relations of silver-using countries with the rest of the world were much more disturbed by fluctuations than by mere low prices of the metal.

The silver industry in the United States, though not large in any national view, was nevertheless important in the West, and significant politically because it spread over so many states whose chief income was from mining. The industry suffered in the general decline even prior to 1929, and more heavily afterward. The Western representatives in Congress offered some startling figures to justify their programs for relief. For example, in 1925, when the average price of silver was at a mid-point (sixty-nine cents) between the high of 1920 and the low of 1931, the national production exceeded 66,000,000 ounces with a value of almost $46,000,000. One state, Utah, produced 21,250,000 ounces with a value of $14,750,000; seven states claimed at least a two-million-dollar industry. The four states of Arizona, Idaho, Montana, and Nevada ranked silver second in value of their mineral produce, and a fifth, Utah, ranked it third in value.

But in 1931 silver production was about 31,000,000 ounces, valued at less than $9,000,000. Compared to 1925 production was just under one-half and value about one-fifth. Furthermore, Utah, the leading producer, mined only 8,000,000 ounces at a value of $2,250,000. Only two states still had a two-million-dollar industry and only four a value of more than a million dollars. Only one state, Idaho, still listed silver as second in value of her minerals; Arizona's silver had slipped to third place, while Montana, Nevada, and Utah did not even show silver among their first three minerals.[4]

The depression also reduced the production of other minerals in these states. There was abundant reason for the West, in common with all other sections of the country, to seek remedies in Washington for their diminishing income and their mounting unemployment. But the Western states, with a longing glance back to the "good old days," selected the time-tested path of government action in behalf of silver alone as politically the most expedient.

This choice was largely promoted by the Western mining concerns, which thought they discerned a way of getting their industries into the black again. It has been noted that 80 percent of American silver is a by-product in the mining of other metals, so that its production is relatively inflexible. In the boom year of 1929 large output of the baser metals was feasible. But the resultant large production of silver came at a time when the markets and the price were diminishing.

For example, in 1929 the American Smelting and Refining Company produced at home and abroad 89,000,000 ounces of the metal; the output of the United States Smelting, Refining, and Mining Company was 25,500,000 ounces; that of Cerro de Pasco, chiefly from Peru, 15,700,000 ounces; and Anaconda Copper Mining Company, 7,800,000 ounces. All these companies except Cerro de Pasco had large foreign holdings as well as extensive interests in the West. All operated primarily to mine copper, lead, zinc, or all three. These and other large mining concerns in 1929 obtained 10 percent of their gross receipts from silver.[5] In some mines silver production constituted a sufficient percentage to make a margin of profit for the whole mine if silver prices were adequate. Fluctuations in its price often made the difference between profit and loss, although the same was true of prices for the baser metals.

To this group of large mining concerns should be added the smaller companies, especially in Idaho and Nevada, which mined silver alone where it was found in a relatively pure state. These mines exerted great influence locally, always on the side of a resuscitation of the metal on which their business solely depended.

When the depression forced a restriction in output of all metals, the future of silver therefore received careful study by the interested companies. By 1932 the silver production of most of these concerns had fallen sharply. The American Smelting and Refining Company had reduced its output by one-half, Cerro de Pasco by two-thirds, the Anaconda Copper Mining Company by four-fifths, and only the United States Smelting, Refining, and Mining Corporation remained fairly stable. Furthermore, silver averaged only 27.8 cents for the entire year.[6]

The story of the pressure that these companies brought to bear in the states and in Washington requires a separate study. Suffice it here to say that Francis H. Brownell, chairman of the board of directors of American Smelting and Refining, early assumed the role of public spokesman for silver. He appeared before Congressional committees, made several public addresses, and saw some of his remarks inserted in the Congressional Record.

It is no more remarkable that Western legislators and mining concerns should agitate for their interests than that mid-Western and Southern Congressmen should press for aid to their agricultural constituents. The chief difference lay in the fact that agricultural production was a leading item in the nation's economy, while the normal year's output of silver was worth much less than the peanut crop, and averaged only one percent of all commodity exports. Nevertheless, the time came when the silver and agricultural regions again realized their common needs and pooled their energies in programs believed to be mutually beneficial.

MOOD OF A NATION IN DEPRESSION

In order to comprehend the amazing results of the silver campaign, it is necessary to recall the climate of opinion after 1929. The agitation for silver coincided with many other proposals from various groups of people who sought to wrestle with the deepening depression in which they found themselves.

The economic disturbance that started as a collapse of the stock market in the fall of 1929 was widely regarded as transient in character, affecting chiefly speculators and financiers. The business structure, it was felt, was basically sound. However, when 1930 brought a widening of the economic collapse, when 1931 and 1932 saw no end to the misery, unemployment, and stagnation, everyone from the President down was forced to admit that a major crisis demanded action.

But there was no agreement on what direction that action should take. One segment of opinion held that a restoration of foreign trade was necessary to bring an upswing of economic activity at home. Its proposals embraced tariff revision, the purchase of silver and the loan of more money abroad. Another felt that the banking and currency laws needed an overhauling. For the lack of other purchasing media, a movement started in the West and extended into parts of twenty-nine states to use barter, wooden money, and printed scrip in business transactions.

By 1932 the sufferings of great numbers of confused, desperate, and restive people were impelling them to action and agitation. In a now famous petition to President Hoover, the railway brotherhoods stated the temper of the times:

> Mr. President, we have come here to tell you that unless something is done to provide employment and relieve distress among the families of the unemployed, we cannot be responsible for the orderly operations of the railroads of this country.... We are not Socialists, we are not Communists, nor are we anarchists.... There is a growing demand that the entire business and social structure be changed because of the general dissatisfaction with the present system.[7]

Mr. Hoover took a number of steps consistent with his cautious economic philosophy, yet nevertheless radical departures from previous practice. Whether the measures

were too little or too late is beyond the scope of this study.
The fact remains that they did not produce rapid results,
with the consequence that the election year of 1932 found the
nation still deeply mired in economic stagnation. The mood
was one of searching, doubting, hoping, and planning. "The
recital of facts riddled the validity of old formulas," wrote
the Beards. "Slogans tinctured with radicalism were uttered
in all parts of the country. Under powerful and respectable
auspices comprehensive plans had been put forward for over-
coming the ills of the panic and preventing such black plagues
in the future." [8]

One of the first popular reactions to this as to other depressions was an inflationary sentiment, a mood of readiness
to experiment with monetary cures. "Powerful and respectable auspices" began to question how a gold standard and a
Federal Reserve System could have allowed an economic
collapse to occur; otherwise, how could money be so scarce,
credit so nearly nonexistent, prices so low?

THE APPEARANCE OF SILVER IN POLITICS

In view of the traditional attempts to broaden the American monetary base by the extensive use of two metals instead
of one, a reappearance of the silver agitation in the depression years was entirely natural. In the current crisis, the
silver forces had the stage setting of a national willingness
to experiment; they used the Pittman Act of 1918 as a guide-
post; and they gradually acquired numerous allies in their
attempt to rescue the country's economy. Indeed, the fact
that much of their program was eventually adopted speaks
volumes for what those who voted for it thought and intended
it would achieve.

Yet underneath all the verbiage, the side issues that were
brought in and the ambitious claims and platforms that confused the uninformed, the movement for silver had two very
simple aims that even some of its naive supporters failed to
grasp. One was that by one means or another the mining interests sought a "restoration of silver," meaning simply a
higher price for their product. The other was that the debtor
sections of the country hoped to wrest financial control from
the grasp of the East, which, they had long felt, maintained
an exclusive grip on the purse strings of the nation and determined in its own interest the amount of money in circulation. Time after time in the coming months these sections
lashed out at the demon Wall Street. Their basic belief in

silver was that of their fathers; it was "the vehicle through
which the agricultural states have expressed the age-old demand of the agrarian debtor for an increase in currency."[9]

The myriad of proposals concerning silver pertained both
to foreign and domestic affairs. In general, they may be
grouped around four basic aims:

1. To seek international agreement on silver. The chief
hope was to outlaw demonetization by foreign governments
and the dumping of bullion on the world market; a subsidiary intent was to make silver acceptable, especially in the
United States, in payment of war debts.

2. To raise the world price of silver. This was to be
achieved in some degree through international action, but
chiefly through the assumption of responsibility by the United
States government. One motive was the expansion of the purchasing power of silver-using countries, particularly in the
Orient and Latin America. Silver advocates liked to quote
the sentiments of Julius H. Barnes, chairman of President
Hoover's national business survey commission and head of
the United States Chamber of Commerce:

> The final mistake was made of treating silver as a com-
> modity although it still represented resources and capital
> and credit to more than half the population of the world....
> A price of silver which fluctuated from $1.35 some few
> years ago to 35 cents today, and yet symbolized the credit
> and resources of a great people, could not but harm the
> business structure of the world.[10]

3. To guarantee a market for American silver, presumably through its purchase by the government. Above all else,
the American producer must be provided for.

4. To expand the currency base of the country, chiefly by
the increased use of silver as backing for large issues of
silver certificates. If the gold standard had failed to keep
the country supplied with money and credit, the answer was
a broader monetary base. More money in circulation meant
higher prices, it was asserted, and presently the depression
would be cured.

These claims appealed to a wide variety of interests. The
arguments were carefully planned to gain adherents by offer-
ing tangible and attainable means for remedying the depression. However, the proponents failed to anticipate the changes
toward greater flexibility in the Federal Reserve System,

and the tremendous gold-purchasing program undertaken
somewhat later, whereby the aims which the silverites had
set for their metal were partially achieved.

Silver proposals began to appear in both houses of Congress early in 1930. Western legislators were the spearheads,
and although they at first attracted little support, the proposals were indicative of those to follow. The early emphasis
was on international action as the only way of rectifying the
glut of the world's silver markets. The President was urged
to sound out foreign governments on a silver conference and
the Senate in 1931 adopted a resolution to that effect.

Half-hearted efforts were made to interest other governments, without result. The Administration was not convinced
of the desirability of a conference, particularly to the extent
of assuming the initiative in calling it. The United States had
no official solution to offer on silver and feared the proposals
other countries might make. Furthermore, the government
was aware that any monetary conference ran the risk of becoming entangled with the problem of war debts that were
then plaguing American foreign relations.

Yet as the agitation continued, and as the election of 1932
approached, the Administration came gradually to feel the
political advisability of acceding to these demands. In July,
1932, the British government invited the United States to join
in preparations for a monetary and economic conference.
This move resulted from the Lausanne Conference, which
had adopted a resolution on a world gathering to which the
United States was to be invited. The government accepted,
but specified that the agenda must include a consideration of
the American silver proposals and exclude any treatment of
war debts.

Under these conditions, the Republican as well as the Democratic platform in 1932 took a stand in favor of the conference. Yet extreme proposals found no place in either. Both
advocated sound money and ignored Congressional requests
for currency inflation. The Democratic convention flatly rejected silver remonetization or distribution of new currency
issues to veterans. The chief difference in the two planks
was that the Democrats alone promised American initiative,
if necessary, to bring about a world conference. The New
York Times declared that "the fact seems to be that both political parties and most candidates for office feel it necessary to butter the silver parsnips with fine words, but feel
in their hearts that no practical plan has been devised, or
can be devised, to restore silver to the place which it once
held in the currency of many nations."[11]

Since silver agitation knows no party lines, President Hoover found it expedient to "butter the silver parsnips" as a part of his Western campaign. For example, at Salt Lake City he voiced a personal liking for miners, especially of silver, and went on: "Increase in the value of silver would relieve us from strain of cheap production of goods which flow over our borders. It would rehabilitate the buying power of many foreign nations for our goods."[12] Since Governor Roosevelt also expressed his faith in the Democratic platform, both parties were committed to the idea of an international conference.

Meanwhile, agitation on the other aspects of silver gathered momentum. In 1932 Senator Carl Hayden, of Arizona, with the help of the State and Commerce departments, investigated the possibility of paying in silver the war debts due this country. His report showed that all the nations indebted to the United States had taken part in the "flight from silver" since the war; that American acceptance of silver in payment would not only raise its price in world markets, but also help the British and Indian governments to get rid of silver they did not want.[13] He introduced a bill that proposed accepting silver on such favorable terms as would tempt debtor nations to restore the silver content of their own coins or start new silver coinage. As with all the silver proposals, action was delayed until after the election.

By 1932 outright demands for bimetallism at the old ratio of 16 to 1 were heard in Congress. Senator Burton Wheeler, of Montana, the chief advocate, announced apropos of the depression: "The nation must adopt bimetallism or face bolshevism." However, the silver proponents themselves were divided on the issue, with most of them at first favoring a less radical proposal, one more certain of passage. Moderates led by Senator Key Pittman, of Nevada, were unenthusiastic for bimetallism unless it was international.

One of the early all-purpose measures was a Senate bill requiring the purchase by the government of American-produced silver at the current market price. Payment would be made by the issuance of silver certificates. In extensive hearings on the bill, its aims were summarized as (a) withdrawing American production from the world supply; (b) furnishing a broader circulating currency in the United States; (c) enlarging the legal tender qualifications of silver certificates.[14] The measure failed of passage, but succeeding bills down to and including the Silver Purchase Act of 1934 followed a similar pattern. All were more or less modeled after the Sherman Purchase Act of 1890.

In the first half of 1932 both houses of Congress held public hearings on silver. The Senate hearings were published under the title Purchase of Silver. The House hearings, published as The Effect of Low Silver, were much more ambitious in scope. All the known silver arguments and most of the silver fallacies were voiced in accents designed to attract the attention of the world. They filled 530 pages, received much newspaper publicity, and were printed for wide dissemination. Correspondence from foreign silver enthusiasts was included. Members of Parliament, economists, business men, and industrialists of Great Britain and the Netherlands were all represented. Winston Churchill registered his approval of an international conference. Indeed, at a later date he was quoted as saying: "Silver is the money of all Asia. Silver is the money of a billion human beings, and it ought not to be treated with as little regard as if it were a sack of potatoes. Silver has always been the comrade and ally of gold. Surely, we would do well to consider more carefully the part it has to play in our World Housekeeping." [15]

III. NEW EFFORTS IN OLD DIRECTIONS

*I readily admit that the mass of the citizens sincerely wish
to promote the welfare of the country...but it is always more
or less difficult for them to discern the best means of attaining the end which they sincerely desire.... Hence it
often happens that mountebanks of all sorts are able to
please the people, while their truest friends frequently
fail to gain their confidence.*

Tocqueville, I, 201

CHANGES IN NATIONAL LEADERSHIP

March 4, 1933, represented not only a complete turnover
in government, but also a tremendous psychological crisis.
The accumulated fears and agitations, dammed up during a
depression now in its fourth year, and brought to a head by
a banking crisis at the very time of the inauguration, were
suddenly let loose like a flood and only partially channeled
by the master strategist who had become the national leader.
For in at least one respect, the new President did not so
much formulate the policies as compromise or accept the
plans of others; even during the first few months, in the
treatment of silver accompanied by all kinds of inflationary
proposals, he was either unwilling or unable to control the
monetary program, which at times threatened to run away
with him.

Franklin D. Roosevelt was a product of his times, a man
who rose to the challenge of the climactic events which
swirled around him. If the financial system had been as
sound as President Hoover claimed during the campaign,
or if there had been no economic crisis in the weeks after
the election, the Roosevelt Administration might have followed the traditional path that party politicians expected --
some mildly corrective laws would have made the New Deal
difficult to distinguish from the programs of several preceding presidents. But none of these conditions prevailed,
and consequently a knowledge of the ideas and motives of
the President and his close advisers is necessary to an understanding of what happened to money under his guidance.

Government," Roosevelt told the Commonwealth Club of

San Francisco, "includes the art of formulating a policy
and using the political technique to attain so much of that
policy as will receive general support; persuading, leading
sacrificing, teaching always, because the greatest duty of a
statesman is to educate."[1] In such a frank and positive
promise of action Roosevelt gave the country a clew to his
two great political gifts: the ability to seize and maintain
the offensive, and a realization of the strategic importance
of compromise.

With his election, probably the ablest politician since
Lincoln appeared. A great part of his leadership, like that
of his predecessor's, consisted of direct appeals to the people. If he was definitely committed to some course of action,
he could be formidable; if he was crossed, he could be hard,
stubborn, and resourceful. Nevertheless, he thoroughly understood the political necessity of retreating on occasion in
order to go forward. With a perfect sense of timing, he knew
the point at which compromise must begin, and he usually
was able to advance one part of his program at the expense
of concessions in some other direction.

During the campaign the country became aware of Roosevelt as the chief Democratic exponent of a modern liberalism whose core was the willingness to use governmental
power to correct the lack of balance in the economic life of
the nation. Contrary to current opinion, he had developed a
general political philosophy long before the depression or
before contact with the "brains trust." His subsequent advisers merely helped apply that philosophy to the specific
conditions of 1933.

Yet being primarily a man of decision and action, Roosevelt at no time either subscribed to or formulated a finished
system of thought. He had no sympathy with codified schools
of political economy or rigid social plans. Rather, he sought
facts, for which he usually was prepared to sacrifice theory.
His mind was quick, his memory excellent, and his capacity
to comprehend new material unusual. Yet this intellectual
equipment was often impeded by a strong emotional inter-
ference, by conscious and subconscious likes and dislikes.
He gave superficial treatment to many subjects relating to
economics, especially to finance, not from inability to grasp
them, but from an aversion which prevented his making the
necessary effort. He thought in terms of people. His decisions were never abstract, but were generally couched in
terms of the probable effect upon one group or another. In
fact, his political skill was such that it sometimes inclined

him to play politics rather than take a direct and forthright course.

Roosevelt's liberalism was grounded on a firm belief in the good sense and rights of the average man, which led him to seek ways of raising the larger good above privilege. He leaned slightly toward a decentralization of industry, and he had an emotional attachment to an economic pattern based on the small individual farmer. Probably the most persistent legacy of his life as a resident of a small community was his concept of America as a congeries of such communities whose individual uplift would lead logically to the uplift of the nation as a whole. His sights were so completely trained on the home scene that the conviction grew on him that the depression would not be cured by international action. In his inaugural address he favored a revival of foreign trade by international agreements; yet such activities, "though vastly important, are in point of time and necessity secondary to the establishment of a sound national economy. I favor as a practical policy the putting of first things first. I shall spare no effort to restore world trade by international economic readjustment, but the emergency at home cannot wait on that accomplishment." [2]

In embarking on his tremendous social and economic program, he frankly called himself an experimenter and his program an experiment. Improvisation became for him a conscious technique, and his tentative and unorthodox temperament was reflected in those of his advisers who were able to endure the tempo of the New Deal for any length of time.

The Democratic platform called for support of the gold standard and of sound money, while the national convention resisted all proposals for tampering with the currency. Candidate Roosevelt did not mention the gold standard during the campaign, although he did promise to follow a "sound money" policy. Yet his pledge was a little less than a promise to maintain the gold standard. Rather, it was a compromising verbiage aimed at leaving the door open.

Roosevelt's sights even before the inauguration were primarily fixed on increasing employment, raising prices and lightening the debt load. He regarded currency as one device for achieving these goals, and maintained a complete freedom of action both on silver and gold until some of his price-raising schemes, later embodied in such legislation as the NRA and AAA, could be tried.

After the election, rumors were rife that Roosevelt was

thinking of devaluation and some kind of inflation of the currency. Senator Carter Glass made a determined effort to get a commitment from the President-elect on sound and conservative monetary practises. At one time Roosevelt offered the post of Secretary of the Treasury to Glass. The Senator made a final effort to obtain a promise of maintenance of the gold standard, but Roosevelt refused to discard ideas merely because they had inflationary labels. Under these conditions Glass refused the appointment, and Roosevelt's refusal was blamed by the Republicans for the banking crisis that shortly ensued.

The President-elect, even if he had desired to, could not suggest that he believed a "sound money" would necessitate devaluation of the dollar, because of the probable panic and speculation in gold. Instead, he quietly maintained his freedom of action and showed interest in the various methods for achieving his ultimate goal.

The quality of the men around the President was significant for two reasons. One was Roosevelt's strong will and desire to set the pace. From that will sprang his self-confidence, his rapid and explicit decisions, occasionally his abrupt orders and snap judgments. But as a consequence, he drew to himself men partly because he wanted their points of view, more because their views agreed generally with his own. He did not care to entertain outspoken opposition in his entourage, and he was somewhat suspicious of recognized eminence.

The other factor that influenced the President's choice of advisers was the nature of his program, which, to the worldly and seasoned members of his own party, whether politicians or businessmen, entered fields from which democratic government was supposed to remain aloof. Hence Roosevelt as a critic of the exploiting society he knew was forced to form his Administration from men whose opinions had prevented their gaining practical experience in government or business, men who had consequently remained detached enough to see the weaknesses of that society.

Senator Pittman proved politically useful on the Western campaign trip. Lean, gray, and canny, he was possessed of an abundance of Wilsonian liberalism which at this state of political events coincided with many of the sentiments of the group around the candidate. Consequently, he was for a time after the trip included in the regular membership of the "brains trust," where, however, there is little evidence that he made progress with his designs for silver. Pittman was

seriously considered for a cabinet post. Roosevelt appreci-
ated his years of experience but felt he would have the power
and influence of a cabinet member if he were allowed to become chairman of the Senate Foreign Relations Committee.
The choice of Senator Claude Swanson for cabinet office
opened Pittman's path to the Senate post, and thus set in
motion the chain of events that took him to London and resulted in an international silver agreement.

Within forty-eight hours after the inauguration, a national
bank holiday was proclaimed. The Treasury Department
immediately assumed an importance in the government second only to the White House itself. Consequently, the post of
Secretary of the Treasury took on new significance, and
here the President, given his aims and objectives, was in-
consistent in his selection. His first choice was Senator
Glass, who refused. He next offered the post to William
Woodin, president of the American Car and Foundry Com--
pany. It is doubtful if the President had any premonition of
the nature and extent of the Treasury operations in the next
few years, for in both cases he picked men known to favor
sound money and conservative practises. Mr. Woodin, who
accepted the post, was a business man and musician, not a
financier or banker. He was intensely loyal to the President
but came to disagree with some of the Administration's
monetary policies. However, he had contributed to the election of the President. Furthermore, he was respected by big
business and his appointment was bound to be reassuring.
Yet his nomination was almost rejected in Congress because
of evidence that he was one of the friends of the House of
Morgan.

Woodin's reaction to silver is illustrated by his composi-
tion of "Lullaby in Silver" one night late in February. He
had just been exposed to three hours of exposition by silver
enthusiasts on the glorious benefits of bimetallism. He named
his piece as he did, he asserted, because he wrote it to get
the silver talk off his mind before he went to bed.

Yet as Secretary, Woodin showed that he was a hardheaded
business man with a flexible mind. Untrained for the job
even if it had been normal times, he found himself at the
center of the biggest financial crisis the country had ever
faced. He showed more than average competence in those
first desperate weeks. But the strain aggravated an ailment
that grew worse until by summer he played a small role in
the affairs of his department. The situation in his sphere of
the government as early as April moved Walter Lippmann

to write: "The Treasury, which is undermanned, overworked and so busy pruning the trees that it does not see the woods, has been too unsure of itself to adopt a policy which required courage and technical competence. The Federal Reserve system has been without leadership and has had no policy worthy of the name for the past eight weeks."[3]

Dean Acheson, Under-Secretary of the Treasury beginning in May, had one of the most astute minds at the American bar. However, on matters financial, he, too, was rated a "sound-money" man. The fact that the top men of the Treasury were out of sympathy with some of the currency proposals of the Administration helps to explain why President Roosevelt early became his own Secretary of Treasury and why the entire department was revolutionized toward the end of the year.

The consideration of the President as the spark plug of Treasury operations raises the question of the sources of his ideas. Prior to his inauguration, he had made no statement of his monetary intentions. For an understanding of his motivation, three factors seem significant:

1. The critical events at the time of his inauguration forced a major change not only in the tempo but also in the direction of his thinking. He faced a nation panic-stricken by the banking crisis and increasingly fearful of its capacity to right itself. The fifteen million unemployed felt no more hopeless than the business men, lawyers, and labor leaders. Bankers were in no position to resist any action he might choose to wrest control of finance from them, yet he merely declared a holiday, and set about reforming their practises. Meanwhile, he suspended a decision on any inflationary move until he could see the results of the banking acts. The impact of his first weeks in office made him even more receptive to the next two considerations.

2. Two financial advisers exerted considerable influence over Roosevelt's policies during his first year of office. When he left the gold standard early in 1933, the President had no monetary expert sympathetic to the idea, or acquainted with currency not anchored to gold. As a result, George F. Warren, Professor of Agricultural Economics at Cornell, and James Harvey Rogers, Sterling Professor of Political Economy at Yale, were brought to the White House for the first of many conferences in June, 1933, and were put to work immediately on plans for a managed currency.

Of the two men, Professor Warren was more influential. He was no stranger to the President. As economist of the

Committee for the Nation, an organization of business men
and farm organizations favoring a 40 percent reduction in
the content of the gold dollar, his views had already been
placed before the country. Roosevelt had also known Warren
and his ideas in Albany, where Henry Morgenthau, Jr., had
summoned him for assistance in agriculture and conservation.

The Warren theory embraced the commodity dollar. He
believed that gold, on which the currency is based, is not
an immutable symbol of value, but itself a commodity, subject to the laws of supply and demand. When the supply of
gold is great at any given time or place, prices are high because each dollar based on that gold is cheaper. If gold were
as plentiful as coal, the dollar would become as cheap and
would buy correspondingly little. Likewise, when the supply
of gold is scarce, prices fall. Warren believed that the depression resulted from a scarcity of gold.[4]

Applying this theory to the immediate American problem,
Warren proposed an artificial raising of the price of gold
through government purchases of the metal at increasing
dollar prices. The result would be a devalued or cheaper
dollar that would force commodity prices upward as the
gold value of the dollar fell. Devaluation of the dollar would
thus painlessly be accomplished, and the depression price
level raised. Furthermore, the theory suggested that a
cheaper American dollar would stimulate American exports
at the same time that it erected an effective barrier to imports from the rest of the world.

Warren proposed his policy on a national scale only, independent of the actions of other countries. Its nationalistic
scope coincided with the President's concept of domestic
apart from international action to meet the depression. Professor Rogers tried to warn that prices would not rise automatically under gold purchases, that devaluation should be
accompanied by public works on a large scale and by simultaneous international action toward the same goal. Nevertheless, the commodity dollar won support at the White
House. During the spring and summer Roosevelt's chief interest in it was simply that it offered him one more technique for raising prices, the central purpose of his first
months in office. Late in the year he accepted the Warren
plan completely when he embarked on the double policy of
large purchases of gold at advancing prices.

3. The most impelling and immediate influence on the
President, at least politically, was the tremendous surge of

agitation and public opinion, culminating in a strongly inflationary Congress.

These ingredients taken together -- a desperate populace
with a deeply inflationary sentiment, a President willing to
experiment and surrounded by men of similar inclinations,
a President who knew when and how to compromise -- set
the stage for the effective entrance of silver on the national
scene.

THE ENTERING WEDGE

The new Congress that convened on March 9, 1933, seethed
with plans and proposals to cure the depression. Between
March and May at least twenty-four different bills were introduced involving an expanded monetary use of silver. Silver arguments were being increasingly accepted by people
who now believed that somehow their individual purchasing
power depended upon the country's total stock of precious
metals and currency. To meet the great issue of the depression, apparently Congress was committed to only one positive course, the "hoary program of currency inflation in
some form."[5]

No one in the Administration doubted that inflation com-
manded a majority in the new House, but its strength in the
Senate was unknown. No test of sentiment had been made
there since the defeat of bimetalism in January, when only
eighteen Senators had voted for it. Therefore, on April 17
Senator Wheeler obtained a vote on another bimetallic amendment. The tally was forty-three against and thirty-three for
the measure. White House opposition, voiced through Majority Leader Robinson, helped prevent its passage, for members were reluctant to defy the President, and hesitated to
embarrass the Administration as it entertained foreign
heads of states preparatory to the coming world conference.

Equally effective was the counsel that Administration advisers gave those Senators who sought help in escaping a
dilemma. Some of them were not sure bimetallism was
sound, but had the "folks back home" to think about, and disliked being recorded in opposition to any inflationary proposal. They were told to absent themselves until the end of
the roll call, when they should vote against the bill if there
were already thirty votes for free silver, and when they
might safely vote for it if there were under thirty votes.[6]

Hence the Administration knew that at least ten Senators
failed to help the amendment, although they favored inflation

of some sort. Since that many additional votes would have secured passage, there was no longer doubt about the inflationary majority in the Senate.

Directly after the vote on the Wheeler proposal, Senator Elmer Thomas, of Oklahoma, introduced his amendment to the Agricultural Adjustment Act. It was flagrantly inflationary, and sentiment began immediately to crystallize around it. With the farm belt on the warpath, inflationists out to solve the farm problem in their own way, and silverites eager to support any legislation that would advance their interests, it became obvious that the President could not get his agricultural program through Congress without an inflationary rider. Both Senators Bulkley, of Ohio, and Byrnes, of South Carolina, individually reported to the White House that the amendment was certain to be passed, and that at the most the President might persuade Congress to vest the inflationary powers in him.

The time for decision had finally arrived, and on April 18 the President openly embraced the principle of inflation. It is not certain that he could have avoided such action even if he had wanted to. With the immense amount of prestige and good will he had accumulated, he probably could have applied pressure enough to postpone the issue; his veto power alone could have accomplished that. Yet as a president of only six weeks, as the sponsor of a tremendous legislative program in Congress, as an open-minded executive who probably had already realized that eventual inflation might be necessary to accomplish his main objectives, his agreement is understandable partly as conviction, partly as political pressure. The price of his support was a rewriting of the bill to give him the inflationary powers, and to make them permissive rather than mandatory. In these respects he gained a major victory in his compromise.

The Thomas Amendment passed both the Senate and the House by large majorities. In both cases conservative Eastern Republicans and "sound money" Democrats were snowed under in their first vigorous opposition of the Congressional session. They fought chiefly the fantastically broad powers over money that the amendment gave the President.

One provision was primarily a result of the pioneer work of Senator Hayden. It provided for the acceptance of silver at a valuation of not over fifty cents an ounce as payment on war debts to become due in June. The silver thus received was to be coined into silver dollars as Treasury backing for a new issue of silver certificates. Yet on June 15 all the war

debts were defaulted except about 8 percent, which were paid
in fifty-cent silver. Since the market price for the metal was
then less than thirty-six cents, the debtor countries saved
over twenty-eight cents on a dollar by paying in silver. For
example, Great Britain saved about $2,750,000 on the $10,
000,000 she paid. Czechoslovakia, Finland, Italy, Lithuania,
and Rumania made similar payments.[7]

Furthermore, the President was given a wide discretionary control over money. The biggest inflationary power was
permission for the Federal Reserve to purchase government
securities up to $3,000,000,000 and to issue greenbacks up
to the same amount. The President might also set the weight
of the gold and silver dollars at a fixed ratio and order unlimited coinage of both metals at that ratio. The sole limitation in this sweeping authority was a prohibition against reducing the gold dollar by more than half. Frankly bimetallic
in purpose, the law never brought the country to a double
monetary base only because the President refused to use
his powers in that direction.

Among the blessings of the law may be mentioned the additional bargaining power given the President as the international monetary conference approached; the collection of
a few war debts that might have been defaulted entirely; the
near unity of Congress on the bill and the cessation of agitation for a time; and the opportunity it gave Roosevelt, because of its permissive features, to pursue an entirely different but logical and consistent policy of raising prices.
The disadvantages are obvious. Its acceptance was proof
that the President could be influenced by the exertion of sufficient pressure; his failure to execute its provisions served
to irritate the extremists, who remained dissatisfied until
the passage of a mandatory law; finally, it confused the public mind simply because the Administration could not be
frank about its future plans without playing into the hands of
speculators.

THE LONDON ECONOMIC CONFERENCE

American participation in the London Conference resulted
from correspondence between the United Kingdom and the
United States. The latter made its acceptance dependent on
the inclusion of silver on the agenda, and the exclusion of
reparations, intergovernmental debts and specific tariff
rates.

With his accustomed vigor President Roosevelt cham-

pioned the cause of international economic deliberations at
the same time that he was embarking on a tremendous national program of his own. Early in April the State Department undertook to formulate its conference program, which
contained extensive plans for the enhancement of silver in
the monetary systems of the world. Yet at no time did the
planners take seriously the Senate-adopted Wheeler resolution that directed the delegates to "work unceasingly for an
international agreement to remonetize silver on a basis of
a definite fixed ratio of not to exceed sixteen fine ounces of
silver to one fine ounce of gold." [8]

The conference labored under grave disabilities from the
start. The nations of the world had no intention of dissociat-
ing themselves from their old nationalistic treatment of economic problems. Furthermore, the American delegation was
hopelessly divided in sentiment, with its chairman, Secretary of State Cordell Hull, staking everything on the revival
of international laissez-faire, and the President inclining
increasingly toward his domestic program, which assumed
considerable insulation of national economy. So many opinions were represented and so much dissension aroused that
on the trip to London the news reporters spoke among themselves of the "Funeral Ship." Secretary Hull later wrote:
"Few mistakes can be more unfortunate than for the official
head of a delegation to a world conference not to have a
chance to consult with the President on the selection of the
entire personnel -- or at least let the personnel have that
distinct impression. Otherwise, there is little sense of loyalty or teamwork on the part of some, and open defiance
from others." [9]

For three weeks the London Conference worked chiefly
on stabilization. Its efforts were abruptly terminated when
President Roosevelt, in his famous "bombshell" message,
rejected currency stabilization as artificial, temporary, and
helpful to a few nations only. He wrote in part: "Let me be
frank in saying that the United States seeks the kind of dollar which a generation hence will have the same purchasing
and debt-paying power as the dollar value we hope to attain
in the near future. That objective means more to the good
of other nations than a fixed ratio for a month or two in
terms of the pound or franc." [10]

Professor Warren, financial adviser to the President,
and his collaborator, Professor Pearson, used the President's message as an opportunity to publicize their ideas.
Emphasizing the President's search for a dollar with an

even purchasing and debt-paying power, they believed that their compensated dollar answered the specifications.[11]

The President was already under the influence of the commodity theory of money. Moreover, the "bombshell" message was dispatched by the President from the cruiser "Indianapolis." Accompanying the Chief Executive were his secretary, Louis Howe, and his good friend, Henry Morgenthau, Jr. Howe was strongly opposed to stabilization because of its unforeseeable cost to the United States. He drafted a message to London, but the President completely rewrote it and eventually sent his own version. It was a statement of his firm conviction that the American dollar must be devalued further and prices raised before he would be ready to discuss international action.[12]

Nevertheless, the conference was kept in session for another three weeks through the herculean efforts of Secretary Hull. This period of the gradual demise was of vital importance to the silver group if it was to accomplish anything. The subject of silver had been treated as an international joke, and of all the topics on the agenda this one had been expected to yield the least results. But Senator Pittman, neglecting all other aspects of the conference, turned this prophecy into the conference's only agreement in a way which reads something like "a mining camp romance," behind which lay "the hard persistent work that those romances hide."[13]

When Pittman presented the American silver proposals, Secretary Hull announced that they had the approval of the President. Pittman asked for (a) limiting arbitrary sales of silver, (b) outlawing the debasement of coins, (c) remonetizing up to a fineness of at least eight-tenths, and (d) maintaining an optional 20 percent silver reserve in Central Banks. The first two were generally acceptable, but the others occasioned weeks of argument, chiefly in a Silver Subcommittee headed by Pittman.[14]

The dying conference was the scene of intense proselyting by the American Senator and his cohorts. They strained to produce a resolution that the sixty-six nations would find innocuous enough to adopt. In this they were successful, for most of their proposals were merely recommendations which did not bind the signatories. One paragraph alone was the germ for further action on silver, for it recommended an agreement between silver-using and silver-producing nations to stabilize world markets.[15]

The silver countries, prodded by Senator Pittman, pro-

ceeded to take this paragraph seriously and produced a sup-
plemental agreement of much more definite and binding
terms. On the one hand, China, India, and Spain as large
holders of silver, and on the other hand, Australia, Canada,
Mexico, Peru, and the United States as large producers of
the metal, arrived at the so-called "London Silver Agreement."

In the first place the silver-holding countries agreed on
certain sales quotas for a four-year period. China promised
not to dispose of any silver by melting coins; but she was
one of the few large nations that had not engaged in this
practise; furthermore, she was the chief silver importer
in the world by this time, and had not sold the metal for
many years. Spain, which had not sold silver since the war,
professed herself agreeable to a restriction of sales to 5,-
000,000 ounces a year. India consented to a quota of 35,000,-
000 ounces annually, much less than she had ever attempted.
Indeed, she gained practically a guarantee of a market for
that quantity of sales each year. In all three cases, the "concessions" were but promises not to do things that were not
likely in the foreseeable future.

For their part, the silver-producing countries agreed to
consume certain quotas each year for four years. In return
for silver users confining their sales to 40,000,000 ounces,
the producers agreed to withdraw from the market 35,000,-
000 ounces annually.

Allotment

	Ounces [a]	Percent of 5-country total	Percent of obligation to 1932 production [b]
United States	24,421,410	69.78	98.5
Mexico	7,159,108	20.45	13.3
Canada	1,671,802	4.78	10.1
Peru	1,095,325	3.13	17.4
Australia	652,355	1.86	10.0
Total	35,000,000	100.00	

[a] For the full text, see Silver, Memorandum of Agreement..., Executive Agreement Series, pp. 4 ff.

[b] Based on world production figures as given in Bratter,
Monetary Use of Silver in 1933, p. 14.

From this table two facts are obvious. One is that almost singlehanded Pittman committed his country to the purchase of the current output of American mines, an objective that the silver interests had never succeeded in reaching through Congress. The other is that the agreement was entirely one-sided in favor of the six nations that stood to gain from the magnanimity of the United States in assuming 70 percent of the burden, India and Mexico were particularly pleased at the outcome, and the former publicly commended Pittman on his great efforts. Only the Chinese saw their interests endangered as the specter of a rising price of silver assumed more definite outlines.

Even after adoption in London, the Silver Agreement had to be ratified by each of the eight governments before it was binding on them, unless, as the Agreement carefully provided, only one of the producing countries ratified but was willing to buy the entire 35,000,000 ounces. Since the greatest commitment was American, the other countries waited to see what action the United States would take.

In October the President put the Warren theory into practice by starting large-scale purchases of gold in an effort to raise commodity prices. He also attempted to split the silverites and the inflationists in Congress by inferring that if only the Silver Senators would form a coalition with sound-money advocates so as to defeat printing-press inflation, they "could write their own ticket."[16] He was said privately to have stated that he would support such an alliance, but his bid failed to break up silver-inflationist unity.

On the contrary, Senator Wheeler, disappointed with the results of the London Conference, again proposed bimetallism in the Senate, and with the full support of the inflationist forces he had reason, by December, to be certain of its acceptance. For the second time in nine months the President realized the need for compromise, and he used the London Silver Agreement as a vehicle.

Roosevelt found it easy to consider a silver-purchasing program as an adjunct to his gold-buying scheme of raising prices. He thought it was politically necessary to draw off Congressional support of more radical monetary legislation. He also had come to view the desirability of economic aid to the Western states by a domestic silver program.

Consequently, the United States was the first country officially to accept the Silver Agreement. By presidential proclamation of December 21, 1933, the Secretary of the Treasury was directed for four years to purchase newly mined American silver and coin it into silver dollars. Whereas the London Agreement had allocated 24,400,000 ounces as the American share, the President's directive applied to all new silver, which in 1932 approximated the amount mentioned at London, but which in 1929 had been some 60,000,000 ounces.

Furthermore, the proclamation directed that 50 percent of all silver be retained in the Treasury as seigniorage, and that the silver producers be reimbursed for the remaining 50 percent only. Since the statutory price of silver was still $1.29 an ounce, the proclamation meant that the government would pay silver producers 64.5 cents an ounce. The market price of silver on the day before the proclamation had been about forty-three cents, with the result that the government undertook to pay a bonus to silver producers of twenty-one cents, or about 50 percent above the market. Yet the price was a compromise, for Pittman had expected free coinage of silver with no deduction for seigniorage, while the President refused to pay producers such a large bonus.

As phrased by the President, the aims behind the proclamation were overambitious and fell far short of fulfilling expectations. The program was dwarfed by more extensive and striking governmental activities such as the huge gold-buying program, although in both cases the metals were purchased without an actual drain on current receipts merely by monetizing the purchases. They were to be less than those under either the Bland-Allison Act of 1878 or the Sherman Purchase Act of 1890. Yet they were important to silver proponents as one more milestone in the accomplishment of their objectives. Indeed, Senator Pittman enthusiastically reported that the proclamation would "bring happiness to millions dependent on mining."[18] Yet during 1933 only twenty-five companies produced 86 percent of the total American output.[19]

The proclamation required neither the remonetization of silver nor bimetallism; it proclaimed free but not unlimited coinage, for it was limited to one half the domestic production; nor did it fix any coinage ratio with gold. Nevertheless, it proposed to add some new money to the currency, although in infinitesimal quantities. It was estimated that after four years of the program the currency stock would be increased by only about one percent. Yet this fact was not generally realized, and inflationists and silverites alike heralded the President's gesture.

Roosevelt expected to elevate the depression price level by his purchase of gold and silver, and by the artificial raising of their prices. The programs proved only mildly inflationary, far from the prognostications of their proponents. Yet for several months the President persisted before he realized that the results were not commensurate with the cost and effort involved.

The immediate result of the silver program was its buoyant effect on world silver prices. In view of the paternalistic concern of the United States for the metal, world markets responded with a continuing price recovery during most of 1933. Indeed the specter of rising silver almost prevented the Chinese from ratifying the London Agreement, which they did only with reservations. By late April, 1934, all eight nations had agreed to conform to their quotas until December 31, 1937.

The American program was immediately recognized as bearing the seeds of further agitation. The government undertook to purchase only newly mined silver. Old bullion was not provided for, and must therefore be sold on the market subject to supply and demand. Speculators and hoarders were estimated to have stored 180,000,000 ounces of the metal.[20] It had been accumulated in warehouses, where it was overflowing the vaults. Here was a special silver interest that the government would be under pressure to recognize.

REVOLUTION IN THE TREASURY DEPARTMENT

As 1933 wore on, changes in the Treasury were indicated. The department was increasingly the center of governmental activity. Yet for months, with the developing illness of Secretary Woodin, it had no effective head outside the White House. It was held together by the able Under-Secretary, Dean Acheson, who performed an extremely difficult task. He and the junior members of the department had been forced to manufacture policies to meet the various situations as they arose.

After July, 1933, despite the NRA and AAA, a renewed fall in prices took place. Widespread agricultural unrest gave force to the demands of the inflationists. As a partial response the President on October 17 issued an order to Henry Morgenthau, Jr., at his post in the Farm Credit Administration, to start the purchase of wheat for the Emergency Relief program, with the primary aim of raising and sustaining its price.

On Sunday, October 22, a distinguished White House gathering of Oliphant, Warren, Rogers, Morgenthau, Wallace, Hopkins, Moley, and others learned that the President had accepted the idea of a managed currency. His thinking traversed the whole extent of the Warren theory, even brushing aside the last-minute remonstrances of Professor Rogers, who tried to caution that prices of gold and commodities did not vary in exact proportion.

This concept of money and prices was not new to Morgenthau. Therefore, as a result of Acheson's opposition on legal and practical grounds to the purchase of gold, Roosevelt accepted Morgenthau's help in handling the transactions. He found himself conferring daily with his chief about the new price to be bid for the metal, which consistently took an upward direction.

Late in October the President broached the matter of action on silver in conformity with the London Agreement. Morgenthau offered his services to ascertain what moves were necessary. He also became involved in buying corn and oats in an effort to raise their price. Yet early in November he counseled the President against further governmental purchases of commodities until the effects of the new gold program could be seen. At any rate the anomaly developed of Morgenthau at his desk at Farm Credit carrying on several Treasury activities. He seems not to have been so much ambitious for advancement as sympathetic to the program and desirous of helping his chief in the face of Treasury opposition.

The time finally arrived when Roosevelt ordered Acheson and the Treasury to purchase gold as a matter of Administration policy. The former greatly angered the President by requesting a personal letter to protect himself. Continued lack of co-operation on the gold program created an impossible situation within the Administration.

On November 13 the President notified Morgenthau of his appointment as Acting Secretary of the Treasury. Following the immediate departure of Dean Acheson and the eventual resignation of Woodin, Morgenthau became Secretary on January 1, 1934. His accession to the Treasury position was generally welcomed. Mark Sullivan summarized the prevailing opinion in writing of him as "conservative in a sense which, relative to the times, connotes many sound principles of finance and government, even though Mr. Morgenthau is also a supporter of some startling innovations.... He regards the innovations as for the emergency only and not for permanent change in the social system."[21]

One current theory was that Morgenthau was put in charge to help the Treasury digest managed currency. There was some truth in this viewpoint, but it omitted from the picture the relationship between the President and his new Secretary. Their association went far back to their days of neighborliness on their Duchess County farms, and continued on to Albany. There farmer Morgenthau became enthusiastic over Governor Roosevelt's program, in which he soon had á part. Morgenthau at one time headed the Governor's Agricultural Advisory Commission, at another the State Conservation Department, and on both jobs he had the help of a brilliant trio from Cornell -- William S. Myers, Carl Ladd, and George F. Warren. At the age of forty-two he was put in charge of the huge new Farm Credit Administration, a four-billion-dollar "Federal Reserve system for agriculture." He proved himself in the position by considerable administrative ability and by his loyalty to the Administration.

Morgenthau was a hard-working, honest, pleasant individual with a flair for administration that enabled him to impart considerable order and integrity to the running of his department. He was sensitive to criticism, chiefly because he felt the President was being attacked through him. Yet Morgenthau and the Treasury "brain trust" of experts and specialists assumed the function of preparing policies and details to submit to the President for final decision.

He consulted the President frequently, even on such matters as the daily change in the government's bid for silver. He had weekly business lunches with Roosevelt, and for a long period was at the White House almost every day. The informal morning conferences inevitably started with the easy bantering of two good friends. On one occasion the President entertained him in the bathroom while he shaved. Morgenthau recorded that he was now a member of the "bathroom cabinet." Each visit developed shortly to serious terms, including a discussion of action for the day.

Although the Secretary sometimes asked his chief for too much guidance on details, he in turn was able to counsel the President. Being conservative in most money matters, and preferring to proceed cautiously, he sometimes exercised the persuasive powers of which he was capable.

Morgenthau depended on the help of his general counsel, Herman Oliphant. When the President notified Morgenthau of his appointment as head of the Farm Credit Administration, he also laid down his prescription for the general counsel. The President wanted a lawyer who "had been brought

up on a farm, had not been in a Wall Street office, had a
broad social viewpoint including understanding problems of
the farmer, was an outstanding lawyer and highly respected
at the Bar." [22]

In despair at filling the office, Morgenthau consulted his
friend and counsel, Edward S. Greenbaum, of New York.
Overnight Greenbaum thought of Herman Oliphant and with
difficulty persuaded the latter to leave his work at Johns
Hopkins long enough to talk to Morgenthau. Oliphant and
Morgenthau liked each other, and Oliphant was persuaded to
undertake the work. He stayed with Morgenthau until his
death in 1939. Morgenthau later made him general counsel
at the Treasury, where the Secretary relied constantly on
his legal knowledge, and general advice. Oliphant was present at important monetary conferences in the White House.
In connection with the Silver Purchase Act, Oliphant carried
the chief burden of preparing and explaining the legislation.

While still in Farm Credit, Oliphant made himself valuable as a wizard at finding precedents for unconventional
undertakings. When the President decided in the fall to buy
gold, he was told by the Treasury that there was no legal
sanction for such activity. Although the subject was outside
the scope of the Farm Credit Administration, Oliphant prepared a memorandum suggesting various ways in which gold
could be purchased; it went directly to the President by way
of Mr. Morgenthau. He also discovered in a currency law of
the early Civil War period authority for the President's devaluation of gold.

Thus it came about that the Treasury was in the hands of
men who would allow no obstacle to stand in the way of the
operation of the Administration's price-raising activities.
Early in December a news ticker was installed next to the
Secretary's office, and it became an invaluable adjunct to
the Treasury's purchasing programs. After December 21
these activities were expanded by the new silver purchases.
Meanwhile the Administration scanned the statistics to learn
the effects of the Warren theory.

These effects were at first a matter of controversy. In
mid-December the Brookings Institution called gold buying
a fickle price aid and attacked the gold theory of commodity
prices as "wholly inapplicable to the complex modern
world." [23] But Morgenthau expressed satisfaction with the
reported rise in commodity prices of one third the rise in
the price of gold during November; [24] yet the Labor Department wholesale price index showed a decrease of one-tenth

of one percent for the same month. Other indices tended
to show either little or no rise in the general price level.

Yet devaluation must be given considerable credit for
stemming the serious decline in commodity prices of the
summer and fall. The trend was reversed after November.
In the foreign field, the commodity-dollar experiment won
an advantageous position for the dollar in relation to foreign
currencies. The cheaper American money stimulated exports
at the same time that it insulated the American market from
foreign dumping. Furthermore, through the purchase of foreign gold at high prices the government program in effect
was providing foreign buyers with purchasing power for
American goods, thus subsidizing increased exports.

Therefore, at the beginning of 1934 the President prepared
to abandon his extreme economic nationalism by making
ready to talk international stabilization on more even terms
with other nations. He asked Congress to set limits of 40
and 50 percent devaluation of the gold content of the dollar,
within which he might fix the value as the occasion arose.
Congress gave the authority in the Gold Reserve Act, and
the President stabilized the devalued gold dollar at 40.94
percent below its former gold content.

Under the enthusiasm for the commodity theory of money,
a frame of mind was created favorable to a whole series of
monetary acts. It is necessary to view the President's proclamation for purchasing silver under the London Agreement
in that light His proclamation fitted into the monetary ideas
and aspirations of the particular time in which it was made,
as did his acceptance of the silver provisions of the Gold
Reserve Act and later the Silver Purchase Act.

THE SILVER PURCHASE ACT OF 1934

The year 1934 witnessed the climax of the silver agitation
and brought the achievement of the chief silver proposals.
Perhaps these results were not inevitable in specific details,
but some degree of inevitability is obvious from a glance at
the forces at work in Congress and the country.

Twice during 1933, Roosevelt had interfered with the intentions of the legislature by interjecting silver compromises. In his December proclamation, he hoped he had sufficiently split the silverites from the "cheap money" party
to forestall further radical proposals. Under this delusion
he stated in his annual message in January that he was "withholding any recommendation to the Congress looking to fur-

ther extension of the monetary use of silver because I believe that we should gain more knowledge of the results of the London agreement and of our other monetary measures."

Yet within twelve days from the date of the message he had to intervene vigorously to prevent the passage of Wheeler's proposal for the mandatory purchase of 50,000,000 ounces of silver monthly until a billion ounces had been acquired. Senator Wheeler adroitly appealed to the cotton, tobacco, and Republican Senators on the ground that his bill would help their interests. The President voiced his vehement opposition to the measure through Majority Leader Robinson, who also recited Treasury objections and ended by showing that the bill, far from helping China, would cause a violent deflation there.[27] Even then the amendment was defeated by a vote of only forty-five to forty-three. Congress was obviously pushing toward a complete showdown with the Chief Executive.

The first of the "compromises of 1934" came in the Gold Reserve Act, of January, which had an important silver amendment. The President was given the same power to reduce the weight of the silver dollar that he held over the gold dollar, and the inflationary authority to issue paper money against all silver not already held as backing by the Treasury. Since it was permissive in nature, the amendment was accepted in the spirit of compromise by an Administration that had achieved a doubtful victory in heading off the Wheeler proposal. However, most of the amendment remained inoperative and merely stirred Congressional determination to force action by means of a mandatory law.

Congress needed little new stimulus, because for almost a year it had been predominantly silver and inflation-minded. Its opinion was being formed with the aid of increasing public participation in the argument. Although it never reached the proportions of the popular agitation of the period of the 1890's, the crusade was nonetheless carried on by pamphlet and press, radio and club. Of the organized efforts to sway opinion, two stand out as the most efficient and effective.

The Committee for the Nation had carried on a persistent campaign for its objectives. Organized early in 1933 by a group of industrial and agricultural leaders who were alarmed over the dangerous trends in business, it had taken a stand for price inflation. It accepted most of their economist Warren's theory and strongly advocated devaluation. In general the Committee approved the Roosevelt policies and claimed proudly that many of them were advocated first

by the Committee before being made Administration doc-
trine. Its chief objection was that the President was proceed-
ing too slowly. Through an active press department and a
large mailing list the group spread its platform far and wide,
while some of its members were active in the silver agitation.

Probably more effective because reaching more people
were the efforts of the radio priest, Charles E. Coughlin.
During 1933 he built up a large following in his radio ser-
mons on social justice. Having embraced the cause of cheap
money, he adopted the silver program with as great avidity
as its Congressional proponents, and was one of the leading
forces in building up public support for silver.

His appeal was chiefly emotional, with tremendous claims
for the benefits of restored silver. During the winter of 1933-
34 his radio lectures were a strange blending of religion and
money, sprinkled with exhortations to "play the good Samar-
itan to the lowly Oriental," or to end the "flat tire currency
doled out to us by the Federal Reserve bankers," or to stop
imitating England where "the liars and the Judases, the high
priests, Annas and Caiphas were at work crucifying silver,"
or to write to Congressmen, for which purpose he conveni-
ently furnished lists.[28]

His contribution to the hearings of the Coinage Committee
of the House contained much cheap exhortation: "Let us restore the purchasing power of the Orient, of 800 million
people so that our farmers, our industrialists, our laborers
will not have to look forward to the tragic spectacle of being
servants under the C.W.A. for the rest of their lives."[29] Yet
Marquis Childs decided that "He gave expression to the in-
articulate discontent of thousands upon thousands of Americans.... He was speaking to the great middle class.... He
believes that the New Deal has only made a start in the direction of shorter hours, higher wages, cheaper money, and
general redistribution of the nation's wealth."[30]

The struggle between the executive and the legislative
branches over the treatment of silver broke into the open
following the defeat of the Wheeler amendment. Both sides
threw all their weight into the fight, which, as it progressed,
assumed increasingly the characteristics of a political tus-
sle, and was less and less based on the economic program
of the original silver proposals. The renewed interest in
silver was due not so much to concern for the silver producers, who had received compensation already, as to a revitalized alliance of forces. When the interest in the metal

appeared to be diminishing, the connections among silver, farm relief, and inflation were strengthened to such an extent that in the course of time the three had become inseparable. Small wonder that the President had failed to detach one group from the others by his acceptance of parts of their· programs.

Roosevelt's antisilver policy during these months was passive in nature, because he hoped to avoid making enemies for his domestic program, and because his mind was taken up with what he considered more important legislation. He disappointed silver hopes when he did not use his great powers under the two preceding laws. He relied on his political popularity to check undesirable legislation merely by the nod of the head that had proved successful on previous occasions. And he left to his Secretary of the Treasury the thankless task of being front man, of making the investigations and announcements that were so offensive to the silver group. If its members ever realized the fact, they never acknowledged that the Secretary was merely carrying out the President's wishes on silver. Even after Roosevelt capitulated, Senator Pittman stated when he presented the final compromise to Congress: "The Secretary of the Treasury and his expert advisers...desired there be no mandatory features.... They know little about silver. They suspect much with regard to silver. They are misadvised by distinguished and learned professors who know less about silver."[31]

For several months Morgenthau led the offensive for his chief. Yet he made a sincere effort to learn the other point of view. He went to Senator Ashurst, of Arizona, for a little basic instruction in silver, asking the Senator why he felt so strongly about the subject. All he got for his pains was the reply: "My boy, I was brought up from my mother's knee on silver and I can't discuss that any more with you than you can discuss your religion with me."[32]

Morgenthau sent Professor Rogers on a fact-finding trip to the Orient. Its avowed purpose was to ascertain which of two schools of thought on silver should govern Treasury actions -- one, that the increased price of silver would mean greater exports from the United States to China and, the other, that China would be forced to curtail her imports. For this move Morgenthau was accused of stalling for time, particularly since the announcement of the trip came on the day of the House vote on the Dies silver bill. One Senator went so far as to say that it was "the height of asininity" to interview Chinese coolies regarding the metal, that the Professor "started with a prejudice."[33] If the Administration intended the Rogers mission as a delaying tactic, it was disappointed. Irritated silver proponents merely became more determined than before, and they succeeded in achieving their goal long before the Professor returned in October.

On March 15, in opposition to any further silver legislation, Morgenthau announced a policy of sitting tight, with the comment: "I still have to be shown that silver alone is a cure-all."[34] He hinted broadly that a Treasury investigation of silver speculation had implicated some silver advocates in the activity. The uproar in Congress after this statement led him hastily to exonerate all legislators from suspicion, but resulted in Congressional demand for all the facts.

This investigation was the Administration's chief attempt to take the offensive in the fight. The Treasury believed a check of silver speculation would prove that much of the silver agitation had the backing of financially interested individuals. Stirred by the reports of vast hoards of silver in New York bank vaults, Morgenthau early in February ordered Treasury agents to obtain from the Commodity Exchange and the banks connected with it the names of large holders of the metal.

The buying and selling of silver for profit had long been practiced in the London and Oriental markets. But similar American activity dated from 1931 and the establishment in New York, under the impetus of the silver agitation, of the National Metal Exchange, later the Commodity Exchange. Probably the underlying cause of speculation, at home and abroad, was the belief that some action would be taken to improve the price of the white metal. American trading increased rapidly to a peak of 262,000,000 ounces in November, 1933.[35] It was obviously a profitable venture, as illustrated by the fluctuation in the price of silver between 26.7 cents in February, 1931, and 42.9 cents in November, 1933.

Yet the Administration considered itself directly concerned with the activity, knowing that no small part of the increase in price resulted from past or potential legislative measures on silver and from the government's general inflationary program. Furthermore, its leaders recognized the inevitable tendency of the speculative interests to promote the demand for action in favor of the metal. Finally, they realized the contradiction of silver as a commodity subject to speculative enterprise, and silver as a basic monetary metal.

The investigation was made on a national scale and was

not complete when the Senate, following Morgenthau's reference to speculation in high places, requested the findings. The Senators resented the implication that their own body was influenced by speculation, and they developed a strong antipathy to the investigation and to the Treasury for sponsoring it.

Meanwhile in February a poll of members of the American Economic Association showed that more than 85 percent opposed the increased use of silver. On April 26 the Economists' National Committee stated that no additional silver should be purchased at any price, for it "will not promote sound recovery, but will add to the liabilities of government and reduce confidence in the nation's currency. A rise in the price of silver benefits materially neither domestic industry nor the foreign trade of the United States."[36]

The legislative side of the battle on silver was fought entirely with heavy artillery. The tactics included special dinners, Congressional hearings, and conferences at the White House and the Treasury, to say nothing of numerous proposals for legislation. Typical of White House conferences of the period was one on April 19 with Senator King's silver delegation. Even at this late date the President was hopeful of holding out -- to the comment that the meeting had accomplished nothing, the President replied that he had not intended it should. Of the Treasury conferences, an example was the one on April 25 in which Senator Pittman, fortified by an expert from the Bureau of Standards and some fifty charts, tried to prove that an advance in the price of silver was always followed by an advance in the price of other commodities.

In Congress, the defeat of the Wheeler amendment was a signal for the introduction of more measures. Almost every active silverite sponsored a bill, so that for a time over forty proposals were in the legislative mill. The chief cause for delay was the inability of either house to agree on what it wanted. Gradually sentiment in the House crystallized around two measures. The Fiesinger bill proposed the purchase of 1,500,000,000 ounces of silver. But it lost out in the parliamentary precedence granted another measure. The Dies bill was probably the most perfect expression of the combined interests of silverites, farmers, and inflationists that Congress ever formulated. It proposed the acceptance of silver at not above a 25 percent premium over its world market price in payment for American farm products. The premium, to be paid by the government, was not to exceed

$400,000,000 a year, which meant acceptance of a minimum
of $1,600,000,000 and a maximum of $4,000,000,000 in silver annually. The magnitude of the plan is indicated by the
fact that the world output of the metal in 1934 was worth
about $92,000,000. The bill passed the House by a large ma-
jority, and the Administration became fully alarmed.

The Dies measure went next to the Senate Committee on
Agriculture and Forestry, where some additional projects
were added. As rewritten, it retained the farm surplus provision, but also called for the nationalization of silver and
for the mandatory monthly purchase of 50,000,000 ounces by
the government. Its passage was practically assured by its
appeal to the three groups. On April 21 the President vigorously repeated his repudiation of any mandatory legislation.

In this situation, the Treasury list of speculators was
made to play its role. On April 23 Morgenthau suggested to
the President that the time had come to "spring our silver
list."[37] The President not only assented, but suggested that
publication be dragged out over a period of several days.
Beginning on the twenty-fourth, and in three installments,
the Senate published the Treasury lists in twenty-six pages
of closely printed type.[38]

The lists contained the names of no Congressmen, but
they included banks, corporations, and business men, two of
whom had helped give a dinner on April 23 for Congressmen
interested in silver. The most sensational revelation was
that a half million ounces of silver futures were owned by
"A. Collins, Royal Oak, Michigan." Miss Collins turned out
to be secretary of Father Coughlin's Radio League, and the
priest felt obliged to explain her purchases with funds of
the League and to denounce both Mr. Morgenthau and his
investigation, which, he added, "smells to high heaven."[39]
Indeed, the decline of the priest as a power in Washington
dated from this savage partisan attack.

For a few days the lists and Presidential opposition slowed
down the legislative plans of the silverites, and silver
dropped so sharply that the Treasury steadied the market
by purchases. Yet Congress, which might have been expected
to demand a more complete investigation of the speculation,
especially after Morgenthau had specifically recommended
it, allowed the matter to subside into silence. As strategy
for delaying action on silver, the lists proved a disappoint-
ment, for pressure from Congress resumed almost immediately.

Meanwhile, the Administration's retreat to a new line of

resistance was unobtrusively taking place. Accepting the inevitability of some legislation, the President thought again
in terms of compromise. At his cabinet meeting on April
27, impending silver legislation was discussed and the group
was asked whether he should compromise with Congress or
attempt to prevent all legislation. The political instinct of
the members produced a recommendation for compromise,
since they felt that a veto by the President of another important measure would be "most embarrassing for Congressmen at election time."[40]

Even after the decision to compromise, the President held
out for three weeks over the crucial mandatory feature. He
viewed silver as a small part of his currency schemes; he
feared the loss of independent action on the management of
the dollar; and in the mandatory purchase of silver he saw
his financial program endangered by the necessity for a
rigid, predictable program. He felt his Administration had
done a great deal for silver, and he correctly reasoned that
he already had sufficient authority to do anything he wanted
in regard to buying the metal and devaluing the silver dollar.
He had evidence from the Treasury that silver producers
were not turning in their silver under present purchase
plans, probably in a gamble on something better. And with
the achievement of his gold objectives in January, he wanted
a period of "wait and see." Finally, he did not like to be told
what he must do in any legislation. The battle of wills was
supplemented on the silver side by numerical superiority,
where victory was gradually won.

The last phase of the fight began on May 5, when a silver
conference was held on the train en route to the funeral of
the late Secretary Woodin. The President agreed to study
the silver proposals. Yet the mandatory feature was still
the stumbling block for a number of very confusing days. A
White House conference on May 8 advanced the field of
agreement but excluded any mandatory feature. The Treasury drafted the Administration's version of these agreements. When Morgenthau read it at a capitol conference,
Senator Borah walked out of the meeting in protest against
the lack of mandatory provisions.

A deadlock had been reached. Finally, at a White House
conference on May 16 the President gave way in his "second
compromise of 1934." It was a true compromise, as will be
seen, since neither side obtained all of its original demands.

The factors that led the President to this final action were
at least six in number. In the first place, he hesitated to

veto a **mandatory** bill because of the enemies it would create, and the embarrassment it would give campaigning Congressmen in the fall. In this he had the support of his cabinet. Second, he was highly desirous of keeping Congress in session for action on controversial labor and housing legislation that some of his own leaders opposed, and which, by prolonging the session, would probably prolong and intensify the silver agitation. Third, he was faced with threats that Senators Thomas, Borah, and others would make a campaign issue of remonetization and would filibuster on all Administration measures in Congress. Fourth, the President believed that by compromise he could still retain the power to dictate some terms, and thereby salvage principles that might be lost in a Congressional bill passed in revolt. Fifth, he was disappointed in the inflationary results of his gold program. He was vulnerable to those Congressmen who quoted statistics showing that the wholesale price commodity index had risen in thirteen months from 60.3 to 73.4, only 21.5 percent, while the gold content of the dollar had been reduced 41 percent.[41]

Finally, the timely article by Walter Lippmann on May 15 provided a formula for the compromise not yet reached. Senator Borah had it inserted in the Congressional Record, and the President is known to have read it. It called for some mandatory features, but proposed that the "execution of the policy should be permissive because Congress, when it adjourns in a few weeks, cannot hope to foresee all that may happen in the world until next January."[42]

On May 22 Congressional ears were treated to the sweet music of a presidential message on silver, the most musical part of which was that "the Executive Authority should be authorized and directed to make the purchases of silver necessary to attain this ultimate objective."[43]

The Silver Purchase Act was introduced immediately. Senator Thomas assailed it for not going far enough and Senator Long called it a "baby rattle," "another all-day sucker."[44] But as an Administration measure it received the rapid action of "must" legislation. The House held desultory hearings to which no opponent of the measure was called; they were noteworthy for Morgenthau's strong plea for the speculator's tax as an Administration policy.

There was small but violent opposition in both houses of Congress, where some felt the measure was inimical, not only to the public interest, but to the best interests of the Administration itself. Nevertheless, the bill was adopted

substantially as submitted. On May 31 the House voted its
approval by 263 to 77, and on June 11 the Senate accepted it
by a vote of 54 to 25. The opposition here numbered six
Democrats and nineteen Republicans. On June 19 President
Roosevelt affixed his signature.

Congressional majorities had spoken. Yet their vote is
difficult to reconcile with a later speech by Senator Pittman
in which he admitted: "A great majority of the people of our
country were imbued with the idea, by reason of the debates
in the 'Bryan Age,' that silver was a dishonest money....
whether they were right or wrong, that was their opinion,
and that is still largely the opinion of the majority of the
people of this country and majority of the economists of this
country."[45]

A summary of the Silver Purchase Act reveals its compromise nature:

1. The proportion of silver to gold in the monetary stocks
of the country was to be augmented so that ultimately one
fourth of the monetary value would be in silver. The fulfillment of the requirement meant the acquisition of more than
1,200,000 ounces of silver to match the current holdings of
gold. Yet before the year was over, the gold stocks had increased to such an extent that 125,000,000 additional ounces
of silver were needed to attain the required goal.[46]

2. The Secretary of the Treasury was to purchase silver
until this objective was reached. However, a permissive victory for the Administration left the rates, times, and conditions of purchase to the discretion of the Treasury. The one
exception was that no more than fifty cents an ounce be paid
for silver located in the country on May 1, 1934. An Administration provision, it represented an attempt to avoid rewarding those who had hoarded silver since the purchase
proclamation of December, in anticipation of further government activity. The December purchase price of 64.5 cents
for newly mined silver was not affected; nor did the Act put
any limit on the price for foreign silver.

3. The Treasury might sell its silver only when the metal
exceeded one fourth of the country's total stocks or when the
market price of silver exceeded its monetary value of $1.29.
In view of the large-scale gold purchases, the attainment of
the first condition was extremely unlikely; as for the second,
many Congressmen expected that a logical result of the Act
would be this maximum price.

4. The Treasury was directed to issue and circulate silver
certificates with a face value of the cost of all silver pur-

chased under the Act. One hundred percent silver backing was required in the form of new silver dollars, and all such certificates were to be legal tender. This part of the law was vague on the question whether certificates were to be based on the actual cost price of the silver or on its legal valuation of $1.29 an ounce.

5. The Treasury was given power to regulate silver trading. The Act provided for a 50 percent tax on the profits from silver-trading. Unpopular with many of the silverites, this provision was insisted upon by the Administration, with the purpose of limiting undue profits to any individual who bought silver speculatively in anticipation of government purchase at a higher price.

6. The Treasury might at its discretion nationalize all silver in the country.

EARLY EXECUTION OF THE ACT

At first glance the Act appeared to be a major victory for the Administration with its preponderance of permissive features, particularly on the purchase of silver. Some of the silver advocates objected to it on this basis, and the suspicion was widespread that the President would disregard it as he had previous silver legislation. This suspicion persisted even after the President, as part of his compromise, verbally committed himself to execute the Act "enthusiastically and in the spirit in which it was enacted," in exchange for exclusion of quantities and time limit for the purchase program.[47]

The suspicion gained new impetus with the early announcement by the Treasury of its minimum compliance with some features of the law: (a) its anti-inflationary decision to issue the new silver certificates on the basis of the actual cost of the metal, not on $1.29; (b) its determination to avoid excess inflation by retiring Federal Reserve notes to match every new issue of silver certificates.[48]

Yet the silverites needed to have no fear about the purchase program. Not only had the President made his "gentleman's agreement," but the Secretary of the Treasury took the cue from his chief and promised also to carry out the spirit of the bill enthusiastically. He came to look on his function as a direct mandate from Congress that he was obligated to carry out.

For a time he actually did enter into the spirit of the Act. He took great satisfaction in watching silver rise under the stimulus of his purchases. He described the nationalization of silver as the most exciting day he had experienced. But aside from the thrill of undertaking a big project, most of his enthusiasm was summed up in his own words: "...this was an obligation which the President had placed on me and I would feel that the President had every right to criticize me on his return if he found that we had bought so little silver."[49] A year later, when Senator Walsh, of Massachusetts, protested against the effect of the silver purchases on silver manufacturers, the Treasury Secretary replied that while the act was on the books he could do no differently, that "the silver law was started by the senators and not by the Administration."[50]

The Administration's insistence on equity was a role it played stubbornly and consistently. In most phases it was bitterly opposed by many Congressional silverites. But the course was based on the simple formula that no individuals were to be enriched as a result of any governmental action on silver, while the resistance was based on the belief in the freedom of silver to seek its own unrestricted markets.

The first evidence of government interest in fair play manifested itself at the time of the investigation into silver speculation. The second was in the Silver Purchase Act itself, through the limitation on the price of silver bullion already in the country, through the speculator's tax, and through the authority to nationalize. The third and fourth, still to be described, were the embargo on silver exports and the actual nationalization of the metal. In many other small ways the Treasury's execution of the Act sustained the principle of opposition to speculative benefits from government action, as well as to any semblance of runaway inflation.

On June 28 the Treasury suddenly clamped an embargo on the shipment of silver from the country except by government license. The move was the result of the realization that quantities of the metal were being shipped abroad where it could be kept safe from possible nationalization, and be allowed to reap the inevitable profit resulting from large-scale American buying. How far this export business had proceeded was not known, the Treasury merely reacting to reports of its agents in foreign silver centers.

Prior to his summer vacation President Roosevelt issued confidential instructions on the nationalization of silver, which was to be accomplished as soon as the price reached 49.5 cents, just short of the fifty-cent maximum provided for the purchase of American bullion. The time arrived on the morning of August 9, when the Treasury, in a dramatic series of purchases, forced the market up to the necessary level. Nationalization called in all the loose silver bullion of the country within ninety days, at a price of fifty cents and to a total of some 112,000,000 ounces.[51] The move seemed necessary to head off profits that would have accrued from raising the world price of the metal.

Even before the passage of the Act, the Treasury had bought in an effort to stabilize the silver. Now the Administration must start the wheels of silver purchases on a large scale and over a long period of time. Since Morgenthau was to be in Montana for the month of July, the President personally instructed Under-Secretary Coolidge to purchase at least one and a half million ounces a day. Then the President also departed from the capital.

Yet when Morgenthau returned on August 1, he found that in four weeks only 5,100,000 ounces had been purchased. Coolidge pleaded the great difficulties, disagreed with the entire program, and argued against aggressive buying that would draw on the Chinese and Indian supply. Thereupon Morgenthau took over the buying and continued at the helm through all the succeeding months of large purchases.

But the delay had caused the damage. Senator Thomas on August 1 opened a long series of agitations by the silver forces to compel maximum compliance with the silver acts. He charged especially that silver certificates were not being put into circulation as rapidly as currency expansion demanded, and he threatened to carry the issue to the people if the Administration did not take action.[52]

Secretary Morgenthau immediately announced that new methods for designing and printing had cut the time by two thirds, that already the one-dollar and five-dollar bills were rolling off the presses, and that the other denominations would follow in the near future. But he also asserted that it was not inflation to issue certificates only on the cost of silver.[53]

Yet the printing of new money was only one part of the mandate, which also required its immediate circulation. The President wanted some novel method such as distribution through a bank near Boulder Dam for the cashing of the workers' pay checks. He thought this would both dramatize the new issue and head off further criticism from Thomas. Such a procedure was not adopted, nor was it necessary to resort to the aid of William Elmer Mead. The so-called

"Christian Kid," arrested in 1936 after a profitable career of counterfeiting and confidence games, on his own assertion was commissioned by the President and the Treasury to help circulate new bills by selecting "worthy" citizens to buy at fifty cents on the dollar.

Rather, the Secretary of the Treasury chose to force them out through the Federal Reserve Banks, chiefly in exchange for other forms of money. During the year June, 1934, to June, 1935, the per capita circulation of silver certificates increased 74 percent from $3.17 to $5.52, and the total quantity from $493,000,000 to $810,000,000 or 64 percent. But by persistent Treasury policy, enough gold certificates, Federal Reserve bank notes and national bank notes were retired so that the total monetary stocks of the country increased only 11 percent and the total per capita circulation only 3 percent. Between 1934 and 1936 the monetary stocks increased 28 percent and the per capita circulation 11 percent.[54] This represented only a mild inflation, far from the hopes of Senator Thomas and his group. Furthermore, some of this increase in money resulted from the Administration's gold policy, the inflationary effects of which are difficult to distinguish from those of silver.

During this period of silver purchases, their quantity, cost, and source were secrets of the Treasury Department. Two considerations guided Morgenthau in concealing these details. One was the fear of the effect abroad, where exact knowledge of American intentions might promote speculation and other obstacles to the program. The other was the political aspect of the program at home, where the Silver Bloc never missed an opportunity to prod the Administration into a more zealous performance.

Realizing that swelling gold stocks inevitably raised the silver requirements for attaining a three-to-one ratio, Morgenthau in August tried two methods for slowing down the importation of gold. One was to bring over enough silver to equal the $300,000,000 favorable balance of trade and thereby "stop bleeding the rest of the world of its gold." The other was the attempt to prevent gold from leaving Europe at existing exchange rates, and even to foster the selling of gold abroad in exchange for silver.

Morgenthau's intention during this brief period was to reconcile the reserve requirements of the Silver Purchase Act with the seriously unbalanced distribution of the world's gold supply. But he soon realized that gold flowing out of the country was an unnatural movement which usually expressed a lack of confidence in the future dollar, and he shortly terminated all efforts to regulate the flow of gold, Its importation was resumed, and it continued at such a rate that after six years of large-scale silver buying, that metal was farther from its one-to-three ratio with gold than at the time of the passage of the Silver Purchase Act.

August became the starting point for heavy silver purchases on the open market, with more than 48,000,000 ounces acquired from nationalized and domestically mined supplies. During the next six months the average open-market purchase was 24,000,000 ounces. Purchases were made all over the world through various New York agencies such as the Chase National Bank and the firm of Handy and Harman. Only in the case of Mexico did the Treasury deal directly with a government.

These purchases slowly forced up the world price, with the United States in almost complete control of the buyer's market, and with Morgenthau in direct charge of the American program. By mid-October the price passed fifty-five cents, partly as a result of the new Chinese tax on silver exports. It remained at this price for several weeks; meanwhile the President intimated that he wanted the price up to 64.5 cents by the time Congress next met. He did not get the complete fulfillment of his wish, for more time was required. However, heavy purchases continued, bringing a serious dislocation of finances in China, Mexico, and Peru, of which the details will be explored later.

IV. DISILLUSIONMENT AT HOME

In a democratic country, like the United States, a represent-
ative has hardly ever a lasting hold on the minds of his con-
stituents.... Thus it is natural that...the members of poli-
tical assemblies should think more of their constituents than
of their party.

Tocqueville, II, 90.

To silverites and inflationists early in 1935 the millenium
appeared to be well on its way, and to be assured if the
Treasury could be stampeded into a one-hundred-percent
execution of the Silver Purchase Act and if some of the restrictions on silver trading could be eradicated. The story
of silver during the next six years is consequently the dis-
mal recital of the threats and investigations employed to co-
erce the Treasury into maximum compliance; the terrifying
effects of the American silver program on foreign countries;
and the growing disillusionment over the program among
large numbers of people, who were joined, as early as December, 1935, by the Secretary of the Treasury himself.

The Treasury's silver purchases had gradually pushed an
optimistic world market upward until, early in April, 1935,
the price approached 64.5 cents. By the proclamation of 1933,
this was the maximum the government could pay for new
domestic silver. But the Administration was willing to guarantee American producers at least as much as the world
price for their output. Thus there was general agreement
that the domestic price should be raised, but no consensus
of opinion on the amount. Morgenthau favored a 5 percent
raise to 71.11 cents, which could be made by lowering the
seigniorage rate from 50 to 45 percent. He wanted to keep
below seventy-two cents, since the Mexican peso was based
on that valuation, and a higher price would be devastating to
that country. His proposal carried the day and the proclamation was issued.[1]

This American advance of the domestic price stimulated
speculation in the London market, where a new high price
was reached. The rise was speeded along by the belief that
the metal had an important benefactor in the United States
government, whose actions were bound to raise silver to

$1.29 an ounce. The American advance also brought forth
large quantities of the metal at home, where American producers had held back in hopes of a better price from the
government.

Speculation began to concern the Treasury. However, as
the world price again approached the new legal limit for
domestic silver, the President and the Treasury were faced
with another decision. On the evening of April 24, upon hearing the garbled contents of a United Press release, an angry
Secretary of the Treasury recommended a further price
rise to the President, and within half an hour the necessary
papers were signed. The rise was to 77.57 cents. Asked
next day by newsmen if he always raised the price of silver
when he was aroused, Morgenthau replied good-naturedly,
"If they knew that they would know how to raise the price of
silver."[2]

The world market price reacted from this tonic as might
have been expected. On April 25 it jumped five cents, and
on April 26 it reached eighty-one cents, considerably above
the new American price. For the first time the Administration was confronted with serious doubts about executing the
price-raising requirements of the Silver Act.

The President realized that the American program promoted a speculative market. Morgenthau suggested $1.29
as the most likely price at which to shake out the speculators, and proposed a bargain with the Silver Senators by
which, in return for that price, they would promise no more
silver legislation during the current session of Congress.
The President emphatically rejected the proposal for the
two reasons that "I have at least 65 votes. I can positively
defeat any silver legislation, so the question of more silver
legislation does not need to be considered," and "the Administration would be criticized for giving the mining interests too big a subsidy."[3]

In that case Morgenthau preferred to use about seventy-
five cents as a maximum for a few months, since he felt
the advance had been entirely too rapid. They agreed to
hold the price, and to confer with the Silver Senators. For
the first time since the start of the program, the domestic
price was to be allowed to lag behind the artificially high
world price.

Morgenthau immediately called Pittman to ask what "sympathetic" Silver Senators should be called together. The resulting conference included Adams, King, Wheeler, Borah,
and Pittman. Morgenthau presented to the group a picture

of the silver situation. He admitted loss of control of the silver market and asked for advice on his next move. Even these "sympathetic" men split among themselves, though not seriously. While agreeing that speculation and an unnatural rise in price were undesirable, they differed on future procedure. The group finally agreed on Morgenthau's policy of "sitting tight," and broke up with an informal silverite-Treasury understanding.[4]

Significantly, however, Senator McCarran had not been invited. Later in the day he telephoned Morgenthau to bemoan the fact, whereupon the Secretary obligingly arranged a meeting at his home and answered the Senator's questions. However, McCarran did not consider himself bound by the conference agreement, as will be seen.

During the next few days Morgenthau embarked on a plan of lowering prices by making progressively lower bids in London. Only small amounts were offered for sale, until on April 30 no silver at all was obtainable. Morgenthau's common sense impelled him to sell some silver; he realized the law did not allow it, yet he recalled that the Stabilization Fund was provided to stabilize currency. The President agreed, thought the procedure legitimate, and authorized the sale of the previous day's purchase of 250,000 ounces. The scheme helped bring down the price slightly, and not more than two or three people in the Treasury knew of the operation. Thereafter, Morgenthau kept a million ounces in London in case of a sudden need to sell. The occasion arose again on May 14, when silver jumped three cents, and Morgenthau, with the President's consent, sold another 250,000 ounces.[5]

During these hectic days in which the Treasury was trying to re-establish control of the silver market, the program was faced with other crises. One was a revolt within Morgenthau's official family, when Under-Secretary Coolidge protested against the rumored rise in price to $1.29 and tried to make Morgenthau promise not to raise silver above seventy-five cents. When he threatened to resign, Morgenthau finally asked the President to explain the program to him. Coolidge stayed on.

Another disturbance was the continued agitation by the Silver Bloc. Senator Thomas had fired the first gun of a new silver-inflation campaign in August, 1934. During the fall he kept up a barrage of agitation in preparation for inflationary legislation in the next session of Congress. His appeal was chiefly to the debtor interests, and the key to his theme, "A falling price level has always brought unemployment, stagnation and depression."[6] In December the restive Bloc asked the Treasury for an accounting of its performance under the silver law, motivated by the conviction that the Treasury was not energetic enough in building up stocks of the metal.

Meanwhile, in view of the promise of high prices for silver, American production had begun to expand. From a low of 23,400,000 ounces in 1932, and even lower in 1933, it started its upward trend in 1934, and was to mushroom to 68,400,000 ounces in 1937. Copper mines that had been closed during the depression resumed operations. Although the prices of copper, lead, and zinc improved only slowly, mining companies found it profitable to increase their production in order to benefit from the price of silver that had nearly tripled since 1931.

For example, the Anaconda Copper Mining Company found it worthwhile to expand its great plants around Butte, Montana. The ore it treated contained 4 percent copper, and there were but two and one-half ounces of silver to a ton of ore.[7] However, the large quantity of ore handled made such operations feasible when prices of one or more of the metals were good. Anaconda operated on a deficit in 1931, 1932, and 1933, and not until 1934 did it show a profit.

The American Smelting and Refining Company illustrated the trend in an extreme form. It owned or managed mines in Idaho, Arizona, New Mexico, Utah, Colorado, Canada, Newfoundland, Mexico, and Peru, plus scattered interests elsewhere. Its low silver production of 44,900,000 ounces in 1932 grew to 76,300,000 ounces in 1934, and was to reach its peak expansion of 197,500,000 ounces in 1937.[8] Anaconda grew from 1,550,000 ounces in 1932 to 16,000,000 ounces in 1937;[9] and the Cerro de Pasco Copper Corporation went from 4,900,000 ounces to 9,800,000 ounces.[10] In 1934 and 1935 it reported that the value of its gold and silver production exceeded that of its base metals. Its agent, Bryan, Penington, and Colket, of New York, frankly observed that current silver prices and demand were increasing Cerro de Pasco's earnings, and that prospects of increased dividends appeared favorable. Even a concern such as the United States Smelting, Refining, and Mining Company, which did not increase its silver output, stated in its report for 1934 that its higher earnings were due to the increase in gold and silver prices at a time when prices for lead, zinc, and other of their products were "abnormally low."[11]

Altogether, the silver program perhaps helped all mines

producing that metal to recover somewhat more quickly from the effects of the depression than otherwise would have been possible and, furthermore, gave them confidence in continued aid for the future. Yet in estimating the exact benefits, a later study by the Treasury's Division of Monetary Research must be kept in mind. It suggested that the output of silver between 1924 and 1940 varied with a number of factors. For example, silver production increased most rapidly with general industrial production, with a coefficient of correlation of .86; copper production and silver production correlated at .85; price of silver and silver production, .81; lead production and silver production, .60. In other words, despite assertions by the Silver Senators and the mining companies, the price of silver was only a factor of third rank in encouraging silver production, while general business recovery stood first. [12]

The Seventy-fourth Congress met on January 3, 1935, and the first session ended in August. During that period a number of bills dealing with silver were submitted, but the subject failed to arouse much enthusiasm.

The Thomas proposal as whittled down in the Senate called principally for the issuance of silver certificates to the full monetary value of silver rather than its cost, and for Treasury authority to exchange gold for silver and to accept silver on account from other countries. The proposal was tacked to the Administration's $4,880,000,000 works relief bill, and passed the Senate. Despite Administration disapproval, the rider appeared likely to gain acceptance in the House. A five-minute speech by Chairman O'Connor of the Rules Committee apparently turned the tide. He appealed to the House to maintain its dignity, refuse to emulate the Senate, where minorities could control, throw out a rider that had no place in a relief bill, and not be stampeded by Senate threats of a filibuster. [13] The House refused to concur on the amendment, and it was deleted in conference.

Senator McCarran proposed the repeal of three sections of the Silver Purchase Act, which provided respectively for Treasury regulation of all silver transactions, the nationalization of silver, and the tax on profits from silver trading. Secretary Morgenthau vigorously defended the first two sections as necessary for the proper execution of the rest of the Act. On the speculator's tax he wrote the Senator categorically that "no responsible and just policy could have disregarded the question as to who should reap the advantage flowing from the Government's monetary action with reference to silver."[14] Nevertheless, the McCarran proposals were later passed by the Senate, and not until the next session of Congress were they rejected by the House, which considered them out of order since all revenue bills must originate in the lower house.

Consequently, no silver legislation passed Congress in 1935, just as Roosevelt had predicted. The inflationary sentiment of the previous year had relaxed slightly; agricultural support of silver measures had been partially diverted by the Administration's generous bounties to farmers under the Agricultural Adjustment Act.

Furthermore, the Silver Bloc had lost some of its earlier cohesiveness. There was no conservative wing of the group, since every member still kept his original aim of restoring silver completely to its former place in the monetary system. But the moderates were those possessing the patience to wait and see how the Silver Purchase Act worked out, having a little consideration for its foreign effects, and giving general support to the current Administration policy. The radical group now focussed much attention on the inflationary aspects of the silver program. They were the irreconcilables who were unsympathetic to the Administration's execution of the Act, favored repeal of the tax and other features of the bill, and wanted the price pushed to $1.29 immediately so that the next session of Congress could achieve complete bimetallism.

In general the Congressional groups of this period corresponded roughly to the currents of Western opinion:

a) the bimetallists, dating back to Bryan. They were interested in monetary theories rather than metal prices. They would be satisfied with nothing less than free coinage at sixteen to one.

b) the mining interests, who were hopefully waiting to open new mines until silver reached one dollar and stayed there

c) the rest of the population who had no interest in Bryan's economic theories or a financial stake in mining. They favored silver only because they had been told it would be a boon to the West. Only they were unqualifiedly satisfied with Roosevelt's silver policy. To date silver advances by Congress had not resulted in any great upturn of business in the West, but the assertion was made so often that higher silver prices would produce good times that a boom was seen just around the corner.[15]

At any rate, failing in its legislative objectives, the extreme silver wing resorted to other methods of pressing its demands. In June McCarran ended the silverite-Treasury understanding of April by calling a series of meetings to work for $1.29 silver. He requested Secretary Morgenthau to explain the recent drop in silver from its high of eighty-one cents, and asked him about rumors of silver sales. The Treasury answer, on which Pittman was consulted, called the disappearance of the speculative influences "a wholesome development," and added that the acquisition of 420,000,000 ounces in the last ten months spoke for itself.[16] Silent on silver sales, the letter dissatisfied McCarran, who demanded more explicit answers to his questions.

McCarran proceeded to call together two dozen Senators who set up a five-man committee to prod the Treasury. Significantly, the name of Senator Pittman was omitted from the list of those invited, indicating that his decisive support of the President's veto of the inflationary Patman Bonus Bill and his general backing of the Administration's silver policy had alienated him from the radicals. The distrust was mutual. Pittman once told Morgenthau that Wheeler, McCarran, and Thomas were unpredictable; that Thomas had no interest in silver except from an inflationary standpoint; that when he got a bright idea he "just shoots his mouth off;" that Thomas was back of much of McCarran's agitation; and that he, Pittman, would never let the Thomas amendment pass.[17]

The name of Senator King was also omitted, and here again the antagonism was outspoken. His moderation and his "Well, I'm standing by you, Mr. Secretary" set him apart from his more zealous colleagues. Of these men King sadly commented: "I don't know what...in the devil's getting the matter with those fellows.... the President and you did such a magnificent work and gave us that Silver Bill."[18]

In July forty-six senators appealed to the President for aid to silver; Roosevelt answered that the Act was being carried out vigorously and in good faith.

Meanwhile, revolt against the silver program had developed from the silverware industry of the country, which was effectively barred from purchasing domestic metal. Calling the high price of silver disproportionate to the general price level, Representative Joseph W. Martin, of Massachusetts, asserted that it would cause higher retail prices for silverware and a consequent reduction of sales. He asserted that 70,000 men, women, and children were directly dependent upon the manufacture of silverware, and that through 20,000 retail outlets a total of 225,000 more were dependent upon the silver industry for a living.[19]

Martin and Senator David I. Walsh, also of Massachusetts, introduced bills calling for a large annual allotment of silver for commercial purposes from the Treasury's stocks, at prices in line with the silver industry's ability to pay. The Senator's request for Morgenthau's support of the measure brought the famous reply that the silver law was started by the Senators and not by the Administration, and that Walsh should approach his capitol colleagues.

Nothing came of these bills in Congress. Their urgency disappeared with the falling price of silver during the summer, and not until the war situation several years later did the silverware industry face serious difficulty in obtaining its supplies from foreign sources.

The Treasury's buying policy during these months was notable for the reassertion of control over the world silver market. After the April crisis, silver dropped through the refusal of the United States to buy at speculative prices. During this period the President expressed satisfaction with the execution of the silver purchases. He stated a preference for the importation of silver in small weekly amounts rather than in large shipments that would "tip our hands to the world."

But in July disequilibrium again threatened the world market. Speculative interests probably caused a break in the price with the intention of smoking out the American policy. A collapse of the market was likely until Morgenthau stabilized it by large purchases. However, he bought at prices considerably below the open market price -- indeed, below the price many of the speculators themselves paid for the metal. He was criticized at the time for squandering government money in the old game of trying to save silver. Yet he was still operating seriously under the mandate of the Silver Purchase Act. Since he felt obliged to purchase, his manner of going about it had much to commend itself. It consisted of a continuation of his day-to-day policy designed to keep silver interests guessing and, incidentally, conducive to his acquiring silver as cheaply as possible.

At about the time of this flurry, Morgenthau broached to some of the silverites the idea of pegging the price of silver. But he ran into the alliance between silverites and Southern cotton interests, for whom Senator Bankhead believed he saw a higher cotton price resulting from higher silver. Therefore, Morgenthau had to be content with a policy of careful purchasing and a refusal to buy at certain prices, by which means he did in fact peg at various levels.

A sudden drop of about two cents in mid-August was apparently the result of the selling of "stale" holdings by speculative interests in London. Just as before, Morgenthau bought heavily during falling prices. On August 14, he acquired about 27,000,000 ounces, the largest day's activity to date under the program. By heavy purchases over a three-day period, he managed to stabilize silver at 65.375 cents, where it remained for a number of months.

However, the fall in price stirred a violent storm of protest from the Senate. Criticism of the Treasury program was so severe that Morgenthau broke his long-standing silence on purchases to give a clew to the magnitude of his recent activities. Thereupon, both McCarran and Thomas denounced purchases in a falling market as contrary to the purpose of the Silver Act, while Thomas, even after a conference with Morgenthau, promised a senatorial investigation of the drop.

At this juncture Morgenthau took the offensive. On August 14 he gained the sympathetic understanding of Senators Robinson and McNary, majority and minority leaders, and of Senator Pittman. He explained to each his concept of an "international battle between Great Britain, Japan and ourselves and China is the bone in the middle." The Chinese situation regarding silver will be explored in detail in another place. At any rate, Morgenthau believed that continued secrecy was essential for his program, and he pleaded to be spared an investigation that would publicize his purchases and tip off the world market.

Pittman obligingly promised to try to submit his own resolution for a senatorial silver committee of investigation so as to circumvent Thomas' threat. But the Senate campaign was being spearheaded by Thomas and McCarran, whom Morgenthau frankly admitted he could not satisfy, or even talk to because they were so unreasonable. In his extremity he called for help from George L. LeBlanc, a New York banker. LeBlanc was considered the one man who could reason with Thomas, and Morgenthau saw a way of diverting the Senator. As for McCarran, the Secretary was not so concerned in the present crisis over the Senator's drive to repeal the silver tax. And besides, as LeBlanc told him over the telephone, it was Thomas who was egging on McCarran; in addition, Pittman felt that McCarran acted more for the sake of publicity than anything else.

LeBlanc proved sympathetic to the Treasury position and

made a night trip to Washington to see Thomas on August 15, having first exacted the Senator's promise to postpone action in Congress until after their meeting. He did not alter Thomas' opinions on declining silver, nor was McCarran deterred from his repeal of the silver tax, which was adopted by the Senate on the same day. But by persuading Thomas to refrain from Congressional action for one day, he enabled Pittman to introduce a prior resolution for investigation. Thus a predominantly "friendly" committee was named, headed by Pittman, and Thomas had to be satisfied with being merely a member.

However, the creation of a Senate Special Silver Committee had a long-term significance. It did not hold hearings until 1939, but its existence was used constantly as a threat of hearings and investigations of Treasury policy. Furthermore, it became the special, yet official citadel of the Silver Bloc, which the Senate thoughtfully established for its members. All bills pertaining to silver were referred to it, where the majority of silverites were able to dispose of everything exactly as they wanted. The economist Walter E. Spahr later pointed out that there was no Senate Gold Committee or Paper-Money Committee or Peanut Committee or committee for any of the hundreds of industries that outproduced silver on the American scene.[20]

The foreign implications of the silver program became more painfully apparent during the fall of 1935. In November Hong Kong tried to sell 100,000,000 ounces to the United States, preparatory to adopting a managed currency. Although the offer was refused, Hong Kong nationalized silver early in December, and began to sell heavily on the London market.

China also offered up to 200,000,000 ounces as a prelude to leaving silver. Alarmed, Morgenthau in November proposed dropping the price to a point where neither Hong Kong nor China would find it profitable to dump their stocks. But the President, still attached to the idea of a high price, rejected the plan.

By early December Morgenthau had decided that the silver purchasing policy was increasingly futile. In surveying world currencies he found that all but one country had abandoned silver as a basic standard, and he termed absurd a silver-purchasing program for the sake of the silver standard of Ethiopia. At the present rate he saw the United States buying up all the free metal in the world and driving every silver-using country to paper money. He desired to take the artificial support away from the silver market and try to reach a price which would be supported by its intrinsic value, apart from the American program.

Morgenthau believed that he could "pretty nearly prove that two or three large corporations know several senators. One big official in a mining corporation said that they knew everything we are doing; that they learn it directly from the senators every time we do something on silver."[21] He had already come to view the silver program as the only monetary policy he could not explain or justify as Secretary of the Treasury, and he thought that exposing it would save the Administration much grief in the coming presidential election.

Although the President was not prepared to see the silver program exposed, he agreed that it was time to drop the price of silver. Morgenthau was surprised at his quick acquiescence but decided that perhaps he was also becoming disillusioned.

On Monday, December 9, the new policy was inaugurated. At the President's instigation, Morgenthau proposed to change the method of fixing the world price. Hitherto London had awaited American bids before setting its price for the day. Now the tables were to be turned; London must submit its offerings and price to the Treasury first, where they might be accepted or rejected at will.

A panic gripped the silver markets of the world, with a complete breakdown in the routine channels of trading. Panicky selling took place in India and Canada, while Mexico underwent a financial crisis. But the Treasury calmly went about its business, and between December 9, 1935, and January 20, 1936, worked the world price from sixty-five down to forty-five cents.

Senator Pittman welcomed the new program as an attack on British financial dominance. Since American producers were still getting seventy-seven cents for their silver, he told the Treasury he did not care what happened to the world price. Thomas, on the other hand, felt that the Treasury had lost money by the drop in price, and again threatened an investigation.

Gradually world markets settled to a semblance of normality. The United States was the chief buyer of silver during these days and so almost all her offers were accepted, even though at progressively lower prices. Meanwhile, Morgenthau listened to Mexican cries for help, worried about Hong Kong's dumping of large quantities of silver, and puzzled over which of China's requests he should honor.

Once the price of silver was on the run, the President wanted to pursue it aggressively. This operation represented a complete denial of the Administration's philosophy back of its acceptance of the Silver Purchase Act -- that of raising commodity prices by raising the price of silver. The Administration publicly abandoned the theory when Morgenthau announced that during the period of falling silver, commodity indexes had increased. He showed the President a chart that proved his assertion.

The second session of the Seventy-fourth Congress convened in January, 1936. Morgenthau's public relations stood him in good stead, for he was spared the newly threatened investigation of his silver policy. Senators Pittman and McNary, of the Silver Committee, had approved the price-dropping scheme, as well as the new schedule for buying Mexican silver. Even Senator Wheeler told Morgenthau he was entirely satisfied and would have done exactly the same.

Therefore, Senator Thomas was able to make little headway in getting more inflationary silver legislation through Congress, although he tried hard. To finance part of the proposed soldier's bonus, he suggested the seigniorage from the issuance of silver certificates to the full monetary value ($1.29) of all Treasury silver. The proposal would have been mildly inflationary by providing several hundred million new dollars. Secretary Morgenthau had always avoided this method of valuation, and the Senate followed suit by defeating the Thomas proposal in January. Thereupon Thomas introduced a bill proposing the retirement of the Civil War greenbacks by silver certificates based on a new big purchase of silver. This bill never left committee. Other measures, including a first attempt at the repeal of the Silver Purchase Act, likewise made no progress.

In May the Economists' National Committee on Monetary Policy recommended to Congress the cessation of silver purchases and the repeal of the silver acts, together with the disposal, as advantageously as possible over a period of eight years, of the silver held by the Treasury. The report was signed by a long list of the country's leading economists.[22] Senator Pittman took the occasion of its publication to make one of his long speeches in Congress. He spoke of the great benefit to China of American purchases of silver, failing to mention that the American policy had first prostrated her, and omitting a list of all the other failures of the Act to do what had been claimed for it.

Although President Roosevelt had once desired to maintain seventy-five-cent silver into the election year, he had long since changed his mind. The Democratic platform called for "sound currency" without mentioning gold or silver. The nearest to a silver speech that campaigner Roosevelt made was at Denver when he said: "When we laid the ghost of the old gold parity of the dollar, when we purchased gold and purchased silver too, you in the mountains felt the old thrill of the search for precious metal. Old developments again became profitable. New developments sprang up. Mining became again an industry where men could find jobs."[23] Morgenthau later admitted that both he and the President avoided silver during the campaign. For a year the Secretary had felt the Treasury's silver policy was the least defensible of its activities.

But the Republicans dared not raise such a minor issue which might lose them votes in the mining and agricultural states. Their platform was as noncommittal as that of the Democrats. Candidate Alfred M. Landon favored a return to the gold standard but had nothing to say about silver, deliberately side-stepping a reporter's question in Denver in favor of a discussion of fishing.[24]

Consequently the election could in no way be considered a referendum on the silver policy. Most of the nation was still unaware that there was a silver issue, concealed as it was by so much other New Deal legislation. Those parts of the voting population directly concerned with silver undoubtedly voted for the re-election of Roosevelt, but other issues claimed their support as well, so that the silver vote was difficult to distinguish. At any rate, the election brought no immediate change either in the executive or legislative attitude toward the Silver Purchase Act.

Silver received little attention during the first session of the Seventy-fifth Congress in 1937. Bills for repeal of the Silver Act were introduced into both branches of Congress but did not get out of committee. On this occasion Senator John G. Townsend, Delaware Republican, made his first appearance as sponsor of the antisilver legislation that was to be connected with his name for several years.

The rumor was circulated that the Administration would try to repeal the Silver Act. Senator Wheeler telephoned Morgenthau to learn if there was any truth in the story and to threaten a fight. The Secretary reassured him by promising that if he ever decided to work for repeal, he would call the Silver Committee together and announce his intentions expressly.[25]

Congress in August passed legislation providing for a silver storage vault on the military reservation at West Point, New York. Ever since the accumulation of the Treasury's silver hoard, storage had presented a serious problem, and the Treasury had temporarily solved it by renting vaults in New York City. But it had wanted a silver depository similar to the one for gold at Fort Knox, Kentucky. As early as 1935 Morgenthau asked the Army for its ideas on such a vault at either Philadelphia or Albany. The President favored purchasing the Rogers estate adjoining his Hyde Park home and using the depository to house the records of the Rogers forest that were being maintained for twenty-five years. Morgenthau had doubts about public reaction to a location so close to the President's home and the jokes that would circulate about the President's billion-ounce hoard in his back yard.

The War Department made a counterproposal for locating the depository at West Point, listing eight possible sites. The Treasury was immediately interested and started investigating the possibilities. The matter dragged on during 1936, and early in 1937, Nellie Tayloe Ross, director of the Mint, attempted to confer with some Treasury assistants on a definite location. The Treasury officials refused, on Morgenthau's word that the matter rested between the President and himself.

The long delay over location was caused in part by the interest in the Rogers estate of the Duke of Windsor and his wife, the former Wallis Simpson. As a friend of some members of the Rogers family, the Duchess was being offered the property. Morgenthau was not greatly disturbed, for he had never changed his opposition to the Treasury's use of the site. Finally, on March 1, 1937, he obtained the President's approval of a depository at West Point. Congressional action in August was followed quickly by construction during the winter.

This session of Congress was noteworthy for one other action regarding silver. During the previous two years a racket had developed in commemorative coins, which their sponsors insisted should be made of silver rather than base metals. Most of the coins were fifty-cent pieces which were sold at a premium to raise money for local anniversaries. The Treasury had protested against these special issues because they complicated the bookkeeping of currency in use, and suggested medals as an alternative. Finally, with a huge backlog of proposals for silver coins before it, Congress in June approved three that were holdovers from the previous session with the understanding that no more would be accepted, and the practice subsided.

As the end of the year approached, blood pressures began to mount over the future of domestic silver after December 31. On that day expired the operation of the London Agreement and the President's proclamations on the purchase of newly mined silver. The Administration renounced any effort to renew the international agreement, so the discussions in Washington centered around the government's continued purchase of new American silver. The debate waxed hot with Morgenthau's privately expressed opinion that all subsidies, silver or otherwise, should be stopped and the budget balanced.[26]

However, Senator Pittman took another view and disseminated it widely. He pointed out that the recession, which started in October, plus the uncertainty over silver, was causing fears and stagnation in the mining industry, and that the purchase of American silver must continue. He told Congress that 400,000 people had been given employment through government action on the metal.[27] Senator Alvah Adams, of Colorado, carried the statement further. He asserted that the government annually spent at least $800 for each person on relief, a total for the miners if they were unemployed of $320,000,000. But the government had wisely kept them employed at the bargain rate of $112,700,000, its expenditure to that date for the American silver output.[28]

Pittman's statements were challenged by the Economists' National Committee on Monetary Policy, while Morgenthau sent researchers to the Bureau of Mines to learn the correct employment, which he thought was about eight thousand. But he inadvertently revealed that the President was preparing a proclamation on silver purchases in 1938. Since such a move was unnecessary if the program was to be terminated, the silverites took heart that buying would be continued. Then a hue and cry arose over the price, while considerable editorial opinion was expressed, mostly in opposition to an extension of silver subsidies.

The American debate worried the chief foreign beneficiaries of the policy. Mexico began to experience another financial crisis, while Canada and China both let their anxiety be known at the Treasury.

As the controversy raged over the proper price of silver,

Morgenthau and the President quietly settled the question in the White House. Each wrote down a price and compared notes. Each had written 64.5 cents. The President's proclamation extended the purchase of newly mined American silver for one year. In the face of pressure from Capitol Hill, courage was required to lower the price from seventy-seven to 64.5 cents. The silverites protested loudly, but in view of their fears of a lower rate, they were probably satisfied with the compromise the President offered. On the other hand, many thought Roosevelt should have used this opportunity to lower the price much more, or even to terminate this unpopular subsidy to a small group.

The year 1938 was notable for a re-evaluation of the silver program and a study of ways to remedy the harm already done. During the previous year some silver producers had inaugurated a program of research into new uses of the metal; they were impressed by the decline in the monetary demand for silver, and feared the eventual termination of support from the government. The so-called "Silver Producers Research Project" sponsored work at the National Bureau of Standards and at several universities and research institutions. Investigations had revealed many promising uses such as the lining for containers used in the food, drink, and chemical industries; bearings for airplane parts; bactericide and fungicide for purifying drinking water and fish hatcheries; electrical contacts; and brushes. Even at the current price of $6 a pound, silver was considered as adaptable to industry as tungsten at $9, platinum at $525 and other industrial metals at even higher prices.[29] But the tremendous value of this research became fully evident only under wartime shortages.

The silver program itself underwent increasingly serious scrutiny and attack. Some of the Silver Senators began to question foreign buying, especially from Mexico where American oil wells were expropriated and high tariffs enacted. Senator Arthur H. Vandenberg, of Michigan, introduced a resolution requesting information on the Mexican silver purchases, which, however, was not adopted. Representatives John Taber and Bruce Barton, of New York, labored against the silver program without results.

The Treasury had maintained its price for foreign silver at forty-five cents since January, 1936. Late in March the London market dropped somewhat and Morgenthau lowered his price to forty-three cents, which he maintained for the rest of the year. This step was not taken without considerable soul searching in the Treasury. A careful study of the status of the silver program concluded that the original objectives were attainable only through maintaining or raising the price of silver. But Morgenthau rejected any such course of action, although he was still plagued with the moral obligation of executing a mandate from Congress.

A proposal to help world silver emanated from the Treasury, where Harry White, of the Monetary Research Division, proposed the establishment of an Inter-American Silver Bank. Though never adopted, the plan was significant as an attempt to salvage a program that was being maintained only through the organized vigilance of Congress, but that had long since been despaired of by its administrator, the Secretary of the Treasury.

Yet the irony of the situation was enhanced by the fact that 1938 became the peak year for silver purchases, with acquisitions of more than 400,000,000 ounces, nearly seven-eighths from foreign sources. Morgenthau had decided that the original purposes of the silver laws were either undesirable or unattainable, and that under the circumstances he could not possibly promote the world use of silver. However, since he was still charged with the execution of the program, he found new and to him much more important objectives for his silver purchases. In his dealings with Canada, Mexico, Peru, China, Spain, India, Siam, and many smaller countries, he brought the silver program forward as a major weapon of diplomacy, details of which are reserved for separate treatment. In the Western Hemisphere he saw an opportunity to implement the Good Neighbor policy, to bolster progressive governments, especially in Mexico, and to tie the American republics together financially. Elsewhere he saw a way, despite the Neutrality Law, of giving aid and comfort to those legitimate Chinese and Spanish governments with which the Administration sympathized in their fights for survival.

During the spring of 1938 the new depository was completed at West Point, and the Treasury contracted with a New York trucking firm to transport about 1,000,000,000 ounces of silver. The actual transfer started in July and continued for more than seven months. A long convoy of trucks traversed the fifty miles between New York and West Point early each morning, carrying fifty-six Coast Guardsmen in the procession. The route was changed from time to time and every possible precaution was taken to protect the silver in transit.

The metal was innocuous in appearance, a dull white without any of the glitter of polished silverware. The silver bricks, each about a foot long, five inches across the top, and four inches at the bottom, weighed seventy-two pounds and were worth $430 at the market price, or $1,290 at the statutory price. Every truck carried 320 bars, giving the load a value of $412,800 in government figures.[30] By the following February, when the 40,000 tons had all been moved, the government had a hoard at West Point worth more than $1,500,000,000.

Senator Pittman in September proposed to sell abroad the huge stocks of surplus cotton at a rate of ten pounds of cotton to one ounce of silver, with the government coining silver dollars to pay the cotton farmers.[31] At prevailing commodity prices, both the foreign buyers and the cotton sellers would benefit enormously, with the government footing the bill of administration and coinage. The proposal met little response.

Otherwise during 1938 nothing affected the silver program until the end of the year, when continued purchase of new American silver became an issue. In a frank appraisal of the arguments, Harry White concluded in a memo to his chief that the program should be renewed. He thought the decisive considerations were political because the current program of increasing Western buying power, while not as good as other methods suggested by critics of the program, was the only one "politically available" and therefore justified the silver subsidy.

But he reasoned that economic considerations, although of secondary importance, also favored the continuation of the 64.5-cent price. Admitting that most of the government's largesse went to the stockholders of a few mining companies, yet he pointed out the certain if small drop in national income, employment, and plant usage during the current recession. He also recalled that the purchase of domestic silver did not add to the government debt, since the Treasury actually made a 50 percent profit from seigniorage. He therefore concluded that economically, the weight of the argument tipped slightly in favor of continued subsidy. But he called it the least justified of "public-work expenditures," and the first one that should be curtailed as full employment was achieved.[33]

Consequently, Morgenthau recommended continuation through June, 1939, at the same price. The date coincided with the expiration of the President's broader powers over

gold and silver as originally set forth in the Thomas Amendment to the Agricultural Adjustment Act of 1933. The President agreed, and on December 31 the appropriate proclamation was forthcoming.

Meanwhile, storm clouds began to gather. The mid-term
elections of 1938 returned a strong Republican minority, together with some Democrats not particularly close to the
Administration. Among the latter were the survivors of the
President's attempted party purge, including some Southern
Senators and Pat McCarran, of Nevada. With the opening of
the Seventy-sixth Congress in January, 1939, the Administration was thus faced with a more determined opposition, which
on one extreme attacked the silver purchase program, and
on the other worked for even higher benefits to the silver
miners.

Senator John G. Townsend, spearhead of the attack during
the next two years, introduced a resolution calling for investigation of the silver problem, listing fifty-two objections
to the existing policy, and recommending suspension of foreign purchases of silver in the meantime.[33]

Pittman attempted to head off the creation of another, and
possibly unfriendly, silver committee by having Townsend
and three others named to his old Senate Special Silver Committee. This enlarged group of nine started hearings immediately. Nevertheless, Townsend introduced a bill to repeal
the Silver Purchase Act, to dispose of the surplus stocks of
silver, and to appropriate money for research into possible
industrial uses of the metal. Pittman countered with a bill
that would advance silver to $1.29 and limit foreign pur-
chases. Even Senator McCarran proposed a bill to abolish
foreign acquisitions. The considerable antiforeign sentiment
was directed chiefly at unreconstructed Mexico, with whom
the State Department was still struggling for a settlement.

Goaded by Townsend and other Republican members, the
Silver Committee opened a general discussion of the silver
program. One of Pittman's aces was a statistician who had
"some magnificent curves" to prove that the proceeds of all
silver purchased abroad had been used to buy exports in the
United States. His other ace was Secretary Morgenthau, who
was expected at least to be sympathetically neutral.

In clarifying his thinking for the hearing, Morgenthau
knew he opposed all government subsidies, including silver;
but he decided to revert to his old stand of carrying out
Congressional orders. Yet he had become so caustic of the

program that he feared under questioning that he would be diverted from noncommittal answers.

Morgenthau's fears were groundless. He attended what he called a humorous hearing on February 7. The brief farce was enacted along the lines laid down by its chairman, Senator Pittman. Since Townsend had decided he would not be present, Pittman seized the opportunity to table Townsend's repeal bill, "now that he's a member of our Committee." In their questioning of the Secretary, the Senators were so fearful he would trip that they treated him like a piece of glass five thousand years old and likely to break.[34]

Marriner S. Eccles, chairman of the Federal Reserve Board, did not fare so happily. During his appearance before the Committee, Federal Reserve policy was attacked as anti-inflationary to a harmful degree and therefore a drag on the improvement in business and industry. Tempers ran short as charges and denials followed, and Eccles attempted to show that prosperity depended not so much on the volume of money as on its turnover. He denounced the silver-buying program, even though, as he pointed out, he was from the important silver state of Utah.

Congressional attacks on the Silver Purchase Act continued throughout the winter and spring. Representative Taber lost a fight to reduce Treasury appropriations for execution of the silver and gold acts. Defeat resulted partly from an appeal by Representative Compton I. White, of Idaho, to save the only Administration monetary policy that had produced a profit.

Yet apparently public opinion was overwhelmingly in favor of an end to the silver legislation. During the winter a former member of the Literary Digest staff conducted a survey of editorial opinion on the subject of relations with expropriation-minded Mexico.[35] An incidental part of his work was the revelation that the country's newspapers were almost unanimous in condemning all the silver laws, particularly that part which called for continued purchases from Mexico. He quoted the opinions of some seventy-five representative organs in the East, South, and Far West, and even a few in the silver stronghold of the mountain states. His study showed that Southern opinion took no notice of the old alliance between cotton and silver, although Southern Senators had not changed their ideas.

Congress meanwhile started hearings on the extension beyond June 30 of the President's power over the dollar, linking it to a discussion of the termination of the silver pro-

gram. Senator Carter Glass, of Virginia, led the attack
against the President's authority and he was ably assisted
by Senator Robert Taft, of Ohio, who especially wanted to
abolish Roosevelt's powers under the Thomas Amendment
of 1933 to issue $3,000,000,000 in additional paper money
backed by silver, and which Roosevelt was quoted as calling
a desirable club to have tucked away in the closet. Morgenthau appeared before Senate and House committees to appeal for both the continuation of the President's authority
over the dollar and the permanence of the Stabilization Fund,
which, he pointed out, had been the instrument for stabilizing the dollar-yuan and the dollar-peso exchange by means
of silver and gold collateral.[36]

The fight continued through June, with a number of conservative Democrats and nearly all Republicans opposed to
extension. However, one argument began to prevail above
others -- that in view of the increasingly troubled status of
world affairs, the United States would be at a disadvantage
in dealing with foreign governments, most of which had cen-
tralized monetary powers, if the President lost his authority for prompt action. Consequently the House approved extension in April. Sentiment in the Senate favored continuance
of the Stabilization Fund but was opposed to other monetary
powers, although the Silver Bloc was willing to support them
if a higher price was promised for domestic silver. Chiefly
under Pittman's tutelage the Bloc was made to realize that
the enhancement of silver could not wait. He explained to
the Treasury that the copper mining companies had been
operating with a slight deficit pending a restoration of the
former price of seventy-seven cents; if this was not done,
these mines would close down on July 1 and send their employees on relief.

But at the end of June the news from Congress was encouraging, and yet the stocks of Anaconda Copper and of
Phelps-Dodge dropped 2 percent. Harry White saw evidence
that silver was now a negligible factor to the copper companies in view of improved markets for copper, lead, and
zinc. White felt that Pittman would have been more nearly
correct if he had confined his attention to those few small
companies producing only silver, for they were directly
concerned over its price. The largest and most profitable
was the Sunshine Mining Company, of Shouts, Idaho, which
produced one-fifth of all the metal in the country. For political reasons it proclaimed a shut down on June 30 in protest
against Congressional failure to raise silver. Yet it employed

only 550 workers. Furthermore, at sixty-four cents, the mine made a net profit of forty-five cents on every ounce of silver produced; at seventy-one cents it would make about fifty cents, and would increase its revenues by more than $500,000. Between June 1 and July 6, when Congress raised silver to seventy-one cents, the company's stock rose 50 percent, benefiting about 2,200 shareholders. After Congressional action, mine officials announced a resumption of business and a twenty-five-cent increase in the daily wages of its 550 employees. With company revenue raised by half a million dollars, this advance accounted for only 10 percent of the increase, leaving 90 percent to accrue to the mine owners in the form of earnings. White's conclusion was that the silver program directly helped only a very small number of people, all out of proportion to the cost to the government. [37]

With the silver claims in mind, Morgenthau boiled with anger at the filibustering Silver Bloc and vowed that he would "sit here until Hell freezes over before I buy an ounce of silver." However, his hands were tied, for the President had told him he would make a deal directly with Pittman in order to expedite Senate action on the removal of the mandatory arms embargo from the neutrality law. [38]

For six years the President had been able to command the unswerving support of one member of the Silver Bloc, in return for legislation that dealt kindly with silver. Roosevelt needed such a supporter as head of the Senate Foreign Relations Committee, and Senator Pittman occupied this post during a crucial period of world history. He worked well with the State Department, and responded to Administration calls for help during the long neutrality controversy in Congress, although he could not always swing his own committee into line, to say nothing of the entire Senate. Probably his ultimate service to the President was his introduction in the Senate of the court-packing plan in 1937.

Yet in 1939 Roosevelt was eventually forced to "buy" repeal of the Arms Embargo Act by agreeing to a higher price for domestic silver, since Pittman told him: "We have got 18 votes -- and what are you going to do about it?" [39]

Meanwhile, the President and his Senate leaders were disturbed by the continuation of what the President termed "an unholy alliance between the non-devaluationists and the silver bloc," led by Glass and Pittman, respectively. The President at first rejected higher silver prices. Senators Wagner and Barkley, fresh from brushes with the Silver

Senators, urged the President at least to extend the existing price of 64.5 cents for one year. His stubbornness aroused, the President agreed to make extensions for six months at a time, since he did not like a pistol held to his head and did not want to create the precedent of long extensions. In the end he authorized the Senators to commit him, in an extremity, to a one-year extension. Yet he also pointed out that Congress always had the right to raise the domestic price of silver by statute, and although he thought such an increase was unwarranted, he did not threaten to reject it.[40]

Acting upon this suggestion without making any concession to the President, the Senate on June 26 amended the House bill to discontinue Roosevelt's authority of revaluing the dollar, to increase by law the Treasury's purchase price of newly mined domestic silver from sixty-four to seventy-seven cents, and to prohibit further acquisitions of foreign metal. The silver Democrats were willing to sell the President short for this raise in the metal. Morgenthau replied by threatening that under seventy-seven-cent silver, the 50 percent tax on sales would be applied to domestic producers, hitherto exempt.[41]

· The vote to stop foreign purchases precipitated a panic in the world silver market, and the London price declined. After consultations with the President, who at first favored buying no silver, Morgenthau lowered his offers to match the London price, until on July 10 he renewed his support of the foreign market by adopting a price of thirty-five cents, a figure that prevailed for several years. Meanwhile, the Chinese, Mexican, and Canadian governments became excited at the prospect of the loss of the American market.

Two days later the House rejected the Senate amendments and the bill went to conference, where the fight continued. Its report restored Presidential powers, reduced the price to seventy-one cents and reinstated the authority to purchase foreign silver. The President kept the path to compromise open by rejecting the proposed price, and then promising not to veto it. But the Senate silverites were not satisfied with that price, while the conservatives continued to fight all of Roosevelt's monetary powers. The President was very bitter about the Senate campaign, which he labelled simple blackmail.

On June 30, the day the President's powers were to end, the House accepted the conference report, but a Senate filibuster prevented action before midnight. At 12:30 A.M. of July 1, the President was still waiting to sign the bill if it

passed that night. Both he and Morgenthau were in touch
with the capitol by telephone, ready to promulgate the necessary regulations and proclamations. Yet the vote appeared dangerously close, with opponents claiming the floor
for a series of speeches and emphasizing that the Presidential powers expired at midnight and could not be revived; in
addition, some of the silver Democrats were threatening not
to vote at all. Under the circumstances Leslie L. Biffle,
Secretary to the Majority, suggested that Senator Barkley
postpone a vote until after the long weekend created by Inde-
pendence Day. The Attorney General had prepared in advance an opinion that the President's powers in such a case
were not dead beyond recall, even after the lapse of the old
law. Barkley now had it read to the Senate, and then obtained
agreement for a vote on July 5 at five o'clock.

During this period, Morgenthau decided not to buy any silver, either foreign or domestic, because of the uncertainty
of Congressional intentions. But Roosevelt wanted the
Treasury to buy all day on July 5, at the falling world price,
so that he would have a bargaining point with the Silver Senators. Morgenthau was sure that the President would be
making so many trades before Wednesday that he would need
no additional arguments. Both Morgenthau and Barkley believed that the President's behavior would alienate more
people than it won.

The interim was used to persuade reluctant Senators,
particularly Democrats. Each questionable vote was worked
over. Biffle reported that a North Carolina Senator had
promised to be absent, that an Iowa Senator was safe, but
that some agricultural Senators were doubtful. Morgenthau
actively entered the fray by making suggestions and by asking the Farm Bureau to approach some Senators from the
mid-western agricultural states. He worked not to maintain
the silver program, but to continue the valuable Stabilization Fund and the President's other powers.

All possible support was rounded up, so that the final vote
supported the President by forty-three to thirty-nine. According to Senator Wagner, the opposition included nonde-
valuationists and some of the Silver Bloc, as well as
spokesmen for the oil companies and the Catholic church,
both of whom turned hostile eyes on continued purchases
from Mexico. The Senator told Morgenthau that only his
excellent record in the Treasury Department salvaged
enough votes to pull the bill through.[42]

The new law revived the silver program for another two

years. It continued the Treasury's power to acquire foreign silver merely by leaving all provisions of the Silver Purchase Act unchanged. It made the purchase of domestic silver and the price statutory, not a temporary and discretionary power of the President. Henceforth Congress would dictate the price of American silver. The President was forced to accept this provision despite his earlier rejection of higher silver, in order to keep his wider powers over money.

With the deletion from the final bill of the prohibition against foreign purchases, Senator Glass' subcommittee on Banking and Currency immediately undertook to pass the Townsend Bill outlawing them. It had previously won Senate approval as a part of the larger bill. But the new silver price mollified some members of the coalition and made their opposition to foreign silver less extreme. Furthermore, the President wanted continued authority to make purchases abroad because of their current assistance in Mexican relations and their potential help to Canada in the event of a European war.

In this respect Morgenthau differed widely with his chief. Now that his aid to China was terminated, he strongly opposed further foreign purchases. Politically, he thought it would be wise for the Democratic party to take the initiative for repeal away from the Republicans, since he believed that 95 percent of the people opposed foreign silver. Economically he could not justify its continued purchase, although some of his advisers were prepared to do so in terms of increased trade and employment. Morgenthau was ready to admit that the Administration had made a mistake. But with the adjournment of Congress early in August, attempts at silver legislation subsided for a time.

Congress reconvened early in 1940, and the Banking and Currency subcommittee quickly passed the Townsend bill. The full committee immediately took up the question and was on the verge of approving it also. Only the strenuous efforts of two loyal Administration stalwarts, Chairman Wagner and Majority Leader Barkley, both members of the committee, prevented a vote the same day. Over the telephone, each one learned the President's attitude: that adoption just before an election campaign was an admission of error in a part of the Administration's monetary policy; that the "good neighbor" policy would suffer by repeal.[43] The committee leaders persuaded the group to postpone a vote in order to learn more about the views of the State and Treasury Departments.

Meanwhile Frank L. Peckham, Washington agent for the American Metal Company, as well as several other interested persons, were laboring valiantly for the repeal of the 50 percent tax on silver trading. Silver producers and dealers had always resented this ban on speculative profits and thought that the end of foreign purchases was the natural time to terminate the tax as well. They managed to get tax repeal included in the Townsend measure.

Townsend asked Secretary Hull for his views on the bill. Only with difficulty was the Secretary deterred by his own department from declaring that so far as American foreign policy was concerned, there was no reason why the bill should not pass. After learning the President's ideas and their general support by the Treasury, Hull postponed his answer pending a discussion of the whole subject with the Treasury. However, he believed that the lower price of foreign silver had removed all diplomatic overtones, and thus created a problem primarily for other departments.[44]

The Treasury prepared a consolidated report of its silver activities for Congressional use. It showed that between June 19, 1934, and February 15, 1940, the great majority of the 2,300,000,000 ounces of silver purchased at a cost of $1,143,450,000 had come from foreign countries. It showed, for example, that the United States had spent $143,000,000 in Mexico alone for the purchase of 291,500,000 ounces.[45]

A prolonged discussion ensued within the Treasury over its future policy. The Department appeared almost isolated on foreign purchases with the defection of the State Department, the Federal Reserve and even the Silver Senators. Morgenthau favored the Townsend measure. He was sure that the bill had enough support to pass anyway, and that Administration opposition would result only in a humiliating defeat. He had long felt the silver program was silly -- "that is why I don't want to defend the damn thing."

However, members of his staff, especially Harry White, reviewed the dilemma in which the Department found itself. White pointed out that if the Treasury pushed repeal, it would be open to the accusation of inconsistency for pursuing a discretionary purchasing program so vigorously, and then considering the purchases unsound. Silver might fall as low as twenty cents, and the resulting deflation in the country's silver hoard would be serious. Politically, the purchases would be made to look like a mistake that was not recognized for seven years until Republicans "rammed it down their throats." Furthermore, and most important, the President had already expressed himself against repeal. Yet privately, even White conceived of the silver program as "initiated for rather silly reasons and supported for sillier reasons"; as "invalid, because the people who defended it knew only a little less than the people who criticized it."[46]

Consequently, Morgenthau appeared before the Senate committee to oppose a bill he really favored, a bill whose former friends had deserted it. The State Department was not represented at the hearings, and Pittman was so busy he sent a written memorandum. Morgenthau felt that everyone had left the burden to him: "I never was so lonesome in my life.... there wasn't a single...so-called friend of silver."[47]

After having held up the bill so long, Chairman Wagner allowed a vote on the day following Morgenthau's testimony. As the Secretary had expected, the bill was approved by the overwhelming vote of fourteen to four, nine of the fourteen being Democrats. Fuel was added to the flame of repeal when it became known that during the last quarter of 1939 the Treasury had acquired about $700,000 worth of Japanese silver. Actually the Treasury had not knowingly purchased Japanese silver since 1936, and then only in small amounts. But Morgenthau made little impression when he explained to Pittman that such purchases were unavoidable without specific legislation to prohibit them, and that the imports, moreover, were acquired from intermediate sources. Townsend publicized his estimate of the aid Japan was obtaining under the American silver program.

Senate consideration of the Townsend bill opened on April 30, when the sponsor led the attack on foreign silver. Administration leaders, although they had no enthusiasm for the measure, allowed it to come to the floor because it seemed the lesser of two evils, the other being the Walter-Logan administrative reform bill whose postponement was considered more essential. The Silver Bloc began to sense that repeal of foreign purchases might easily be followed by repeal of domestic purchases, and swung into action against the Townsend measure. Nevertheless, the bill was passed by a vote of forty-five to thirty-six. Administration leaders in the House refused to consider the bill, which they asserted was a usurpation of a constitutional right of their chamber. They held that since the measure included a repeal of the trading tax on silver, the whole bill should have originated in the lower house. Thus the hope of terminating foreign purchases of silver died with the Seventy-sixth Congress.

As a matter of fact, probably the President's only valid reason for wanting continued authority over foreign purchases was to maintain his power of helping those warring nations with whom the United States was in sympathy. Wartime changes in the value of and demand for silver later invalidated even this reason, for little foreign silver was purchased by the Treasury after 1940. Meanwhile, the European war and the defense of the Western hemisphere crowded all other items off the Congressional calendar.

Silver did not figure significantly in the Presidential campaign in which Wendell Willkie attempted to prevent Roosevelt's third term. The Republican platform promised outright repeal of the Thomas Amendment of 1933 and the Silver Purchase Act of 1934, and called on Congress to reclaim its constitutional authority over the currency.[48] The Democratic platform did not mention gold or silver, but made the most of the fact that "the dollar is the most stable and sought-after currency in the world."[49]

In August a significant experiment was undertaken that illustrated the rarity of silver coins in the circulating currency. The Russell Manufacturing Company of Middletown, Connecticut, paid its weekly payroll of $35,000 in silver dollars in order to learn more about the spending habits of its employees. The company was able to trace over 88 percent of the payroll in the Middletown area alone.[50]

The period of American armed neutrality brought continued gold imports far above those of silver, which for 1940 were the smallest since the start of the silver program. In view of the expanding business activity of the times, Harry White concluded that any previous political or economic justification for the purchase of domestic silver had disappeared. He recommended a return to the discretionary silver price as established under presidential authority, so that the price might be reduced.

Thus by early 1941 the whole Treasury Department was united in opposition to the silver program, with Morgenthau openly advocating a repeal of all legislation. Yet his long experience with Congressional vagaries forced him to seek changes in the program within the compass of his own authority. Consequently, during 1941 he gradually developed his wartime policy for the purchase and use of silver.

V. CONFUSION IN LATIN AMERICA

The great privilege of the Americans does not consist in being more enlightened than other nations, but in being able to repair the faults they may commit.

Tocqueville, I, 231.

MEXICO

From the earliest days of the American silver agitation, the position of Mexico was generally misunderstood. She was loosely grouped with the rest of Latin America as a silver-standard country and, therefore, as a sufferer from low silver prices: her purchasing power was reportedly cut in half, her credit destroyed and her trade ruined. It was thought that her plight could be helped only by the enhancement of the metal.

Actually, Mexico after 1931 employed the silver peso as her basic coin, although she fell short of a complete silver standard. Low silver prices never seriously affected the stability of Mexican currency, established as it was in a great silver-producing country where public confidence in the large reserves caused easy acceptance of silver and baser metallic coins of all denominations.

But as the world's largest producer and exporter of silver, she was deeply concerned over its price as a commodity. In 1930 silver constituted 12 percent of the value of her commodity exports.[1] Mexico was in no worse condition than those countries that relied heavily on the export of cotton, rubber, or other items that had felt the heavy hand of depression. Furthermore, a rise in price would directly benefit less than half of her silver industry, because more than half of her mines were in American hands, principally the United States Smelting, Refining, and Mining; the American Smelting and Refining; Cerro de Pasco; American Metal; Anaconda; and Kennecott companies.

A rise was desired by the government for other reasons. Mexican silver mines were much more responsive to the market price than those of most countries, since silver deposits were found in a relatively pure state. Consequently a brisk demand and good price for silver were the best ways of avoiding widespread unemployment in the Mexican mining areas. Furthermore, the government had always depended on its silver industry for large revenues from production and export taxes, which were never more needed than during the depression years.

Altogether, the Mexicans strongly favored both a stabilization of the world silver market and a rise in its price. They collaborated willingly in the London Economic Conference and agreed to purchase 13 percent of their own output of silver with the assurance that the United States was assuming the chief burden. They viewed the passage of the Silver Purchase Act with satisfaction, and by late 1934 much of their production was finding its way to the United States Treasury. Secretary Morgenthau early adopted the practice of dealing direct with the Mexican government, and the arrangement was mutually satisfactory.

Up to a certain point the Mexicans were pleased with the steady rise in silver, but they had a definite limit to which they would willingly see it go. Early in 1934 they had established a parity between their silver peso and the new gold dollar, so that the bullion value of the peso in American money was 71.9 cents an ounce; at that time, when silver was still low, such a parity seemed safe. But if world silver ever reached that level, their coins could more profitably be melted and the bullion sold abroad. It was with some apprehension, therefore, that they saw the American policy forcing the price from forty-five up past sixty cents.

Morgenthau had Mexican parity in mind at the time of the first rise in American domestic silver in April, 1935. He favored a price below seventy-two cents to avoid disaster across the border, and his proposal was adopted. Yet late in the same month the Administration carried the price up past seventy-seven cents and created the groundwork for upheaval in Mexico. Between these two dates several things happened to make Washington somewhat less sympathetic to the Mexican predicament.

Early in 1935 ex-President Abelardo Rodriguez of Mexico was a White House caller, and Morgenthau suggested that his government ponder the rising price of silver. Shortly afterward the Secretary discussed the silver outlook with director Rodriguez of the Central Bank of Mexico; the director obtained Morgenthau's promise of American gold if it was needed to bolster Mexican reserves. In March the Treasury sold 32,000 ounces of gold to Mexico as a "neighborly act" and intimated that more was available at any time.[2]

Morgenthau felt he had given the Mexican government adequate warning about the probable effect of his silver program. Therefore in mid-April Ambassador Najera failed to arouse his sympathy by complaining about the advance in silver. Morgenthau accused him and his government of being equally to blame for the rise in price by hoarding metal which, if sold, would help bring down the price; by buying speculatively in London; of being unappreciative of his good prices and his direct dealings, and of failing to take the steps necessary to meet the inevitable. [3]

Two days later one of Morgenthau's suspicions was confirmed by receipt of information that the Bank of Mexico had made heavy silver purchases in London, either to stimulate the market or to resell to the United States. Shortly it appeared that the purchase lacked the sanction of either the President or the Secretary of the Treasury, and Rodriguez was removed as head of the Bank.

For Mexico the die was cast when the President raised the price above seventy-two cents on the night of April 24. During the days leading up to this crisis great confusion existed in Mexican banking circles. The bullion value of the peso rose above its monetary value. Silver coins were in such demand that they disappeared from circulation. Small shopkeepers were the first to be affected, because silver for making change in ordinary retail trade was almost entirely lacking. The government knew that only a drop in the silver price would bring hoarded silver coins into circulation again, but it also knew that such a drop was unlikely.

Therefore, the Mexican government acted vigorously. On Saturday, April 27, it ordered silver coins to be surrendered to the government in exchange for one-peso notes, in duplication of American treatment of gold two years before. Bronze fractional coins were authorized. A prohibition was laid on the exporting or the melting of silver coins and a bank holiday was declared over the week end.[4] Meanwhile Roberto Lopez, Assistant Secretary of the Treasury, flew to Washington and joined the Mexican Ambassador in a Sunday conference with Mr. Morgenthau.

The Mexicans requested that the price of silver not be raised for one month in order to provide a breathing space for internal adjustment. Morgenthau repeated his charges

of Mexican speculation and manipulation as a cause of the
crisis. However, he promised wholehearted aid from the
Denver and San Francisco mints in stamping new silver
coins, effective speed up of the printing of Mexican paper
money, and regulations to prevent importation of Mexican
coins or silver melted from them. He referred to the President the question of holding the silver price during May.
Roosevelt was troubled about such a commitment, for he
doubted that he could sell the Silver Senators on the idea,
even with the object of keeping Mexico in the dollar bloc.
He finally authorized a promise that the United States would
attempt for one month to buy at no higher than seventy-four
cents. In return, Lopez promised no more speculation, and
in other ways attempted to prove his government's willingness to co-operate on the American program.

Morgenthau tried to convince the Mexicans of the importance of continuing to use silver coins. Learning that their
new law did not provide for a silver peso, he pointed out that
that meant Mexico was withdrawing from the use of the metal.
Sensitive about his mandate to increase the use of silver, he
asserted that many Americans wanted to see his policy fail,
and their argument was that as the price of silver went up
other countries would have to use it less. He reminded his
visitors of their joint responsibility for the future of the
metal.

Morgenthau was careful to keep Secretary of State Hull
abreast of all these conversations. Nevertheless, he soon
realized that the State Department resented his handling of
such affairs, for its officials desired that he make no commitment without consulting them. This conflict of views over
the foreign aspects of the silver program was to recur frequently.

Within the next few days Mexico settled down more nearly
to normal and the year 1935 became one of general prosperity. The country embarked on a managed currency with
confidence in its own silver reserves plus American gold
as needed. Silver sold at a good price, the government col-
lected sizeable taxes, and meanwhile made a profit from
reissuing the old coins with a smaller silver content. Indeed,
although the American program created a temporary crisis,
the danger was over and the country saw only fair days in
prospect.

Suddenly the rosy picture changed. On December 9 **Mr.
Morgenthau** stopped buying in London and deliberately

allowed the price to fall. The Mexican government reacted quickly. Thomas Lockett, American commercial attache in Mexico, telephoned Morgenthau to describe the new crisis and to seek a Treasury exchange of some Mexican silver reserves for gold.

Morgenthau was suspicious of Mexican motives, but in the middle of the call he talked to President Roosevelt and received authority not only to make the exchange, but to allow a premium price for the silver. Morgenthau requested Lockett to pass on this information, emphasizing that "the President of the United States and the Secretary of the Treasury are doing this as a gesture of friendship to the Republic of Mexico." However, he asked time to check the legality of the transfer. According to the London Silver Agreement, no country might sell demonetized silver, although Mexico asked him to waive the Agreement in this emergency.[6]

Subsequent investigation in Washington revealed the one-sided interpretation Lockett had given. Mexico's reserves were not in danger, and she merely wanted to unload silver for gold, for which she was proposing the sale of her entire silver reserve. Consequently, Morgenthau vetoed the whole proposal and suggested a conference with the Mexicans on the future prospects of the metal.

Secretary of the Treasury Suarez flew to Washington and, joined by the Mexican Ambassador, started conferring with Secretary Morgenthau on December 31. The latter first lectured the group on the American silver program, the snags it had hit in various parts of the world, including Mexico, and the Mexican need to co-operate as a matter of self-interest.

Suarez renewed the request for American purchase of Mexican silver reserves. Morgenthau refused until Mexico submitted some plan for an increased use of silver such as a circulating silver peso. But since he was already acquiring most of the current Mexican production, he assented to a definite purchase quota. The United States contracted each month to take 5,000,000 ounces of silver, the agreement to be renewable monthly.

Suarez also asked for some way of acquiring dollar exchange in a hurry. A formula was evolved whereby Mexico would leave a quantity of silver on deposit in the United States on which the Treasury would grant dollar exchange when it was needed. The transactions would not be considered loans, but merely exchanges of pesos for dollars.

Morgenthau further proposed a pooling of statistical information on silver, so that each country would have a maximum of facts on the world situation.

These and other conversations provided the basis for long-range understanding. However, the Mexicans occasionally protested against falling silver and frequently tried to sell their reserves in Washington. Morgenthau remained disappointed that the Mexicans did not help him "carry the burden of the world silver" by using more of it at home.

Consequently, in the spring of 1936 Suarez sent blueprints for some silver currency, and tried to sell 60,000,000 ounces of reserves. Morgenthau declined the purchase until the Mexicans produced something more tangible than plans.

Hence the Mexican government proceeded to execute its plans. At the end of August it replaced one-peso paper with silver coins and five-peso notes with silver certificates redeemable in silver coin or bar silver, while issuing smaller coins of higher silver content to replace current fractional currency.[7]

Several quiet months passed. Suddenly, in November, 1937, the Treasury became aware of a crisis that had been brewing for some time. The Mexicans asked for a loan, American purchase of a large quantity of surplus silver, and the continued monthly purchase of newly mined silver. A small factor in the Mexican crisis was the uncertainty over United States action on silver when the London Agreement ran out at the end of the year. Morgenthau allayed these fears by promising to continue the monthly purchases into 1938.

But the request for loans and surplus silver led to a long investigation of the Mexican internal situation. It was obvious that the country was suffering from a complicated and serious illness that Morgenthau thought, should not be treated as a small scratch "by applying adhesive courtplaster." Therefore, Suarez was welcomed in Washington for conferences in mid-December of 1937. Yet he was made to wait almost three weeks while the American government debated its own policy.

The delay was caused by the differing approach to the Mexican situation by the State and Treasury Departments. State's diplomacy on oil and land rights collided with Treasury's diplomacy on silver and the immediate support of a struggling neighbor. State believed that the Mexican problem was indivisible and that settlement should be general in scope, not piecemeal. Under the influence of this stand, the Treas-

ury reluctantly agreed to withhold concessions to Mexico
pending the outcome of conversations through diplomatic
channels.

The State Department had had a long disagreement with
Mexico since her revolution twenty-five years previously.
Mexico's constitution of 1917 provided for the breaking up
of the great feudal estates, but decreed compensation for
expropriations of agrarian land. The government had not yet
compensated American owners for their land, which was
being taken over in increasing amounts by 1937. American
concern was registered by Secretary Hull's strong condemnation of the expropriations and the assertion that "the sur-
est way of breaking up the good neighbor policy would be to
allow the impression that it permits the disregard of the
just rights of the nationals of one country owning property
in another country."[8]

An even greater cause of friction between the two nations
was the subject of oil property. The new constitution also
sanctioned nationalization of the nation's oil resources. For
more than a decade, it constituted a threat that was not carried out.

During the 1930's the Mexican revolution resumed dynamic
qualities under a Six-Year Program and a new president,
Lazaro Cardenas. This man had for his supreme purpose the
uplifting of the Indian and the restoration of his dignity in
the eyes of foreigners. In 1936 his government sponsored
the formation of one big oil union, the Syndicate of Petroleum
Workers. By autumn of that year the workers, backed by the
government, were strong enough to seek concessions from
the oil concerns.

Responsible Mexicans maintained that they were only trying to do for their workers what the New Deal was doing in
the United States. On the other hand, the companies, both
British and American, declared that the granting of the extensive union demands would make their operations unprofit-
able and would compromise their jurisdiction over their own
industries. Protracted negotiations proved fruitless, and appeals to government boards invariably brought rulings in
favor of the union demands.

The American State Department had been interested from
the beginning in the progress of the oil negotiations. By December the emphasis of the Department was on a general
settlement of the whole Mexican situation, in which concessions should be made first by the Mexicans before financial
aid was extended to them. Economic adviser Herbert Feis

believed that they expected the United States would not refuse them anything they asked because Ambassador Daniels
"has a benevolent outlook on his wards down there so anything they do he perchance has a tendency to approve."[9]
Under-Secretary of State Sumner Welles conceived of the
task of his department as cleaning up all questions between
the two countries, "to give them fair and reasonable treatment, and...the treatment we had given them on various occasions was neither fair nor neither fundamentally conceiv-
able in decent relations with another country." He considered
that the American oil companies had adopted an inept policy
that was creating one more controversy to be settled.[10]

At first Morgenthau was inclined to agree that the problem
was indivisible and that a total solution was desirable. But
gradually he changed his mind and decided that the Treasury
should find some way of helping the Mexicans immediately.
Increasing evidence became available that Mexico was undergoing a serious crisis. Business uncertainty, withdrawal of
foreign capital, slow-down of industrial activity, and unfavorable balance of trade all gave indications of a depression.
The government needed increased revenues, which it proposed to get in part from new high tariffs that would be pre-
judicial to the extensive American trade. The first step toward tariff change was taken while Suarez was in Washington.

Morgenthau became concerned over the seriousness of the
Mexican troubles. He felt that the democratic regime should
be helped over its emergency, and that a long-term adjustment of the relations of the two countries could then proceed
through the State Department. Assistant Secretary Taylor of
his own department thought the emergency did not warrant
separate action and recommended that the Mexicans "cool
their heels for quite a period." Morgenthau resented the suggestion; he also disliked the State Department request that
he refrain from buying Mexican silver until other matters
were settled. He had no patience with Welles' interpretation
that "if the Treasury does not cooperate, the other pieces...
will not be put together."[11]

Morgenthau was caustic of the State Department policy of
delay, which he feared might have disastrous results. "We're
just going to wake up and find inside of a year that Italy, Germany, and Japan have taken over Mexico...it's the richest
-- the greatest store of natural resources close to the ocean
of any country in the world.... They've got everything that
those three countries need."[12] His fears were motivated by
several facts:

It was known that as early as 1935 German firms had attempted to gain barter agreements with Mexico, and that by midsummer of that year the first of them had been concluded.[13] Others were made in the next few years. The Germans wanted oil badly, but had to be satisfied with cotton, rice, and minerals. By 1936 they stood second only to the United States in both Mexican imports and exports.[14]

A powerful group of Mexican critics of their own government consisted of wealthy landowners and aristocrats who favored the Fascist side in the Spanish civil war and looked with delight on German intervention. On the other hand, the Mexican government and the great majority who were benefiting from its program were profoundly committed to the Loyalist side of the struggle.

Mexican intellectuals and liberals believed that friendship with the United States and Britain was of primary importance during the current troubled international situation. A rupture in relations might allow Mexican oil to find its way to Germany.

Finally, the Japanese fishing fleet had an important concession on the west coast of Mexico. It threatened the American fishing industry and, furthermore, caused the American navy considerable concern.[15]

Morgenthau on two occasions reported his fears concerning Mexico to the President. He recommended that the country's rehabilitation should be handled under Roosevelt's prescription for the reorganization of a big public utility: provide aid and charge according to the ability to pay. On both occasions he urged his thesis that if the United States did not help Mexico, Italy, Germany, and Japan would gain a predominant influence there.

Meanwhile, long but fruitless conferences had been going on in Washington between State, Treasury, and Mexican officials. On December 29 Morgenthau decided that his duty lay in helping Mexico immediately by buying her silver, while State continued its own diplomacy. Welles finally agreed with the differentiation between the short and long term aspects of the problem and gave his assent to the purchase of 35,000,000 ounces of silver.

The overwhelming gratitude of the Mexican delegation at the news of the purchase at a good price reassured Morgenthau that his decision was right, "because I think with any kind of sympathetic treatment, intelligent treatment, we may be able to help them pull through and have a friendly neighbor to the south of us. And I think it's terribly important to keep the continents of North and South America from going Fascist."[16]

Admittedly the month-to-month purchase of 5,000,000 ounces of silver and the immediate purchase of 35,000,000 ounces settled none of the basic issues between the two countries. The Mexicans wanted Treasury help in reorganizing their finances. The Americans, on the other hand, were insistent that a settlement on oil was imperative. The oil companies continued to assert that they could not operate under the conditions proposed by the Mexican government.

The dispute raced toward a climax on March 1, 1938, when the supreme court of Mexico supported the previous decisions against the foreign companies. A stalemate was reached, during which the companies refused to obey the order and the government declined to back down. Faltering negotiations continued during which offers and counteroffers were made. Finally, on March 18 Cardenas broadcast the expropriation of those companies involved in the labor troubles, thereby touching off three days of national celebration.

In view of the deadlock, expropriation seems to have been inevitable. But the State Department refused to accept it as final. It set its machinery in motion to get a reconsideration of the decision; barring that, it was prepared to demand adequate compensation. Secretary Hull feared for American oil interests in Columbia and Venezuela if Mexico was allowed to get away with such a coup d'etat.[17] Some elements in the State Department would not have been disappointed at the collapse of the Mexican government, hoping for a new regime that would have been more generous in recompensing Americans for their oil lands.

State's dilemma was, on the one hand, the desire to protect national rights and property and, on the other, the knowledge that the Treasury continued to subsidize and therefore encourage that country by its purchase of silver. Herbert Feis intimated to Morgenthau the desirability of a discontinuance of silver purchases. Feis acknowledged that such a move would be chiefly psychological in its results on Mexico. Therefore, he proposed to fortify it on economic grounds by allowing the world price of silver to decline. His plan amounted to a form of sanctions against Mexico, but Morgenthau was asked to try to consider the entire matter from the point of view of the wrong being done American interests, and to read State's cables on the subject.

Morgenthau spurned the cables. He felt that his silver purchases to date had been handled as a monetary matter and

he did not propose to let silver be used as a political weapon.
If he stopped buying in Mexico, he still could not terminate
the purchase of Mexican silver in London. Therefore, he
felt that the State Department's solution of the problem was
a bluff. He repeated his contention that Mexico's difficulties
could still bring a repetition of the Spanish situation. Yet he
admitted that if American foreign policy was involved, he
must accede to a State Department request, although he insisted on a formal request to that effect.

The request came on March 25 in the form of a suggested
statement of policy: "In view of the decision of the Government of the United States to reexamine certain of its financial and commercial relationships with Mexico, the Treasury
will defer continuation of the monthly silver purchase arrangements with Mexico until further notice."[18]

Morgenthau consulted Senators Pittman and McNary and
was surprised at their concurrence in the move. He wired
the President for approval, and meanwhile gave the State
Department his own reluctant acquiescence. He understood
that the policy entailed a simultaneous announcement by the
two departments, and joint assumption of responsibility.

This understanding was not shared by the State Department,
and consequently the relations with the Treasury were further
strained. Through diplomatic channels the State Department
notified its representatives in Mexico City before any reply
had been received from the President. Inadvertently, the
Mexicans were informed in advance of an announcement in
Washington. From the tone of the Mexican releases, Morgenthau was made to appear entirely responsible for an act of
which he personally disapproved. Furthermore, American
newspapers used the words "reprisals" and "retaliation" in
describing the move.

Morgenthau's ire knew no bounds when he learned of Hull's
press conference from which the following release emanated:
"Secretary Hull said that the suspension of Treasury Mexican silver purchases is primarily a Treasury function ....
He stated Treasury informed State Department of its decision to withhold further purchases before Treasury notified
Mexican Government of this action."[19] Morgenthau obtained
from Welles a promise that his department would correct
this unilateral publicity. Hull later told the press that the
Treasury announcement was the decision of the government
and that it spoke for itself.

The Mexicans were shocked and angry at the suspension
of silver purchases. They were now faced with a loss of mar-

kets for both their oil and silver. Mexican oil firms were already experiencing boycotts by American firms when they tried to order pumps and oil machinery. Ambassador Josephus Daniels described the boycotts as appearing to the Mexicans "items of tough economic pressure from north of the Rio Grande."

On the subject of silver, Daniels wrote Washington that purchases should be considered on their own merits and "should certainly not be made to seem a device for punishment." He recorded that in 1933 Mexico had received twenty-six cents for her silver and in 1938 up to seventy cents. The effect of the cessation of purchases was serious because 100,000 heads of families were employed in the silver mines, whereas the oil industry employed only 16,000. The government received 10 percent of its revenue from silver, and the National Railways obtained 17 percent of their income; silver also provided the major source of foreign exchange. Furthermore, mine owners, mostly American, were infuriated because they felt that they were being made to suffer for the deeds of the oil companies. They raised a loud protest, since they owned 80 percent of the mining industry, which spent millions of dollars in the United States for mining equipment.[20]

On March 30 some of the tension was relieved with Secretary Hull's announcement that "This government has not undertaken and does not undertake to question the right of the Government of Mexico in the exercise of its sovereign power to expropriate properties within its jurisdiction," and that the only problem was now one of proper indemnification.[21] Cardenas immediately wired his gratitude to President Roosevelt, and somewhat later the Mexican Congress also thanked him, adding that world democracy had found its two most vigorous representatives in President Cardenas and President Roosevelt.[22]

Economic conditions within Mexico showed little improvement. The country remained enthusiastic about the oil expropriations but was stunned by the apparent enmity of the United States. Yet a Treasury study by Harry White concluded that there was every reason to expect that Mexico, if helped over a long crisis, would make full restitution to the foreign oil companies; otherwise, adverse American tactics would "result only in driving Mexico to seek assistance elsewhere and/or into political and economic chaos."[23]

Consequently, the Treasury formulated its own solution to the situation. Its main proposal was a large loan of silver to

Mexico at moderate interest, conditioned on the settlement of all the snags in Mexican-American relations. Morgenthau interested the President in the idea. Both of them were especially well-disposed toward the Mexicans after their recent note to England on the subject of expropriations, in which they courteously reminded the British that "even powerful states cannot always pride themselves on punctual payment of all their pecuniary obligations." The President thought it was a "peach."[24]

Feis summarized the objections of the State Department to the Treasury plan. He felt that the Mexican government was irresponsible and could not be trusted to carry through such an agreement. He thought that no settlement of the oil problem was satisfactory that included control over oil operations by the industrially backward Mexicans. He feared the effects of such a precedent on other Latin American governments, and anticipated American public opinion that the government was making a loan in order to bail out the oil companies.[25]

After March, 1938, the most pressing problem for Mexico was the embargo against her oil in all the markets controlled by the British and American companies. This action included the denial to Mexico of about 88 percent of the oil tankers of the world. So effective was this embargo that Mexico was without markets. At the same time she was under considerable pressure from the oil-hungry states of Germany, Italy, and Japan. Together they had sufficient tankers for the Mexican trade, and they offered attractive commercial inducements. But President Cardenas preferred to sell to the democracies as before, and held off a decision on trade with Fascist countries for several months.

Unsuccessful negotiations with Mexico continued. In July a vexed Secretary Hull asked Morgenthau to lower the price of silver about a cent. Hull explained: "Well, we are having lots of trouble in Mexico and you know the President and Daniels have given the Mexicans the impression that they can go right ahead and flaunt everything in our face." Warming to the subject, he continued: "Daniels is down there taking sides with the Mexican Government and I have to deal with these Communists down there and have to carry out international law." He accused Daniels of constantly going over his head to the President, and, by implication, of hamstringing all efforts at a reasonable settlement of the controversy. Morgenthau refused to change the price of silver without some valid excuse, which he did not feel had been made.[26]

Yet Sumner Welles later stated that it was the personal insistence of President Roosevelt that prevented a highhanded and domineering attitude such as the United States would undoubtedly have adopted a few years earlier.[27] Furthermore, the Mexicans were fortunate in having such a walking delegate of the Good Neighbor policy as Josephus Daniels. Through his sympathetic understanding of the goals of the Mexican government, he won a high degree of respect and affection. When the oil dispute reached a crucial stage, he refused to act as a police-court lawyer for the oil companies. With the backing of his government, he admitted the right of expropriation, while insisting upon prompt and adequate compensation to the companies.

American newspapers and magazines clamored for a stronger policy toward Mexico, according to a current survey of editorial opinion.[28] Although the survey was financed by the Standard Oil Company of New Jersey, yet the two hundred and seventy papers and eighteen magazines included in the study represented most of the leading organs of opinion from every part of the country. The Wall Street Journal, the Journal of Commerce, Fortune, and the Annalist all figured in this groundswell of opinion, which was directed against expropriation as well as against the silver policy.

Western opinion indicated intolerance of expropriation and a willingness to stop buying silver from Mexico. The Silver Bloc felt the silver program would not be endangered, since the subsidy to American interests would continue. Acting on the rumor that the United States was again buying Mexican silver, Senator King tried to get the Treasury to stop the practice. The Treasury refused ostensibly because the Silver Purchase Act required silver acquisitions and because the Mexican output would still come to the Treasury by way of London.

Actually, silver purchases had been resumed, but on a different basis. The Mexican government was now placed on the same level as all other sellers of silver, with no guarantee of specific quotas and prices. But the continuity of sales nevertheless helped the government to bridge the gap caused by the reduction in its revenues. Furthermore, Morgenthau saw them as the best and only weapon to use against the economic penetration of Mexico by Germany.

Yet in these months of isolationism, the negotiations between Washington and Mexico City accumulated wide support for Secretary Hull and the State Department policy, whereas the attitude of the Treasury had fewer adherents. The Mex-

icans were more impressed by the continued silver purchases than by the fulminations of the State Department, and
the negotiations were undoubtedly slowed down. The deadlock
arising between the size of the monetary claims of the oil
companies and the Mexican evaluation of the worth of the
property still had three years to run.

In spite of all the assistance the Treasury could give Mexico on silver, it could do nothing to solve her oil problems.
Eventually that country was forced to turn to other markets,
especially Germany. In order to sell to the Germans, barter
methods became necessary. Consequently, Mexico bought
where she sold, and American exporters felt a loss in commerce. The oil companies charged that this new trade in oil
was a betrayal of democracy. In reply, the Mexicans pointed
out that the expropriated British and American companies
were selling Germany 68 percent of her total oil purchases.[29]
So complete was the world-wide embargo against Mexican
oil, and so great her difficulties in oil management, that her
exports for nine months after expropriation decreased 67
percent.[30] Contracts for trucks and oil equipment from
abroad were not honored. When Mexico had tankers built in
Italy, Great Britain refused their passage through her blockade, and they were confiscated by the Italian government after the outbreak of war.

After the start of warfare in 1939 the German market for
oil was lost, but the democracies gradually resumed their
purchase of the Mexican output. However, by the end of the
year another financial crisis was brewing in Mexico. In addition to continuing difficulties with her currency and commerce, she now was faced with the prospect of the complete
discontinuance of American silver purchases.

This situation arose in 1939 from the unsuccessful campaign by the American press and Congress to repeal the Silver Purchase Act. The Mexican crisis, described by Daniels
as "difficult days...while the Senate is discussing the silver
question," quickened with the renewed attempts at repeal in
February and March of 1940. When a Senate subcommittee
approved repeal of foreign purchases, new monetary and
banking flurries occurred in Mexico, and a commission was
created to bolster the nation's banking structure against the
shock of American legislation.

Despite Morgenthau's testimony, the Senate Banking and
Currency committee voted to abolish foreign silver purchases. This vote caused further consternation in Mexico,

where the effects of repeal were direly forecast, Mexicans fell back on the expectation that in an extremity President Roosevelt would veto the measure. In the United States, newspapers editorialized on Mexican relations with reminders of the expropriated properties, and such phrases as "our sympathies are dulled"; "they have been living on our bounty so long that they no doubt would resent being cut off"; "there always remains the question of the value of trade which can only be obtained by bribe"; "Mexico sold us her silver at inflated prices and showed her appreciation by expropriating American...properties."[31]

By late March, Mexico's economy had been stabilized. Officials were confident that the internal situation would not be vitally affected by American action on silver. However, they were spared the trouble because the lower House of Congress, more responsive to presidential desires, checkmated the Senate action on foreign purchases.

In April, 1940, Hull proposed arbitration to break the deadlock on oil. The Mexicans refused, considering "arbitration incompatible therewith, since the matter is domestic in nature and is near solution by the authorities of Mexico."[32] Yet the principals in the dispute were still far apart. The oil companies claimed a loss of $400,000,000, including oil underground; the Mexican government estimated maximum indemnity at $25,000,000, excluding oil underground.

In the summer of 1940 the Federal Bureau of Investigation checked on alien influences in Mexico. It was concerned over Communism in some of the agrarian settlements and with Nazi attempts to create internal chaos and undermine American prestige One FBI report made the future of Mexico largely determined by the "firmly constructive attitude of our Government in its dealing with Mexico"; another pointed out that "the silver purchases by the American Government and the income derived from American tourists constitute the only real income of the country," that the current political setup was based on the fact that "the Mexican people are not getting what they need to exist." The Nazis were being financed by the German government, and both they and the Communists seemed intent on creating such confusion that trouble would be unavoidable. The FBI also revealed the details of a Mexican economic mission to Japan in March, where the fifty members were wined and dined by the Japanese, and exhorted concerning the imperialism of the United States. They returned with large trade agreements involving Mexican oil.[33]

Eventually, the sweep of world affairs broke down the obstacles to a restoration of the friendly relations between the two nations. By the spring of 1941 the subversive work of the Germans and Japanese had conjured before the Mexican government the faint possibility of an invasion as a bridgehead to the western hemisphere. Mexico possessed the will to defend her borders, but neither the materiel nor the means to acquire it. The United States had need of a friendly nation on its flank, but the principal obstacles were the old unsettled controversies. Sumner Welles became increasingly aware of the danger of a situation like that of 1917.

Consequently, in February, 1941, the State Department listened to a Mexican request for American co-operation to purchase her silver and to stabilize her peso. In referring the request to the Treasury, State again attempted the treatment of the entire Mexican situation, and this time with more fortunate results.

Revitalized discussions between State, Treasury, and Mexican officials got under way during the spring, and they covered every claim of one country against the other. By July the United States had agreed to purchase all Mexican strategic materials, in return for which Mexico promised not to sell such items outside the Americas. The oil question was narrowed down to the size of the immediate down payment, for each government had agreed to appoint experts to determine the eventual indemnity.

In the course of the negotiations the Treasury agreed to a $40,000,000 loan for stabilizing the dollar-peso rate. It also assented to a monthly purchase of 6,000,000 ounces of silver, prices to be quoted daily. This was substantially a renewal of the plan of 1936, but included an extra million ounces each month.

The State Department's negotiations were not as quickly concluded, for they embraced several issues. Part of the delay resulted from the refusal of the Standard Oil Company of New Jersey to co-operate in the proposed system of valuation. The formula promised to hurt all the oilmen's coffers, and it was with difficulty that they became reconciled to the idea that their claims and investments must in large part be sacrificed to the war effort, and that they were persuaded to accept the $24,000,000 compensation.

Thus in the final settlement, the United States paid a big price for good will, which, however, turned out to be a good investment. The country had need of some such a demonstration of the Good Neighbor policy. The generous settlement

,fortified the idea of continental solidarity; it bolstered the Mexican government in its fight against Axis sentiment; it later made Mexico the willing partner of the United States at the Rio de Janeiro conference in achieving real continental unity.

These results occurred just in time -- the agreements were finally signed on November 19, three weeks before Pearl Harbor. They dealt with all the outstanding problems between the two countries, and settled them outright or appointed commissions for the purpose.[34] The joint announcement carried the statement: "These arrangements are practical evidence of the good-neighbor policy. These agreements are based upon the principle that the welfare of the two countries is mutual and that common monetary and economic problems can be settled in a spirit of friendly cooperation."[35]

Nevertheless, the Treasury did not again purchase Mexican silver. Domestic wartime uses of the metal had increased so greatly that American dealers protested against the Treasury's proposed monopoly of the Mexican market. Morgenthau willingly cooperated by refusing to pay more than thirty-five cents for foreign silver. Merely by bidding a fraction above that price, industrial users were able to obtain almost the entire Mexican output. The Treasury renewed its bids each month in 1942, but Mexico preferred the slightly higher open market. Throughout the war the Mexicans had no difficulty in selling all the silver they could produce at increasing prices.

Since November, 1941, the mutual problems of the two countries have been settled amicably and relations have become increasingly friendly. The greatest impetus to close understanding was the community of interests created by the war, leading to Mexican entry into the conflict on June 1, 1942 The series of crises in Mexican internal affairs which began in 1935 was now at an end. They varied in seriousness and in some cases turned out to be nothing more than fear of the termination of bounty from the United States. Yet in their inception several of them were the direct consequence of the Silver Purchase Act and the subsequent vagaries of Congressional action, which made impossible any long-term planning by a government that of necessity counted heavily on its most important mineral product.

Furthermore, the Axis threat to Mexico between 1939 and 1941 cannot be over-emphasized; even after the Mexican declaration of war in 1942, many of the people in their confusion rejoiced at the prospects of joining Germany in a war

against the hated gringos to the north. American help and
sympathy was a leading factor in upholding a democratic regime and of preventing the establishment of an unfriendly
government beyond the Rio Grande. In that activity, silver
played an important part. (See Appendix for a summary of
American purchases of Mexican silver)

PERU

As the world's fourth largest silver producer, Peru always
had metal for sale, since her own coinage system employed
it only in a subsidiary capacity. At London in 1933 she committed herself to withhold from the market some 17 percent,
or about 1,000,000 ounces, of her own production.

When silver prices soared in April, 1935, Peru shared the
Mexican experience of silver coins being melted and sold.
Hoarding became serious, while melting and exporting of
silver brought as much as 100 percent premium. Early in
May the situation reached a critical stage, and Peru issued
an emergency prohibition against hoarding, buying, selling,
or exporting silver in any form.[36] On the following day the
shortage of small change became so acute that the government ordered a large number of one-sol notes to be printed
in the United States, and she undertook to print half-sol notes
for herself.

The Treasury started buying Peruvian silver in a small
way in 1935, and during the next and succeeding years stepped
up the purchases considerably, although not under an agreement such as existed for the purchase of Mexican and Canadian silver. However, the dearth of small change continued
during most of 1935, and the situation was aggravated by the
poor quality of the new half-sol notes, which were replaced
by copper coins in September. By December, with the decline
in the price of the metal, silver coins began to reappear in
circulation. But the net result of the year's crisis was an
appreciable decrease in the use of silver in coinage.

Even more than in the case of Mexico the Peruvian silver
mines were owned by foreigners, a fact that made the Treasury ponder the difficulty of helping Peruvian nationals. About
62 percent of the production was owned by an American company, Cerro de Pasco; 18 percent, of which seven was contracted for by Cerro de Pasco, was owned by Peruvians
themselves, and the remaining 20 percent was owned by other
foreign interests, including the American Mining and Metal
Company, a French group and an English group.[37]

Meanwhile, Peru's large production continued undiminished In order to find a steady market, a Colonel Fuchs came to Washington late in 1938 to obtain a monthly sales quota. He was told that the Treasury was not so much interested in purchasing silver as desirous of developing closer monetary co-operation with countries of the western hemisphere. Peru should build up her silver reserves and otherwise increase her use of the metal.[38] Discussions were started, but the Colonel was recalled for a more detailed exploration of the subject at home. An arrangement was never reached, but large purchases by the Treasury continued through 1941. (See Appendix for a summary of American purchases of Peruvian silver.)

CONCLUSIONS

In addition to the large purchases by the Treasury of Mexican and Peruvian silver, somewhat smaller quantities were acquired from other Latin American countries between 1934 and 1941. Substantial amounts were purchased from Honduras Argentina, and Bolivia, with the Dominican Republic, Ecuador Nicaragua, El Salvador, Cuba, and Chile also figuring in the traffic. (See Appendix for a summary of these sales by quantity and cost.)

These purchases, added to those from Mexico and Peru, show that in the seven years prior to Pearl Harbor the United States acquired 388,665,000 ounces of Latin American silver for $181,940,000. The United States in the twentieth century followed in the footsteps of the Spanish conquistadors of the sixteenth century in their insatiable appetite for the silver of Central and South America.

Yet although the United States accomplished its tremendous transfer of the metal in a mere seven years, the earlier Spanish acquisition of an equal amount required a period lasting from 1500 to 1620. During the remainder of their exploitation to 1660, the Spanish added only another 150,000,000 ounces. At that time this quantity of silver caused a revolution in Spanish prices, wages, and economic welfare that permeated all of Western Europe.[39] Yet so large are modern currencies, so high a price was paid by the Americans, and so carefully were the acquisitions controlled, that they caused little more than a ripple in the American price structure.

The modern acquisition of silver was also much more beneficent than the ancient. The Americans not only bought the silver, but they paid artificially high prices for it. The func-

tioning of the Silver Purchase Act coincided with the Roosevelt Administration's attempt to rehabilitate the relations
between the United States and the republics to the south. This
attempt had its diplomatic, economic and cultural aspects,
and came to have the name of the "Good Neighbor Policy,"
from the President's happy choice of words in his first inaugural address.

The policy got under way slowly, for there were many
long-standing prejudices against the United States in Latin
America. The program was retarded as a result of the financial turmoil in almost every country during the first half of
1935, which stemmed directly from the Silver Purchase Act
and its price-raising goals.

Mexico in April became the first nation to be driven to extreme measures. In the next few weeks several other countries found it necessary to call in silver coins, prohibit melting or exportation, and issue new currency of paper or base
metal. Some of the countries were Peru, Costa Rica, Guate-
mala, Columbia, Ecuador, Uruguay, El Salvador, and Bolivia.[40]
Thus the Congressional policy decreased the use of silver in
Latin American countries, where the metal had a long tradition as the chief component of the currency. The policy also
created doubts about the sincerity of the nation that could
cause this inconvenience.

However, opinions changed when it was learned that the
administrator of the silver-buying program would help establish new currencies, print money, and take excess silver
at the current inflated price. Beginning with Mexico, most
of these hard-pressed nations sought advice and help from
Washington. They found a Secretary of the Treasury who was
thoroughly imbued with the Good Neighbor policy. When
Treasury officials told Colonel Fuchs, of Peru, that they
were more interested in close monetary co-operation within
the hemisphere than in purchasing silver, they were imple-
menting the neighborly policy in its financial aspects,

Consequently, the silver program became an important
means of welding a firm hemispheric union that stood the
United States in good stead after Pearl Harbor. Silver buying
continued through 1941. It played a part, between the outbreak
of war in Europe and the attack on Pearl Harbor, in relieving
the economic distress resulting to Latin America from the
loss of her normal markets. For example, in 1938 Peru obtained 25 percent of all her foreign exchange from her cotton
exports.[41] But after the start of war in 1939, her trade was
disrupted and she lost markets. Yet the American silver pur-

chases in Peru from 1939 to 1941 inclusive totaled $10,896,-
000. The amount did not begin to fill Peruvian needs for exchange, nor did silver purchases in any of the other countries. Therefore, resort was made to the facilities of the
Export-Import Bank in Washington to tide over several governments during the period of financial and commercial
strain.

It is small wonder, then, that after Pearl Harbor, Costa
Rica immediately joined the United States in making war,
followed closely by all the other Central American republics,
those of the Caribbean, and Panama. By January, 1942, the
governments of Mexico, Columbia, and Venezuela had broken
diplomatic relations with the Axis. In that month the American countries at Rio de Janeiro adopted a resolution recommending the suspension of relations by each nation. Peru
hastened to carry out the resolution, and she was followed
eventually by the rest of South America.

Undoubtedly, the United States can regard the $180,000,000
spent for Latin American silver as a good investment for the
future. It has already paid dividends in hemispheric solidarity during wartime, and has laid the groundwork for its continuation in peace. More important to this solidarity in the
long run is the new technique of consultation among the Americas. At the same time that the State Department was holding
meetings to reach joint decisions in the face of common
perils, the Treasury was seeking closer monetary co-operation and exchange of information with these same countries.
Neither activity would have been complete without the other.

VI. CONFUSION IN CHINA

*Each citizen is habitually engaged in the contemplation of a
very puny object: namely, himself. If he ever raises his looks
higher, he perceives only the immense form of society at large
or the still more imposing aspect of mankind. His ideas are
all either extremely minute and clear or extremely general
and vague; what lies between is a void.*

Tocqueville, II, 77.

Careless American statements that half the world was on
a silver base were inaccurate in view of the picture by 1930.
India and most other Asiatic nations for various lengths of
time had been on some kind of a gold standard. Therefore,
attention here will be focused on China, where free and unlimited coinage of silver still existed.

By 1930 China had become the leading silver importer of
the world. The metal served chiefly as a medium of exchange
and as a store of value. Since ancient times the Chinese had
regarded it as wealth, and had hoarded it in great quantities
against hard times. Copper and paper circulated for most
small business affairs, but silver had a long tradition as the
chief money for wholesale business and public finances.

As the price of silver dropped to its 1931 nadir, American
interests became convinced that silver-using countries could
not engage in world trade with such a depreciated currency.
The picture of a vast but incapacitated market for American
goods became a rosy glow on the horizon of depression. As
early as 1930 President Hoover told the American Bankers'
Association in Cleveland: "The buying power of India and
China, dependent upon the price of silver, has been affected."[1]
Even a Chinese business man in New York, Mr. K. C. Li,
stated: "The low price of silver is the principal reason why
the American surplus of production cannot be distributed in
Asia, Europe and South America "[2]

The Senate proposed aid for the Chinese at hearings in
1931. The loss of trade with silver-using countries was be-
moaned in this language: "Their purchasing power...has been
reduced one half, their credit destroyed, trade restrained,
and their utter ruin threatened."[3]

The earliest Senate plan was a loan of silver to China, which the Chinese did not want and reportedly would refuse if it was offered. Their country was full of silver, and during 1930 they had even talked of a duty on its importation. It was a proposal, ran one comment, to cure the dog's bite with a hair of the dog itself. Yet the subcommittee that sponsored the proposal sent its chairman, Senator Pittman, to China to study the situation. He returned with much additional information on the subject, none of which changed his opinion of China's needs.

During 1931 and 1932 the correlation between the buying power of silver countries and the world depression received wide publicity in the United States. The Wall Street Journal stated that Chinese exchange would naturally decline with the fall in silver. Dr. Julius Klein, Assistant Secretary of Commerce, blamed the low price of silver for the loss in both import and export trade with China.

Congressional hearings repeatedly attempted to study Chinese economics. It was estimated that with silver at thirty cents an ounce, the Chinese dollar was worth twenty-one cents in international exchange, and five of them were needed to pay for one dollar's worth of American products.

Indeed, there seemed to be no end of the public figures who gained an audience by expounding the nature of the silver crisis in China. Many American business men thought they saw a solution to the problem of world trade, and consequently of the depression. But the silverites, mostly concerned with their own interests, wanted higher silver for other reasons than its commercial advantages to China. Yet only a few people ever considered exactly how their theories applied to China.

To begin with, the low price of the metal was advantageous to a nation that was the world's most important buyer not with, but of silver. China was able to obtain large quantities annually at a saving that was then applied to her purchase of other commodities. To a nation possessing an unfavorable balance of trade that was aggravated by war, flood, and famine, this low price of silver was important.

In the second place, abundant statistics proved that Chinese trade more than maintained itself during the depression. For example, in 1931 the price of silver declined 25 percent from the preceding year; yet the United States actually increased her exports to China by 1.2 percent, although she experienced a decline of 38 percent in her exports to all other countries.[4] The price of silver was only one of many factors in China's trade, for her ultimate purchasing power depended not on the price of silver, but on the goods and services sold by the Chinese to foreigners.

Yet it must also be added that even in 1930 China and Hong Kong absorbed only 2.2 percent of the world's total imports and contributed 1.6 percent of its exports.[5] Even if their international trade could be doubled by raising the price of silver, it was difficult to discern the glorious benefits to American trade and the quick termination of the depression that many Americans proposed.

Third, evidence was available that under low silver China possessed an advantage in relation to the depression-ridden, gold-standard countries. She was undergoing a mild inflation and relatively prosperous times. The index of her cost-of-living items closely paralleled the price of silver.[6] This is best illustrated by a comparison of her price level with that of other countries. The following figures represent the percentage of change in wholesale commodity prices in September, 1931, from the high of 1929. Every country except China showed a greatly reduced level:

United States	-29.5
Canada	-28.9
United Kingdom	-29.2
France	-28.3
Belgium	-31.3
Germany	-22.0
Czechoslovakia	-25.5
Italy	-31.0
Denmark	-31.4
The Netherlands	-38.1
British India	-37.2
Japan	-40.5
China	-20.1

Source: U.S. Bureau of Foreign and Domestic Commerce, Commerce Reports, November 9, 1931, p. 301.

With such facts in mind one American banker asked ironically: "Why should it be good for China to raise her unit's value, if it is good for the United States to depreciate its dollar? If the gold countries want higher price levels, why should the silver countries want lower price levels?"[7] Probably the President himself never understood that raising the price of silver meant to China the exact opposite of raising the price of gold to the United States.

Such facts also caused two economists at the University of Nanking to conclude that "As long as China remains on a fixed silver standard, those who advocate and work for higher silver values are unconsciously working for declining prices and depression in China."[8]

Mr. Li Ming, prominent Shanghai banker, spoke for the businessman: "Instead of proving harmful, low silver prices have been largely beneficial to China. It might not be generally known that China, apart from her many trials due to conditions within her country, has not yet been dragged into the whirlpool of the world crisis. This is due entirely to low silver, a factor which instead of proving a curse to this country, had really been a blessing."[9]

In the fourth place, there was evidence that higher silver would stimulate Chinese imports and destroy exports by raising costs of production in world terms. Then China would have to stop buying silver and export the metal to make up her unfavorable balance of trade, as the British economist, John Maynard Keynes, charged in a letter to a House committee.[10]

Readers of the Department of Commerce's China Monthly Trade Report were constantly being told how a slight rise in silver stimulated Chinese imports of foreign goods at the expense of locally produced material.[11] American merchants saw these sales to China as evidence of an expanding market if only China's "buying power" could be raised; but to the thoughtful person this kind of trade was a forewarning of the troubles China would face under rising silver.

Finally, those who had an informed opinion on the subject realized that China needed steadier rather than higher silver. Most of the Chinese business men, economists, and government officials realized that the rapidly fluctuating exchange rates were doing them grave harm. The American economist E. W. Kemmerer explored the evil effects of fluctuation in exchange. He found that unpredictable changes tended to introduce an unavoidable element of risk and uncertainty into business transactions. The risk arose from the changing price of silver between the time a business contract was made abroad and the time it was concluded. The result was frequently a loss for Chinese business men.[12]

Except in isolated cases the Chinese never joined the cry for higher silver. From the beginning they urged stabilization of its price. Among the early enthusiasts for an international conference, they let it be known that their interest was chiefly in stabilization, and on that basis they would gladly participate.

American silver aims, on the other hand, were fundamentally at variance with those of the Chinese. The Americans were interested in stabilization only at a high level. Many of them never went beyond their elementary conviction that doubling the world price of silver would double the value of China's stocks of the metal and thereby "restore" her purchasing power in world trade. They failed to realize or understand the other factors in the Chinese economic situation. Yet they achieved their goal in the United States and thus helped bring depression and confusion to China.

China reached the peak of her prosperity in 1931 under low silver. Thereafter she entered on a period of deflation, which entailed loss of both export and import trade, and all the appurtenances of a depression lasting through most of 1935. It came late but outlasted that of other countries. It was the result of a series of reverses including Japanese aggression, high tariffs, and other trade restrictions abroad, floods and civil war at home.

Silver activity merely added the crowning blow when, early in 1933, it started its three-year rise. Chinese business was hamstrung by apprehension over American agitation and schemes for enhancing its price, while the Chinese heard with irony that the proposals were supposed to help them.

An American commodity loan in 1933 provided no basic help for China's troubles, so she looked on an international conference as her chief hope for stability in the world's silver currencies. She enthusiastically backed the proposed London Economic Conference. Even after Senator Pittman seized control of the discussions and obtained a Silver Agreement, the Chinese concurred in the hope that it was better than nothing and might help. Actually the London Agreement was potentially a boon to China, since the withholding of silver from world markets by the five producing countries promised to relieve the glut and eventually stabilize the market.

Unfortunately for China, the United States fitted the Agreement into a scheme, not of stabilization alone, but of enhancement of the price of silver, and of co-operation "to augment the purchasing power of peoples in silver-using countries."[13] China had not yet ratified the Agreement. In view of American ratification and of the crescendo of Congressional agitation early in 1934, she communicated her alarm to Washington in February with a request that she be consulted in advance if silver measures that might affect her currency and exchange were contemplated.

This first note of protest from China, like others that followed, was disregarded by the American government. The pressure of politics at home was far too great to allow the Administration to take foreign silver interests into account at that time, even if there had been a real understanding of the implications. However, in April China overcame her qualms and ratified the Agreement, reserving only a freedom of action if adverse conditions arose "contrary to the spirit of stabilizing the price of silver as embodied in the Agreement."[14]

Without this reservation, the London Agreement would have bound China not to demonetize under any circumstances, even if she should want to suspend or abandon the silver standard, as she ultimately did. Her worst fears were realized when, in June, the United States wrote the Silver Purchase Act into law.

During the summer and fall of 1934 China's depression deepened as silver rose under American impetus. Her economic dislocation was made more severe by the great drain of silver from the country, and the consequent contraction of money and credit accompanied by failures of shops and banks. During most of 1934 a record quantity of silver left the country legitimately. Finally, in October, despairing of any relief from the American program, China laid a heavy export tax on the metal, thereby taking the first step away from a full silver standard. This was followed in April, 1935, by a "gentleman's agreement" between foreign and Chinese banks in Shanghai not to participate in the exportation of the metal.

The Chinese furthermore divorced the internal from the external price of silver, in order to protect their currency from the violent fluctuations of the world market. Unfortunately, with the metal worth only forty cents inside China, stimulus was given to smuggling it to foreign markets. Although in 1934 only an estimated 15,000,000 ounces were smuggled, in 1935 the guess was 173,500,000 ounces.[15] One stream of silver left China via Hong Kong, and another via North China railroads and junks to Japan. Efforts of the Chinese government to check the activity were mostly ineffectual against Japanese or Korean citizens in occupied parts of the country, the bases of the lucrative business.

During the last half of 1934 China officially protested against the American silver policy in a series of notes. In one, Minister of Finance H. H. Kung requested that American

silver purchases be restricted for a time to silver already
in America, to avoid draining the metal from China. The
State Department replies promised all possible consideration
of the time, place, and quantities of its purchases, but
stressed the mandatory nature of the silver program.[16]

There was no more that Secretary Hull could say on the
subject of silver. Furthermore, overt Sino-Japanese hostil-
ities had given way to less startling and provocative methods
of conflict, and the attention of the world was centered on
Europe. Hull viewed his position as that of an impartial ob-
server. Repeatedly he refused to take action that might be
construed as anti-Japanese. Therefore, the tradition of friendship for China rested with other members of the Administration. Sumner Welles gave the credit to President Roosevelt,
who, despite the limitations put on him by the neutrality legislation, "never failed in his sympathetic understanding of
Chinese difficulties and of Chinese reactions. In that he has
been greatly assisted by the unflagging interest of his own
Treasury Department, under the inspiration of Henry Morgenthau."[17] Indeed, he might have added that between 1934
and 1937 Morgenthau helped establish the President's understanding through his frequent and highly sympathetic reports
to his chief. The Chinese themselves discovered where they
could expect help, and soon beat a path to the door of the
Treasury.

That Department's initiation into the situation occurred in
November, 1934, when it learned that the Chinese government was selling silver in London to obtain much needed exchange. Partly to help the Chinese and partly to prevent undue disturbance of the silver market, the Treasury agreed
to buy whatever metal they needed to sell. A series of contracts was made totaling 19,000,000 ounces, at a favorable
price. Like most of the later Treasury relations with China,
this first contract was weighted by humanitarian motives.

Morgenthau warned Roosevelt that American policies,
particularly the increased price of silver, were tending to
give maximum assistance to Japan. He reported the smuggling
activities. He obtained the President's permission to stabilize
the price temporarily. He was sure he could sell stabilization
to the Silver Senators by showing them that contrary to prog-
nostication, American exports to China had been falling off,
whereas those of Great Britain and Japan were steadily rising.

The Administration in Washington had a vague understanding of the Chinese situation and some of its members

accepted partial responsibility. Morgenthau was deeply embarrassed by the results of the policy he was required to execute, and began to feel as if he might as well be in the pay of the Japanese. He heard from William Bullitt, one of the roving commissioners in the State Department, that China was faced with complete collapse during the winter unless aid was forthcoming.

Morgenthau in December called together a group of experts to "write a financial program for China." Among the contributors were Dr. Jacob Viner, his special consultant; Professor John H. Williams, of Harvard; and specialists from the New York banks. The result of their labors was a confidential report to the President. Frankly facing the conflicting silver policies of China and the United States, it called attention to the qualitative importance of the Chinese trade to this country, recalled America's traditional role of friendship for China, and made clear that American refusal to help would mean "the withdrawal of the United States as an active influence in Far Eastern affairs, leaving that field to Japan, Great Britain, and other countries."[18] It suggested four broad lines of action, none of which was adopted at the time since the State Department opposed them without suggesting alternatives.

Morgenthau then drew up a program of immediate aid. The Treasury undertook formally to stabilize silver at fifty-five cents and inside of China to buy only from the government. The program could be terminated on one week's notice; meanwhile, the Treasury invited China to send a representative to discuss the silver situation. Stabilization lasted only two weeks, when Morgenthau, prodded by the silver interests, recalled his mandate for silver purchases and gave the Chinese a week's notice. At the protest of the Chinese Ambassador, Morgenthau suggested that he appeal to the Congressmen who were responsible for the law.

The Chinese accepted the Treasury's invitation for discussions, but opposition developed in Washington. Senator Pittman declared that the visit should take place only after a prior understanding that the silver policy would not be discussed. Secretary Hull, for the State Department, suggested either canceling or postponing the visit because of the bad effects of a failure in the conversations. When he heard of the objections, the President called off T. V. Soong's projected visit and explained that it would not accomplish anything that could not be done by cable.

Consequently, the Chinese attempted negotiations by long

distance. Kung sent proposals for adapting his country to
the American silver program, among which was the abandonment of silver in favor of a gold and silver currency linked
to that of the United States, with an American loan to cover
the transition difficulties. The proposals came to naught,
partly because of the friction engendered by the Chinese
notes between the State and Treasury Departments. The
notes came through the Chinese Ambassador to the State
Department. Therefore, Secretary Hull planned to handle
them by the usual diplomatic methods, and he prepared a
noncommittal reply.

When State consulted the Treasury on the communication,
Morgenthau commented that it meant nothing and would not
help China. He declared a policy of hands off unless State
decided it was a monetary matter and should be handled outside diplomatic channels, in which case he was willing to
assume responsibility.

While the answer was still under consideration, Bullitt received a confidential note from the Chinese Ambassador that
he was asked to deliver to the President outside State Department channels. The President learned in this irregular
method that "Japan had told China that she would be willing
to help her provided that Japan would get economic control
of all of China north of the Yellow River. In return for this
she would help China and...would join China in fighting the
United States silver policy." [19]

Next day Roosevelt told Hull that his note to China was
unwise; he also asked him to notify the Chinese that this was
a monetary matter and that the Treasury would handle the
negotiations. Hull apparently did not understand, and the
President did not press the issue at the time.[20] On the contrary, Secretary Hull bitterly resented Morgenthau's efforts
to project himself into the field of foreign affairs. He later
wrote of Morgenthau:

Despite the fact that he was not at all fully or accurately
informed on a number of questions of foreign policy with
which he undertook to interfere, we found from his earliest days in the Government that he seldom lost an opportunity to take long steps across the line of State Department
jurisdiction.... He often sought to induce the President to
anticipate the State Department or act contrary to our better judgment.[21]

Thus China was left to her own devices for a while longer,
with the Treasury and the State Departments unable to reach
accord on basic philosophy, and with the President expecting

agreement among his advisers before he approved a course of action. Meanwhile, China's crisis became worse as the American policy drove silver to its speculative heights in April, 1935.

Facing the Chinese situation more purposefully, the British proposed that the leading governments send experts to investigate the economic and financial ailments of the country. They intended to send Sir Frederick Leith-Ross, economic adviser to their own government, and hoped the United States would act similarly. Asked by Hull for his ideas on the British proposal, Morgenthau answered that since State viewed the subject as primarily political and within its province, the Treasury "does not feel that it is sufficiently informed of the political program to express an opinion." [22]

In July Morgenthau again considered fixing the price of silver more permanently. Pittman vigorously opposed the plan, partly because Morgenthau was now "sitting pretty" on the Hill, partly because Southern Senators were still convinced that rising silver meant rising cotton.

During the spring Roosevelt approved the sending of Professor J. Lossing Buck, economist and statistician, on a "fact-finding" trip to China. In reality Buck served as Treasury envoy in Nanking, where he acted as a clearing house for monetary dealings between the two countries. In July he had an important conference with Chiang Kai-Shek at which the United States again received a direct bid for a currency tie-up. The Chinese ruler stated that the American policy was harming his country, particularly because it allowed the Japanese to disorganize the Chinese financial market and keep China weak and bankrupt. He told Buck that Japan desired China to tie her currency to the yen, but that no negotiations had been initiated. [23]

The summer slipped away with the Washington government unable to come to grips with the problem. For a year and a half China had sought both American aid and information on the silver policy. The Chinese experienced one long financial crisis which they bore with characteristic patience and continued faith in American good will and intentions. The Mexicans, on the other hand, had several sharp crises, more limited in scope, each of which sent their leaders scurrying to Washington.

Late in October, 1935, the Chinese decided they had reached the limits of their endurance. They proposed the sale of a large amount of silver preparatory to going on a paper basis. At last the barriers were down. Morgenthau informed the President that this was the last chance to link the Chinese to the dollar; viewing these talks as purely monetary, Morgenthau proceeded to deal directly with the situation.

When Ambassador Sze proposed selling from one to two hundred million ounces of silver, Morgenthau formulated a five-point basis for doing business: (a) he would buy 100,-000,000 ounces at once and more if the deal was successful; (b) proceeds must be used only for stabilization of Chinese currency; (c) China would set up a stabilization committee of three, two of them Americans; (d) the proceeds of the sale would be kept on deposit in New York; (e) the new yuan would be tied by a fixed ratio to the dollar.[24]

The Chinese thought their crisis demanded action, and they embarked on a managed currency before negotiations were completed with the United States. On November 3 they nationalized all silver, ordered its exchange for legal tender notes, and attempted to stabilize the Chinese yuan at the existing level of about thirty cents American.[25]

The Chinese reply to Morgenthau's terms was a general acceptance of all the points except the last one. On the important issue of linking the yuan to the dollar, China proposed to stabilize at current values, linked to no foreign currency for fear of Japanese pressure and internal disturbances. Morgenthau was dissatisfied, for he was obsessed by the thought that he might finance China only to see her turn to sterling. He had in mind an old directive from the President "to keep a foothold in China." Therefore, he felt justified in insisting on a currency link as a condition for the purchase of silver.

At this juncture Morgenthau received word from the British Embassy in Washington that Hong Kong wanted to abandon silver and sell 100,000,000 ounces to the United States. He experienced a disgust with the whole silver program. Despite the politics of the Silver Bloc, he was sure its members were interested only in American production and did not care about world prices. Therefore, he wanted to let silver fall low enough to remove every reason for the abandonment of the metal by Hong Kong and China, as well as the smuggling from the Orient.

The American dilemma on China had several horns that the Administration tried to seize. The possible departure from silver by the whole of Asia raised the prospect of all the metal coming to the United States. Furthermore, the

New Deal's suspicion of Britain created a deep conviction that Oriental programs had been planned by the British for purposes of their own that included a sterling bloc in most of Asia. Consequently, Washington hesitated to help China leave silver by buying her reserves, or to assist her financially.

Roosevelt, Morgenthau, and Treasury assistants explored the situation in conference. The group became somewhat reconciled to China's refusal to link her currency since the State Department was calling it unnecessary, and since it was realized that if a link took place and anything misfired in Chinese currency, the United States would be blamed. Then several proposals were advanced and rejected. Morgenthau's idea of reducing the price of silver was vetoed by the President as politically inexpedient. A decision was made to purchase 20,000,000 ounces of silver from China, an amount sufficient to help her temporarily without making any commitments.[25]

But the Chinese sent an urgent plea for a larger immediate purchase. A Yokohama bank had just raided the Chinese exchange fund, which was not large enough to stand many such attacks. The Japanese continuously undermined confidence in the Chinese policy through effective propaganda in their newspapers in China. The Chinese desperately needed funds to resist Japan, and they promised special trade advantages in return for more American aid.

Refusing to press for trade privileges at the time, Morgenthau drew up a revised set of four points to cover the transactions. They included the promise of an immediate purchase of 50,000,000 ounces of silver, if the Chinese would use the proceeds for stabilization purposes only, leave them in New York, and keep Professor Buck fully informed of all monetary developments during the next year. The sale was consummated under these conditions. Morgenthau committed himself repeatedly to Chinese aid and left no doubt that he was prepared to defy Japan if necessary in order to achieve it.[27]

In December, Morgenthau finally gained the President's acquiescence in allowing silver to drop. Hong Kong monetary reserves that he had refused to purchase were being pushed on to the London market, and silver was still being siphoned out of China. Morgenthau learned that during recent years average Japanese exports of silver had been between six and nine million ounces annually. Yet for the first nine months of 1935, they reached 60,000,000 ounces, most of it obviously smuggled Chinese silver. He deliberately chose to start lowering silver on December 9, the opening day of the naval conference in London, where, he thought, Japan and England would oppose the United States. By late January, 1936, he had worked the price from sixty-five to forty-five cents. He was gratified when Ambassador Sze shortly reported that smuggling by the Japanese was on the wane.

China's troubles were far from ended. On December 12 the Japanese again raided the Chinese exchange, and China unsuccessfully sought a second American commitment of 50,000,000 ounces of silver. The Chinese frequently tried to get information about the future silver policy in order to protect their currency. Morgenthau was always noncommittal, and he finally explained one of his reasons. He charged, and Sze did not deny, that there was great speculation on silver in China, and that therefore he could never give out figures in advance. Sze explained that the Chinese had so few places to invest that they speculated in land and exchange.

Early in 1936 Morgenthau was disturbed by reports indicating that the Chinese were failing to keep Buck fully informed and that they were considering a diminished use of silver. Therefore, when Sze tried to sell more, Morgenthau announced that he must talk to Kung or Soong. The Secretary became more sympathetic when he heard a few of the Chinese difficulties, the most recent of which was with the State Department. A Chinese debt to the Farm Credit Administration had been due on December 31. In order to avoid the risk of default, China paid the entire amount of $3,000,000 instead of a down payment and interest that the State Department belatedly ruled was sufficient Cried the Ambassador: "Can you help me? When I go to the State Department it is such a long, tedious process I was put in an awful jam."[28]

Secretary Hull objected to the visit. He feared that Soong's anti-Japanese attitude might create serious trouble, but he consented to give way if the President felt the visit was important. The President desired the conference, and Morgenthau informed the Chinese, adding that the visit would be considered a Treasury matter, not a diplomatic mission.

The planning for Soong was premature, however, for he cabled that the political situation kept him at home, and he suggested the sending of the banker K. P. Chen in his place. The President's approval of the mission was immediate, as was his declaration that Morgenthau "does not have to take up with the State Department the matter of Chen's coming here to discuss China's monetary problems."[29]

Kung gave the meeting his blessing and made it clear that since China had now left silver, she would welcome a higher price. He also sent a series of cables that were a primer of Chinese internal problems. China's objective was a stability of exchange and a sound, uniform currency throughout the country. Kung delineated his principal obstacles as the heavy and inevitable budgetary deficit, which threatened inflation, and the political weakness of the currency under a prolonged attack, either from impaired confidence at home or Japanese raids from abroad. Furthermore, the Japanese hindered the progress of monetary reforms by refusing to allow China to recover her silver in the northern occupied territories, and by opposing circulation there of Chinese bank notes. Looking into the future he stated: "If other countries do not attack the bandits (pro-Japanese) now, the bandits will attack them later and Japan will be in a much stronger position after gaining control of China's natural resources and man power." He was fighting against time to establish his new monetary system as a stabilizing influence. For this purpose he must sell silver to acquire a larger stabilization fund for foreign exchange.

The conference started on April 8 between Treasury officials and Mr. Chen, two assistants, and Ambassador Sze. Morgenthau keynoted the discussions by stating that he sought no concessions from China, and by proposing help in order in the long run to aid his own country. He urged China to use more silver, since any other decision would only harm the use and value of the metal in the world. He tried to persuade Chen of the desirability of coins with a high silver content. He clarified his silver activities by explaining his mandate from Congress, under which he had to carry out orders or resign.

The Chinese acknowledged that they had a vital interest in the future of silver, not only because their silver reserves were steadily increasing as the metal was turned in, but also because it constituted the basis for the stability of their currency. They realized the serious results if its price fell below forty cents, the parity of the Chinese silver dollar.

Early in the conferences Morgenthau decided to make monthly silver purchases, as he was already doing from Mexico and Canada. He further suggested that China, like Mexico, might ship some metal to the United States as a basis for loans when she needed dollar exchange in a hurry. He asked that she study Canadian currency with a view to adopting a similar system, which was attached neither to sterling nor to the dollar, but operated in between. He resented the persistent reports that Chinese money was more nearly linked to British than to American currency,

Morgenthau informed the President of the negotiations, and summarized the foreign situation: If Hitler can protect his borders in Europe, he will probably join hands with Japan and attack Russia. China's chances of pulling through are poor unless Japanese activities are diverted through such a conflict with Russia.[31]

The conferences continued for almost six weeks. The Treasury's minimum objectives were a Chinese currency satisfactory to the United States, and the absorption of as much silver as possible. In return the Treasury was prepared to be generous. Its officials soon decided that China's budgetary deficit and unfavorable balance of trade were so large that small monthly silver purchases would be insufficient to strengthen the yuan.

At this stage the Chinese had tentatively advanced three proposals for using silver more extensively. One was to foster its use in the arts and industry by removing the restrictions adopted at the time of the monetary reform. Another was the decision to issue silver yuan and half-yuan coins, experimental dies for which had been ordered from the Philadelphia mint. A third was to adopt a legal minimum requirement of silver in the monetary reserves, probably 25 percent, like the United States. Treasury officials accepted this smaller reserve, although it entailed a reduction by about one half of China's current holdings.

However, the Chinese rejected the suggestion of an independent currency on the Canadian model, asserting that they already had independent money maintained at a definite exchange rate to both the dollar and the pound. When the relationship between the two fluctuated, the Chinese changed their exchange rates in accordance with the foreign currency that was comparatively dearer in value.

By May 12 a preliminary draft of the conversations was ready for refinement. No reference should be made to "credits" or "loans" for China, but rather to the furnishing of "dollar exchange," without naming the amount (actually $20,000,000 on a 50,000,000-ounce silver deposit). To avoid involvement with the State Department, it was decided that the agreement should be made between the Chinese Ministry of Finance and the United States Treasury, not the United States government.[32]

Morgenthau further worked out a formula for buying

75,000,000 ounces of the metal, starting with 12,000,000 ounces for the month ending June 15, and continuing with 9,000,000 ounces during each month through January 15, 1937 The price was to be the current world market, and payment would be made in gold if the Chinese desired. As in previous sales, proceeds were to be left in New York, where the Chinese might use their new dollar balances only to stabilize the external value of their monetary unit. No mention of these amounts, or of the $20,000,000 loan, was made in either country.

Secretary Hull approved the agreements and congratulated Morgenthau on his success. Under-Secretary Phillips praised Morgenthau on "the most important diplomatic step that has been taken. We have been working on this for three years." Silverite Pittman was satisfied with the settlement.

The British press displayed mixed reactions to the arrangements. The responsible Financial News, of London, saw the United States, for a time the only country fighting for the remonetization of silver, now victorious in bribing another nation to adopt her own kind of limited bimetallism and in pulling China out of the sterling bloc.[33] American papers were also divided. Although admitting that it was a good politico-business deal, one leading organ thought it was merely a patching up of the silver program to minimize the damage. Another believed that so far as American needs were concerned, the Treasury might better have invested in Ming vases or Sung paintings. But still another wrote at length about "Morgenthau's Wise Pact" that, to the everlasting benefit of American business, headed off British and Japanese attempts to engulf Chinese finance.[34]

The execution of the agreement soon got under way with the Treasury's first monthly bid for silver. The Treasury agreed to Chinese sales in London, whereupon China placed 2,000,000 ounces in the hands of the Chase National Bank. The market proved slow, for it took eighteen days to dispose of all the metal. Therefore, the Chinese requested and eventually obtained Morgenthau's concurrence in making future London sales under the disguise of an intermediary. The Chinese had no desire to cause silver fluctuations, which might easily result if it were known that China, still next to India and the United States the largest possessor of silver, was selling quantities of her metal in the world market.

After a year of China's new currency, it was estimated that the United States had unintentionally done her a great service by relieving her of an obsolete standard. As the last major nation to leave a silver basis, she jumped to the new managed currency without the trouble of an intermediate gold stage. She had modernized almost overnight. Her currency management had been successful, her people had accepted paper surprisingly well, and she had enjoyed an unparalleled period of stability in both the external and internal values of her money. An accompanying recovery in prices and business conditions, together with unusually good crops, aided the extension of power from Nanking. Chiang Kai-Shek, had spread his authority over the southern Communist areas and Canton, and waged continual warfare against the Communists entrenched in the Northwest. Altogether, the central government had achieved a greater degree of control over what was left of China than had existed for a decade, despite the continuing Japanese pressure for hegemony over North China.

In January, 1937, the Chinese Ambassador asked the Treasury to extend indefinitely the credit arrangements for $20,-000,000. The 50,000,000 ounces of collateral silver were in New York. To date the Chinese had not borrowed, but they wanted the privilege of doing so. In the light of the confused situation Morgenthau extended the credits for one month only, with the promise of review for future months.

In April Finance Minister Kung went to London for the coronation of George VI. There he failed to make the progress he had anticipated on a British loan. Consequently, he came to America, received a degree from Yale University, and then proceeded to Washington where the President told him, "I feel you are an old friend of mine." Afterward Morgenthau assured Kung that Roosevelt was a real friend of China.[35]

Morgenthau welcomed Kung for negotiations on finances. In the first session on June 30, Kung proposed to sell 12,000,-000 ounces of Chinese silver in San Francisco, as well as the 50,000,000 ounces in New York. He protested against the cost of storage and insurance as well as the inconvenience of monthly credit renewals on the New York metal. Since silver was still being turned in to the Chinese Treasury, the government again had a disproportionate supply in relation to its gold and foreign exchange for backing note issues. Morgenthau agreed to consider the proposals before Kung's return from a western trip.

Morgenthau wanted to help China again if American interests could also be promoted. He agreed to longer extensions

of the credit privileges; he was willing immediately to purchase the 12,000,000 ounces in San Francisco, and to consult
the President about the other 50,000,000 ounces. Roosevelt
desired to be generous and go the limit to maintain friendly
relations with China. Thus before further conferences with
Kung, Morgenthau had decided to purchase the entire 62,000,-
000 ounces, for which the Chinese could have gold if they
left it in the United States. Added to their gold already accumulated, they would have $50,000,000 against which the
Treasury would grant dollar exchange until the end of 1937,
subject to renewal at the request of China.[36]

Consequently when Kung returned for a conference on
July 8, the day after the fateful opening of the Sino-Japanese
war at the Marco Polo bridge, he was greeted with exceed-
ingly advantageous proposals from the Treasury. None of the
group yet knew of the Peiping incident of the night before, so
Kung's acceptance "for the sake of a strong China and for
security and peace in the Far East" did not appear ironical
at the time. In his effusive thanks he called Morgenthau "a
far-sighted statesman," to which the latter jokingly replied:
"Listen, Dr. Kung, I bought all your silver; you don't have
to give me anything more."

Not to be outdone, Kung responded, "Well, I sold the silver
to you cheap. I bought your surplus gold."[37]

Kung made an invaluable contribution to his government.
In foreign affairs he stood for a close association with the
western democracies, and he played a large part in the eventual acquisition of economic and political aid from the United
States. He wrote several times in the vein of his message of
June, 1938, in which he called attention to China's courageous
stand against the onward march of brutal force and ruthless
barbarism, and asked if the isolationist policy or the Neutrality Law could protect America from this common men-
ace. Adding that he was told 90 percent of the American
people were in sympathy with China's cause, he hinted that
their government had support for a stronger policy on Japanese aggression.[38]

Such appeals had had an effect in America by 1937. During
the conference with Kung, Morgenthau became profoundly
convinced that his help in making China strong enough to
resist Japan would, in historical perspective, be the most
important thing he did as Secretary of the Treasury. Yet his
attitude was not alone altruism, but a strong admixture of
American self-interest. He was sure that Hull's fears of
British and Japanese predominance in China's trade could be

laid to rest, for the Chinese would never forget what the
Americans were doing for them.

On July 9 reports of the North China incident were being
received and everyone was speculating on the possibility of
renewed Sino-Japanese warfare. Into this situation Morgenthau and Kung issued their announcement of friendship and
collaboration between the United States and China. The only
jarring note in the tea-party atmosphere of the press conference was the explosion of a photographer's bulb that
startled every one present, although pieces of glass landed
on Morgenthau's desk and cut the clothes of some people
near by.

American press opinion was either noncommittal or definitely favorable, with even the New York Times commenting
that if silver must be purchased, a simultaneous redistribution of gold was the best move that could be made.[39] Some
papers stressed the commercial possibilities, and others
saw the great advantage to China of the timely enhancement
of her credit position when a war with Japan was imminent.
Most significantly, several papers called credit on earmarked
gold an effective way to loan money to World War debtor nations which were barred from borrowing by the Johnson Act.

Even as the bonds of trade and collaboration were being
forged between the two nations, a third country decided not
to postpone the fulfillment of its ambitions in Asia. Probably
five years earlier China would have succumbed to such an
attack, but the interim had brought relative stability and
unity to that unhappy land. Even so, an eight-year struggle
gradually enveloped all of China and eventually the world.

The sympathy of the Administration was with the Chinese
from the start, but it found itself impaled on the horns of a
dilemma that was complicated by Japan's blockade of the
Chinese coast. The Neutrality Act applied an arms embargo
whenever the President recognized a state of war between
foreign nations. But Senator Pittman, chairman of the Senate
Foreign Relations Committee, on two occasions stated that
there had been no declaration of war and that the Neutrality
Act should not be applied.[40] On the other hand, Secretary Hull
announced that the government did not believe in "extreme
isolation," but was consulting constantly "with interested
governments directed toward peaceful adjustment."[41] Nevertheless, isolationist and peace sentiment subjected Congress
and the Administration to heavy pressure.

— Consequently, the President saw little chance of granting —

help in the direction of his sympathies. Instead, he warned American nationals that they remained in China at their own risk; he forbade government ships to carry munitions to China or Japan and told private vessels they did so on their own responsibility. Since private shippers ran little risk in the carrying trade to Japan, this warning worked to the dis- advantage of China. However, Roosevelt's directives helped to detract isolationist agitation from the main issue, and he managed never to invoke the Neutrality Act. The result was continued though reduced trade with China, as well as ship- ments of oil and scrap iron to Japan.

The Treasury explored all the ramifications of the war in Asia, and summarized the situation in September: "It would appear then that the peace of the world is tied up with China's ability to win or to prolong its resistance to Japanese aggres- sion. It is our opinion that a Japanese victory increases greatly the chances of a general world war."[42]

The solid relations the Chinese had established in Washing- ton stood them in good stead throughout the years of theoret- ical American neutrality. Repeatedly the Chinese Ambassador or special missions sought to arrange the sale of silver or a loan of money and materials. Because of their previous successes at the Treasury, they pressed their requests in that department, and often opened a conversation with "We always come to you when we need some help."

The first wartime petition came from Ambassador Wang on November 3, 1937. He offered more silver to the Treasury in order to acquire credits for the purchase of ammunition. With a minimum of negotiations, Morgenthau took 10,000,000 ounces immediately and the following week contracted for a similar amount, stipulating only that it come on a different ship.

On the first of December, after Shanghai had fallen and Nanking was under attack, Morgenthau became extremely anxious to help the Chinese before it was too late. He wired the President for permission to purchase 50,000,000 ounces of silver and to extend the foreign exchange agreement for a year. Roosevelt gave his consent, subject only to State De- partment concurrence. Herbert Feis of State agreed to the purchase, and the Treasury took the metal in five lots during the next two months.

State later approved with qualifications the extension of Chinese credits on their earmarked gold. That department felt that extension would not make the United States unneutral at the moment, but that to cover future invocation of neutral-

ity the agreement should state that it was subject to "any
possible questions of neutrality that may arise."[43] When the
President saw this memorandum he termed it stupid and
ordered Morgenthau to draw up an agreement which would
give the Chinese a six-month extension.

At the request of Kung, the Administration decided to continue its schedule of silver purchases. It took another 50,-
000,000 ounces over a two-month period beginning in March,
1938. With its purchase of silver in 1938, the Treasury had
abandoned its insistence that the proceeds be used only for
stabilization. Consequently, the Chinese were currently acquiring enough American exchange to pay for their military
purchases, although they anxiously foresaw a time when
their surplus stocks would be exhausted.

Backed by the President, Morgenthau in May undertook a
third purchase of 50,000,000 ounces on the installment plan.
The Treasury thereby committed itself to continuous bi-
weekly purchases at least between December and July.

During the winter China had broached the subject of a
cash loan in Washington. The State Department brushed the
idea aside by reminding the Chinese of their big proceeds
from silver sales. President Roosevelt also discouraged
them by telling Wang he would put no obstacle in the way of
their raising money elsewhere. But the idea of a loan persisted and by April had been accepted in Washington as a
legitimate topic for discussion. Wang talked to Welles and
Morgenthau about the possibility of China's floating a liberty
loan in the United States, but was discouraged by both men.

In June Morgenthau and Secretary Wallace agreed on a
large loan for the purchase of flour and cotton goods. Morgenthau was committed to aid for the Chinese in almost any
form, while Wallace, although he wanted them to win their
war, also saw great benefits at home from such a program.
But when they consulted Hull, he asserted that a similar
offer must be made to Japan, while his department explored
the subject from the point of view of the Hague Convention,
the Japanese reaction, and the diplomatic and economic risks
involved.[44]

Morgenthau strongly favored some kind of a loan, and he
felt that the objections of the State Department were far from
enough to outweigh the economic, political, and humanitarian
arguments in its favor. To tide the Chinese along, he agreed
to a fourth purchase of 50,000,000 ounces of silver in bi-
weekly amounts, and, almost immediately, the last 19,300,-
000 ounces of free silver in the possession of the Chinese
government.

Ambassador Bullitt in Paris became a sympathetic point of approach for the Chinese. He joined the agitation for a loan by writing the President about the rapid depletion of China's purchasing power and urging a commodity loan. The President favored more help for China, but he expected his department heads to agree first on some principle.

Loan negotiations lagged throughout the fall. Morgenthau felt more and more strongly the need for helping China: "There is no country in the world today, with the exception of Russia, that is doing anything, and we all sit by here, and we are just driving them in the hands of Russia."[45] Yet he was faced with a determined revolt by his own Assistant Secretary Taylor, who eventually resigned over the unneutral foreign policy of the department. Meanwhile, Hull's attitude on Japan was stiffening, as evidenced by a series of "Open Door" communications with that nation concerning her policies in China.

Chiefly through Treasury persistence, an Export-Import Bank credit of $25,000,000 was granted in December to facilitate the export of industrial and agricultural products to China. The purchase of trucks was one of the first uses of the credit. Treasury policy received the hearty endorsement of former Secretary of State Stimson, an early opponent of Japanese designs.

Silver was of no further help to China until March, 1939, when she managed to ship about 14,500,000 ounces of newly acquired metal to Manila. The Treasury immediately bid for it. Yet in June, for the first time in many months, Morgenthau rejected a Chinese offer of 6,000,000 ounces. The Senate was in full cry against foreign silver purchases and Morgenthau told a Congressional committee he had no future silver commitments. If the monetary future was in the laps of the gods, Morgenthau speculated that their laps must be very tired, while the Chinese Ambassador only hoped that "some day in the Senate the Gods may change."[47]

The Chinese offered the same silver somewhat later. In July, while the Townsend Bill to outlaw foreign silver was still pending, Roosevelt approved the transaction. Morgenthau consulted Senator Townsend, sponsor of the repeal bill, who disapproved the purchase on principle but agreed not to force a cancellation of contract in case his bill passed. Then Morgenthau proceeded with the deal.

With the depletion of their stabilization fund the Chinese pressed their demands for help during the summer of 1939. Their serious needs are illustrated by the nature of their proposals, which had to be rejected. They asked the United States to find some way of advancing gold immediately as payment for Chinese silver that would be delivered six to twelve months later. They even tried to sell 200,000,000 ounces of silver at thirty-five cents, to be delivered over a period of years, but to be paid for immediately.

Congress made no change in the Silver Purchase Act of 1939. But in 1940 it tried again to repeal foreign silver purchases. By this time the State Department, Morgenthau, and many silverites were either lukewarm or actively hostile. The day after repeal passed the Senate, the Chinese reported they had 4,300,000 ounces of silver in Rangoon and wanted to sell it. The Treasury bought it, stipulating only that it be shipped immediately before the House also approved the bill. However, the House never did pass the measure, and attempts at repeal died in 1940.

A few small purchases were made from China during the last half of 1940 and during 1941. But her silver had already played its part in the relations of the two countries and in the financing of her war. Henceforth, the semiannual renewal of the stabilization loan, new cash loans, and Lend-Lease took over the spotlight of American aid to China, particularly after the United States became an active ally. The silver purchases helped to create a heritage of good will between the two nations that was often strained on both sides in the next few years but never broken.

One result of the American silver policy should be mentioned in passing. As has been shown, it forced China off silver, whereupon she undertook a managed standard that included the use of paper money. At first all went well under a careful management of her new currency. But after 1937, the Japanese war made large sums of money necessary, and they were not immediately forthcoming. Effective financing of the war would have meant a crackdown on landlords who hoarded grain, and a new graduated tax, together with a better system of collecting all taxes. But the Chinese government refused to sanction such moves. Doing the best he could to obtain foreign loans and to sell silver, Kung saw at hand a new instrument for solving the dilemma; he took the easy way out and printed paper. Circulating currency rose from a billion and a half dollars in 1937 to a trillion in 1946; prices followed a similar trend until at V-J day they stood at 2,500 times the prewar level.[48] This inflation might have been the same or even worse under any other standard in China; yet the fact remains that the Silver Purchase Act

forced her away from her traditional metallic currency
without teaching her how to control her new system. Indeed,
by 1947 proposals were being heard in the United States for
a large loan of silver to China as the only method by which
she could end inflation and, by going back to her traditional
hard money, regain the confidence of 400,000,000 people in
their currency.

Recent writers have charged that American policy in the
Orient was chiefly notable for the sending of scrap iron and
oil to Japan at the same time that Russia was sending gasoline and planes to China. They indicate that whereas Russian
credits to China between 1937 and 1939 totaled $250,000,000,
American aid in the same period was only one-fifth as much.[49]

A summary of silver purchases alone suffices to prove the
exaggeration of this statement. (See Appendix for a summary
by year of quantities and cost of Chinese silver purchases.)
From 1934 through 1941 the United States purchased over
half a billion ounces of Chinese silver, for which she paid
some $260,000,000 During the period of the Russian assist-
ance noted above, the aid to China was $184,000,000 on sil-
ver alone, to which must be added the loan of $25,000,000
in 1938 Some $209,000,000 were made available to China
between 1937 and 1939, which grew by the time of Pearl
Harbor to at least $231,000,000 eighty percent of which re-
sulted from silver sales. This total included another loan
but did not include the many intangibles such as missions to
organize transportation and fight malaria, to say nothing of
General Chennault's American Volunteer Group.

All this activity took place before the United States entered
the war, and most of it was done in the face of repeated en-
actments of neutrality legislation at home. It was a deliberate
attempt on the part of a "neutral" nation to help another nation
engaged in war. It originated with two men -- the President
and the Secretary of the Treasury -- who thought they had
found a practical and humanitarian way of carrying out an
otherwise unpopular mandate for the purchase of silver.
Their policy undoubtedly played a part in bolstering China
against the ravages of Japan, until American entry into the
war made full-scale aid possible.

VII. OTHER FOREIGN RESULTS OF THE AMERICAN PROGRAM

There is doubtless a wide difference between proving that one law is in itself better than another and proving that the former ought to be substituted for the latter. But the imagination of the multitude is very apt to overlook this difference, which is so apparent to the minds of thinking men.
Tocqueville, I, 193.

SPAIN

Spain was one of the world's large holders of silver in 1933. Her stock was in the form of coins, old but still legal tender and mostly idle in the Bank of Spain. The melting point of her silver coins would have been reached at about ninety-four cents an ounce, and in April, 1935, she looked for trouble when American policy pushed the price in world markets to eighty-one cents toward an avowed goal of $1.29.

Other countries also trembled for their monetary future, among them the Philippine Islands, which would be threatened at ninety-seven cents, Siam at $1.04, India at $1.08, Indo-China at $1.12, Australia at $1.17, and Japan at $1.26, before the final American goal was reached.[1] The American policy changed but the tension and uncertainty remained, and although four nations were on a silver standard in 1933, four years later only Ethiopia remained.

Spain, though not on a silver base, gained American attention as a silver user. The Roosevelt Administration first realized Spain's needs in 1935 when Secretary of the Treasury Morgenthau attempted a monetary loan, partly to help redistribute the growing American hoard of silver and gold, partly because Spain seemed to be the neediest prospect in Europe. State Department negotiations for a Spanish trade treaty and other considerations forced postponement of Morgenthau's idea.

With the outbreak of the Spanish civil war in July, 1936, a loan became impossible In the previous year Congress had passed the first of a series of neutrality laws designed to prevent the shipping of munitions to belligerent nations. In 1936 the laws were extended to prohibit loans as well. After

the start of the Spanish conflict, Congress specifically forbade the export of munitions to either faction in Spain.

Determined to avoid a repetition of the experiences of
1914 to 1917, Congress was also under considerable pressure
from those segments of the public that were shocked at the
treatment of the Catholic church in Republican Spain and at
the reports that some of the Loyalist support was derived
from Communists, both Spanish and Russian. Communism
at that time aroused more fears than the unrealized ideol-
ogies of Fascism and Nazism.

Yet a growing number of thinking Americans began to see
the ultimate aims of European Fascism. One of the first to
sense the danger of the Nazi movement, Secretary Morgenthau regarded with horror German and Italian intervention
in Spain and the possibility that Mexico might become a second victim.

Therefore, the Treasury found a way to help the Republican government in spite of the Neutrality Act. Early in 1938,
when Loyalist Ambassador Fernando de los Rios proposed
the sale of some of his hard-pressed government's silver,
he gained a willing ear at the Treasury. When he offered to
sell 55,000,000 ounces in the form of peseta coins, the
Treasury waived its own rule of buying only silver bars by
accepting 5,000,000 ounces, as a trial shipment that the
Spanish might repeat in the future.[2]

This shipment of silver originated considerable trouble
for the American government. When the consignment arrived in New York on May 30, the Federal Reserve Bank as
agent for the Treasury received adverse claims to the
metal from the Franco faction in Spain. It was left on board
while the Treasury decided on the next step. One alternative
was to proceed with the original contract, which would involve the government in possible liabilities. The other was
to refuse to pay for the silver until the title had been cleared
a safer course, but obviously an obstacle to the Treasury's
hopes of aiding the Loyalists. Recognizing the dangers of
the first course, but thinking that he and the President should
accept the representations of the ambassador from a legally
recognized government, Morgenthau on May 31 decided to
conclude the original contract. The Federal Reserve in New
York was instructed to unload the silver, but was reluctant
to do so until the Treasury sent a letter of indemnification
to cover losses. On June 4 Sullivan and Cromwell, represent-
ing the Franco faction, served the Federal Reserve Bank
with a summons in an action entitled Banco de Espana v.
Federal Reserve Bank of New York.

Not to be intimidated, Morgenthau contracted with the
Spanish Ambassador for another 5,000,000 ounces. When it
arrived in New York, the Treasury engaged in a little "hi-
jacking," as Morgenthau called it. This silver had also been
claimed by the rebel Spanish government. Treasury officials
seized the initiative before the ship docked, and prepared to
acquire possession of the metal. A Treasury agent, Mr.
Orre, went to New York, rounded up a number of secret
service men, and in a dramatic move boarded the ship while
it was still in the Hudson River. The United States Lines
protested against every action of the Federal agents. Reluctantly, company representatives showed the officers the
storage place of the silver and saw them guard it during and
after the unloading. No force was used in the transfer of the
metal, for the company agents thought they had no recourse
except protest to demands from the government. They
yielded the pier keys and watched the silver loaded into
trucks and removed. When they even protested to representatives of the United States Trucking Company, Mr. Moran,
a thick-set Irishman who was supervising the work, imper-
turbably asked, "Who cares?" The incident did not deter
Morgenthau from further help for Spain, and he immediately
contracted for a third shipment. He had only praise for the
men who had executed the coup in New York.

When the lawsuit arose over the first shipment, Henry L.
Stimson, of the firm of Winthrop, Stimson, Putnam, and
Roberts, was engaged to represent the Federal Reserve.
Stimson remarked that he always preferred to support the
side with which he could sympathize, and that in the present
war his sympathies were with the established government of
Spain.[3] He and other members of his firm furnished legal
advice on several occasions, including the crisis over the
landing of the second shipment.

Lawsuits were instituted not only against the Federal Reserve of New York but also against the government, the
United States Lines, and the Assay Office in New York which
received the coins for melting. Morgenthau sought and obtained Roosevelt's approval of Stimson's services in all
government suits, including any that might develop in the
future.

The Treasury explored ways of avoiding trouble while continuing to buy Spanish silver. Already the United States was
taking title to a consignment when it was loaded in France,
although payment was made only upon arrival in New York.
The possibility of making payment at the time of loading was

examined and rejected. The Spanish vetoed an American
suggestion to ship by parcel post, but proposed instead the
sale to some French metallurgical firm that would then sell
to the United States Treasury Both the Spanish and the
Americans realized that a secret shipment was out of the
question owing to the alertness of the agents of the rival
Spanish regime.

Other shipping companies besides the United States Lines
were investigated, and it was found that the Franco government had put all Atlantic firms on notice. Therefore, Herman
Oliphant, counsel to the Treasury, appealed to John Franklin,
president of the United States Lines. The result was a formal
commissioning of the line as the agent of the government in
receiving and transporting monetary metals to American
shores. The Treasury arranged to compensate the company
and to relieve it of all liabilities in the execution of the as-
signment. Then Morgenthau bid for a fourth shipment of
Spanish silver.

Meanwhile the ramifications of the lawsuits were growing.
Late in the summer Gonzala Zabala, a Loyalist vice president of the Bank of Spain, came to the United States on business for his government. When Sullivan and Cromwell
learned of the visit, they sought to examine him. The Spanish
Ambassador asked the State Department for diplomatic immunity for Zabala. That Department, considering it a ruse
to trick an American law firm, refused the Spanish request.
When Morgenthau personally intervened to get a reversal,
he was told that no one at State knew the Treasury was interested in Zabala. However, Oliphant in the Treasury recalled at least four occasions on which State had heard or
acknowledged the concern of the Treasury with the whole
Spanish case, including correspondence between John Foster
Dulles, of Sullivan and Cromwell, and the State Department.
Treasury officials were angry that they were not consulted
in advance of a decision adverse to their interests. Nevertheless, Zabala did not get his diplomatic immunity.

On the other hand, Morgenthau continued to assist the
Loyalist government. He helped the Spanish find suitable
counsel for their part of the lawsuits. In October he bid for
10,000,000 additional ounces of silver in a fifth shipment.
However, the assistance he was able to give their cause was
but a pittance compared to the quantities of men and materiel that poured in to Franco from Italy and Germany. American foreign policy was at its most sterile point when the
Loyalists, gradually compressed into small pockets of resistance, were finally ground into defeat.

The United States Treasury during 1938 bought 35,000,000 ounces of Loyalist silver, advancing $14,000,000 toward a war chest. [4] In order to do this it deliberately involved itself in a series of lawsuits covering the whole amount, always with the President's complete approval. With the collapse of the old government in Spain, the suits remained to be settled.

Hopeful that the State Department might offer recognition of Franco conditioned upon the withdrawal of the suits, Treasury officials in February, 1939, reviewed the salient facts of the case. State was particularly interested that only 95 percent of the purchase price had been paid to the Loyalist government. The balance, at least $700,000, had been withheld pending determination of the silver content of the Spanish coins. State thought this balance should be used to satisfy claims by American citizens against Spain. [5] Yet recognition was eventually granted without providing for a settlement of the suits. Sumner Welles explained the failure by quoting Franco's specific refusal under any circumstances to accept conditional recognition.

One of the paradoxes of American foreign policy occurred during the spring and summer when official Washington began to look with favor on help for the Franco government. Application had been made for American credits through the Export-Import Bank to finance Spanish purchase of 300,000 bales of cotton. The proposal met with sympathetic response in the State Department, which had decided to make as quick and friendly an adjustment as possible with the Spanish regime. For various reasons southern agriculturalists and others favored the credits

However, as one of the governors of the Export- Import Bank Morgenthau announced forcefully that he would do everything in his power to prevent such a loan while the Spanish government was suing the United States. He was able to gain the agreement of Jesse Jones, in the Bank, and Sumner Welles, in the State Department. They decided it was desirable to find a market for cotton, but that a loan should also provide for a termination of the lawsuits Morgenthau repeated his opposition at various times during May and June when the State Department and others were pushing the deal. He argued that documents should be demanded from the Bank of Spain and the Minister of Finance guaranteeing that they would never attempt to apply the proceeds of the disputed silver to the bill for the cotton.

In July Morgenthau entertained Juan Negrin of the former Spanish government. Negrin insisted that the constitutional

republic would be re-established and that the present regime had not changed the fundamental laws of the land, one
of which stated that a loan to Spain was illegal unless ratified by Parliament.[6] Subsequently Morgenthau sought to insert into the loan negotiations a provision for ratification.

A decision was finally reached in July on the Spanish suits
involving the first three shipments of silver. The plaintiff
had claimed that the silver was wrongfully taken by the Spanish Republic and that the Treasury, therefore, had acquired
no title. The defendants were the Superintendent of the
United States Assay Office in New York, the Federal Reserve Bank acting for the Treasury, and the United States
Lines. The court decided that the Republican government
had acquired valid title to the silver from the Bank of Spain,
that the Treasury had obtained the metal legitimately, and
that the plaintiff had no case.[7]

The force of this decision caused a lag in the suits involving the other shipments, although the way was somewhat
cleared for the discussion of Spanish aid. Before the end of
the year a cotton loan was arranged. This was merely a
drop in the bucket to war-ravaged Spain, and negotiations
for further help got under way.

In February, 1940, the Franco government offered to sell
the large stock of silver coins that the Loyalist government
had been forced to abandon. Spain had decided to maintain a
gold standard, to replace all its silver coins with nickel, and
to dispose of the 100,000,000 pieces of demonetized silver.
With the proceeds she hoped to pay for Canadian nickel and
the minting in the United States of her new coins. The Treasury was unwilling to discuss helping another country to
abandon silver. Furthermore, the litigation over previous
purchases was still not ended; nor was Congressional agitation against foreign purchases. Therefore, the Treasury rejected the Spanish offer.

Searching for much needed credits, the Spanish applied to
the Treasury for a final settlement of the old purchases.
They asked for payment of the 5 percent that had been withheld pending melting and assaying of the coins. But as late
as June, 1941, the work was not finished, and Morgenthau
promised to notify the Spanish when the various charges, including attorneys' fees and other expenses of litigation, were
more precisely determined.

In November, 1942, the assaying was completed and the
Secretary made his report to Spanish Ambassador Cardenas.[8]

Cost value on assay		$15,149,136.38
Less:		
Advance payments	$13,990,800.00	
Assay office charges	274,409.02	
Cartage charges	7,480.25	
Litigation costs &		
counsel fees	72,728.57	14,345,417.84
Balance		803,718.54

Source: Morgenthau, Diary, November 9, 1942,
   DLXXXII, 356.

However, the ill-fated silver purchases created one final
perplexity for the United States government. When the Spanish Ambassador protested against the inclusion of litigation
fees at the State Department, Secretary Hull wrote Morgenthau that the charging of fees to the unsuccessful litigant was
not in line with American practice, that the tense situation
in the Mediterranean theater of war made unnecessary irri-
tation of the Spanish government undesirable, and that the
item should be eliminated.[8]

Morgenthau reacted strenuously to the suggestion. When
Mr. Stimson, now a member of the war cabinet, offered to
return his share of the fees to the government, Morgenthau
suggested to the President that the Spanish move was blackmail based on a realization of Stimson's patriotism. Roosevelt agreed and decided that if the State Department was so
perturbed, it might use money from its own special fund to
pay the legal fees.

Thereupon Morgenthau, through Dean Acheson, Assistant
Secretary of State, asked for the withdrawal of the original
letter from Hull. Acheson was sympathetic to the idea, and
next day reported the acquiescence of the Secretary. The
correspondence was returned, the request withdrawn and
the matter closed, except for the final settlement with Spain.
Not until December, 1942, did the Spanish government accept Morgenthau's report as the basis for agreement, and
on January 2, 1943, the five-year controversy was terminated by an American check for $803,718.54.[9]

CANADA

Canada's natural resources included rich deposits of silver. In 1933 her production, third largest in the world after
Mexico and the United States, was some 15,000,000 ounces.

At London she promised to withhold 1,600,000 ounces, which she used for her reserves and for subsidiary silver coins.

The rest of Canada's production was for sale, and beginning in 1935 the United States Treasury became her chief customer. Early in 1936 Secretary Morgenthau consulted Hume Wrong, charge d'affaires of the Canadian Legation, about a more permanent arrangement. The secretary suggested a monthly purchase agreement such as he had with the Mexicans. Mr. Wrong was reluctant to negotiate in view of Senator Thomas' statement that the Treasury conference with Mexico was an attempt to "lick the British." Morgenthau argued persuasively to prove that he was not responsible for Thomas' remarks.[10]

Morgenthau's purpose seems to have been the creation of an American silver-producing bloc. He was also deeply interested in hemispheric consultation and co-operation on monetary matters. But he had to overcome Canadian suspicions of the American silver program. For example, the Canadian government reported a loss of $400,000 on silver stocks acquired during the period that the Treasury's policy pushed the price of silver skyward in 1935.[11]

The Canadians eventually assented to definite monthly sales of silver. On February 28, 1936, the Treasury agreed to purchase 1,200,000 ounces of newly mined Canadian silver during March, and to renew the contract monthly upon application of the Canadians.

Yet the program was threatened with an early termination. The Treasury for some time had been attempting to collect unpaid excise and customs taxes from Canadian liquor companies for their shipments into the United States during prohibition. The Treasury sponsored legislation outlawing the importation of any Canadian goods from firms against which suit had been instituted. Stiff Canadian resistance created opposition in the State Department, where there were fears of Canadian abrogation of the new Trade Agreement and an unfavorable attitude concerning the St. Lawrence waterway. The emotions aroused by the problem caused bad feelings both between Washington and Ottawa, and between the Treasury and State Departments. Herman Oliphant began to question the wisdom of continuing to purchase Canadian silver on favorable terms. Extreme measures were obviated, however, when the Canadian companies made a small settlement satisfactory to the Treasury, and the legislation was withdrawn.

The silver agreement was renewed monthly during 1936, 1937, and 1938, but during 1939 and 1940 there were interruptions of the schedule by the Treasury, which was wary of forward commitments during the agitation for legislation on foreign purchases. After the Canadians entered the war, they began to find other uses for their metal. Treasury purchases declined in 1941, and by 1942 had ceased almost completely. However, importations of silver for use in American industry continued in large quantities.

During the war the United States Treasury found a way of making its silver available for nonconsumptive use in war production. The principle was applied in Canada when late in 1942 Morgenthau approved 2,500 tons for use as bus bars by the Aluminum Company of Canada.[12]

The total purchases of silver in Canada, both under agreement and in open market, were considerably lower than those from Mexico, but proportionately the same in comparison with the two production levels. The Treasury spent $53,000-000 for Canadian silver. (See Appendix for a summary of American purchases of Canadian silver.)

INDIA

India, with China, once constituted the greatest market for silver. The two countries during an average year in the 1920's consumed over half of the world output. For a number of reasons their consumption by 1932 was reduced to a fraction of its former level. To early silver protagonists, the restoration of these markets appeared indispensable to a revival of world silver prices. The story of China has already revealed her withdrawal from the buyer's market, and her sale of the metal in vast quantities.

The story of India is different but no less complicated. In 1926 she turned to a gold-bullion standard upon the recommendation of the Hilton-Young commission. This group also suggested reducing the government's hoard of silver rupees by 70 percent. Her consequent sale of large quantities between 1927 and 1932 contributed to the silver depression. Yet at the end of 1932, because of a large net return of rupees from circulation, the government's stock of silver was larger than ever, some 380,000,000 ounces.[13] In addition to this supply, hoarding and silver ornamentation further magnified India's possessions.

India sold about 50,000,000 ounces in 1933, including the 20,000,000 ounces shipped to the United States to apply on the British war debt.[14] In view of the potential avalanche of silver that sudden large Indian sales would create, the

London conferees in 1933 thought they were damming the flood by gaining India's promise not to sell more than 35,000,000 ounces annually during the next four years.

The stabilizing features of the London Agreement and the price-raising objectives of the American program seemed to precipitate a change in the monetary thinking of India. Many of her leaders were pleased with the American policy, which they expected would cause an advance in the value of that part of her national wealth that was in silver. Thus during the next two years she began to have a slight excess of imports over exports of the metal.

In 1936 and succeeding years the Indian demand increased. This is explained by a number of factors, only one of which, the lowering of the wildcat price of the previous year, was related to the silver policy of the United States. Otherwise, until the war years the American Treasury was little interested in, or affected by, the Bombay silver market.

History repeated itself in strange ways in World War II. In mid-1940 a serious situation arose in various parts of India, especially in Bombay, when the hoarding of silver coins and the abnormal demand for rupees occurred. A shortage of change seriously embarrassed the post office, retail shops, and railways, and police were required to regulate the crowds at some banks. An important cause of this panic was the rumor planted by German broadcasts that Indian paper currency would soon be worthless.[15] The crisis subsided somewhat through government steps to prevent speculating and hoarding, and to restore confidence. However, Indian financial troubles persisted, and eventually involved the United States in efforts to cure them by Lend-Lease.

VIII. SILVER IN WARTIME

A great people may be oppressed with impunity by a small faction or by a single individual. Tocqueville, I, 195.

THE INDUSTRIAL CAREER OF SILVER

By 1941 war conditions had deprived the United States of the silver production of Europe, Asia, Africa, and Australia. The Treasury continued to purchase nearly half of the Canadian output, and took all the other foreign silver that was offered. In addition, it bought the entire output of the United States at the mandatory price of seventy-one cents, as distinct from thirty-five cents for foreign acquisitions. Treasury absorption left only the insufficient Mexican and South American production for the expanding industrial demands of the country.

Consequently, American silver users were horrified at the terms of the November rapprochement between the United States and Mexico under which the Treasury promised to purchase almost the entire silver output of Mexico. The firm of Handy and Harman, speaking for industry, protested to the Treasury and State Departments.[1] The basis of its objection was the fact that the use of silver in the arts and industries of the United States and Canada had almost doubled over 1940, and totaled the record sum of 80,000,000 ounces. The firm analyzed this great increase as stemming from the war, which stimulated demand for the metal in three fields:

A) A greater public demand for articles made of silver. Sales of silverware were stimulated by the increase in employment and by greater general prosperity, together with accelerated marriages resulting from enlistments and the Selective Service Act.

B) A growing substitution of silver for nickel, copper, aluminum, and tin under a rationing system established within the silver industry itself. For example, silver alloys containing only small parts of the scarce base metals were being used in place of brass and nickel alloys. Pure silver wire was replacing copper in some electrical appliances and small motors. Silver was being used as a plating mate-

rial to produce corrosion-resistant surfaces on those substitute metals that had only the one defect of being corro-
sive. It was saving tin for other uses by being combined
with lead to make a satisfactory solder.

C) A rapid increase in the use of silver for war materials.
It was already being employed in the construction of ships,
airplanes, tanks, trucks, guns, shells, bombs, torpedoes,
and many other kinds of equipment. It was used most extensively in the form of brazing alloys, but other compositions
were employed to make electrical contacts, while pure silver went into the production of airplane bearings, photographic films, surgical materials, and pharmaceutical
products. Handy and Harman listed several hundred industrial uses of silver wholly connected with defense, together
with the names of dozens of firms engaged in the processes
of manufacture to point up the desperate industrial need of
the Mexican output.

Morgenthau heeded the appeal by declaring that he would
not bid for foreign supplies against industrial users. Therefore, when the Treasury set thirty-five cents for its first
monthly bid to Mexico, Handy and Harman established a
New York price of thirty-five and one-eighth cents. Mexico
chose to sell her silver in December on the open market.
The Treasury continued its monthly bids during 1942, but
throughout the war Mexican silver swelled the total for industrial uses.

The Treasury continued its monthly purchase agreement
with Canada, but bought only a small amount in November.
Instead, it suggested to the Canadians that they offer their
silver to the market instead of to Washington. The Treasury bought no Canadian silver in December, nor after November 28, 1941, did it purchase any foreign silver from any
source. War conditions thus brought about what Congress
had failed to accomplish -- a cessation o. foreign silver
purchases.

In addition to the considerable volume of foreign coins
that were minted in the United States, the American demand
for small coins was so augmented that the mints operated
on a twenty-four-hour schedule. The Director of the Mint
attributed the increased demand to trade expansion under
the impetus of defense, the popularity of vending machines,
and the new sales taxes.[2] A total of 52,000,000 ounces of
Treasury silver was used in subsidiary coinage in 1941.
This figure was greatly increased in each of the succeeding
two years, when the wartime demand for change skyrocketed.

One cause of the increase was the new "silver" nickel,
started in 1942 to conserve other metals. It contained 35
percent silver, 56 percent copper, and 9 percent manga-
nese.[3] The rest of the silver went into half dollars, quarters,
and dimes.

Under the impact of the wartime demands, Morgenthau
told the House Appropriations subcommittee in January that
he favored the repeal of all silver legislation, which, he believed, would help combat inflation and free the metal for
industrial uses. A month later he told the press that the
Treasury was studying repeal and other methods of making
silver available to industry.

Prominent columnists led the condemnation of the government's silver policy and described the Silver Bloc in strong
language as a selfish group working contrary to the best interests of a nation at war. They believed that no legislation
was needed to enable the Treasury to supply industry with
silver. The New York Times later castigated a government
that urged a patriotic public not to hoard sugar, rubber, and
gasoline, only itself to hoard the silver vitally needed for
war. It was a fantastic situation that "could exist only in a
bloc-dominated Capitol."[4]

Meanwhile, the War Production Board had formally asked
the Treasury to find some way of loaning its free silver for
such industrial uses as would not consume the metal, but
that would release copper for other purposes. The silver
would be employed as bus bars at the new government-
owned aluminum and magnesium plants and could be returned after the war. "Free" silver was the government's
uncoined metal that was not held as backing for silver certificates.

Morgenthau obtained favorable opinions from the Treasury's General Counsel, the Attorney General, and the President. Then he sent White and Foley to talk to Congressional
leaders other than silver enthusiasts, and they agreed that
the Treasury should go ahead.

All the hurdles were not yet demolished. Jesse Jones,
Secretary of Commerce and chairman of the Reconstruction
Finance Corporation, announced in cabinet meeting that the
proposed plan would involve a loss to the government of
about $80,000,000, since it was unthinkable that all the sil-
ver could be returned. The Defense Plant Corporation, a
subsidiary of RFC, had agreed to transport the silver, fab-
ricate it for use in the plants, and protect it as much as
possible. Jones thought that nothing more should be required,

particularly a demand for the return to the Treasury of silver of identical weight and fineness.[5]

Morgenthau believed that such a requirement was more reasonable than expecting the Treasury to stand the loss, and he was impatient at the delay in feeding silver into the channels of industry. Jones involved the President and Donald Nelson, of the War Production Board, in the controversy. The latter finally wrote Jones a letter flatly asking that the Defense Plant Corporation assume the risk of the silver. The President approved Nelson's letter, and on May 6 a contract was signed between the Treasury and the Defense Plant Corporation leasing 40,000 of the 47,000 tons of unpledged bullion for nonconsumptive uses, and guaranteeing its return in identical form.[6]

Meanwhile, the War Production Board had put a low priority on the sale of machinery and explosives to silver mines in an attempt to force the mining of more strategic materials, especially copper. Senator McCarran immediately countered with a resolution in Congress calling for an investigation.

Morgenthau continued his attack on the silver program during the spring. On March 30 and again on April 23 he publicly advocated repeal, adding that new domestic silver should be available to industry at the world price. Under such attacks the Silver Bloc prepared for battle. McCarran sounded the first alarms by convening the Silver Committee and asking Morgenthau to attend.

With the death of Senator Pittman in 1940, the chairmanship of the Senate Special Silver Committee had passed to Elmer Thomas, once a fire-eating inflationary silverite. As head also of the Committee on Agriculture and Forestry, Thomas had no trouble during the war years in finding help for agriculture, his first love, whereupon a little of his enthusiasm dwindled for inflationary silver proposals such as he had fathered in the past. Therefore, the Silver Committee often sat with McCarran as presiding officer as well as the most active and vocal of the group. It had been purged of all heretics such as Senator Townsend, so that eight of its nine members were from the Western mining states.

The Committee was at the peak of its power in 1942. With silverites in complete control, it considered all Senate matters that touched its interests. In June it received from the Senate extensive powers to investigate, not only all problems affecting the mining and use of silver, but the mining of gold as well.

Before this solid phalanx of silver, Morgenthau repeated that he felt the silver legislation should be abolished. However, he assured the Committee that his Department did not plan to seek repeal, and that he knew of no such move in Congress. He frankly stated that he liked to pick his fights and that silver was not one of his choices. If he ever changed his mind, he promised to notify that Committee, while the members agreed to refrain from pushing new legislation. An informal truce was again created similar to the one in 1935 between the same adversaries.[7]

The Secretary was involved in silver questions during the rest of the year. Even before the signing of the final contract with the Defense Plant Corporation, Donald Nelson was writing the Treasury about the urgent need for more of the metal. The free silver made available by the agreement was already allocated, and WPB was eyeing the Treasury's large stocks of pledged silver. Morgenthau was not sure the Treasury either could or should touch this metal, which the Silver Purchase Act required as 100 percent backing for silver certificates. Besides, he recalled his promise to the Silver Committee. Consequently, he notified McCarran that he, Nelson, and Jones would like to appear before a subcommittee which was then conducting hearings on silver almost exclusively for the public appearance of mining representatives.

On May 28 the three appeared before the group and made a strong plea. They asked the silverites to authorize the leasing of pledged silver, or at least to recommend Congressional action in this direction. They got nowhere with the group except to receive a promise of collaboration in preparing legislation that would later be considered by the full Committee. But no such collaboration ever took place.

Morgenthau made another effort to free his metallic stocks on June 18, when he again appeared before the Committee. This time he requested Congressional sanction for lend-leasing silver for coinage purposes to allied nations, several of which had requested large quantities. After the meeting McCarran announced his conditions in terms that any blackmailer would understand: sell 500,000,000 ounces to the Allies at one dollar an ounce, then replace it with American-mined silver at the same price.[8] But two days later he reported that the Committee, after mature deliberation, had decided that the Treasury should retain its stocks to back up American currency, since silver sent outside the country might be used to debase the value of United States money. The deliberations of this august group failed to take into account the fact that the bolstering of foreign silver currencies was one of the original aims of the Silver Purchase Act. In repudiating its own measure, the Committee took a shortsighted view of the future of its metal.

At the end of June, McCarran again proposed that the government price for newly mined domestic silver be raised from seventy-one cents to one dollar, asserting that it would stimulate production sufficiently to satisfy all demands. The proposal was an argument in circles, for even if production were stimulated, the government must continue to purchase the entire output, still forcing industry to buy foreign silver.

McCarran also announced that the Committee would postpone consideration of silver proposals for sixty days. The period was to be spent on a junketing expedition through the West by a silver subcommittee. Before the departure of the group, Morgenthau tried again to get a sympathetic response from the silverites. By that time requests for coinage silver had come from six countries. But the Senators insisted on getting the opinion of their constituents before making decisions. They proceeded to hold hearings at Reno, Salt Lake City, and Denver.

The silver crisis to which this small group of Senators held the solution increased in severity during the spring and summer. The story of silver for the greater part of 1942 relates the attempt by the Treasury, OPA, WPB, and the silver manufacturers to channel the supply, to ration its use, and to control its price.

Until July the Treasury bought the entire domestic production at seventy-one cents. Latin American and Canadian silver was acquired by American industry, and there was no excess to provide for the coinage and industrial needs of allied countries. Furthermore, imports into the country were below normal because of shipping difficulties and a reduction in Latin American production resulting from a shortage of mine equipment. Simultaneously, the needs of American art and industry were running farther and farther ahead of the available supply. The silver industry itself took a step toward meeting the problem by rationing foreign silver for all uses other than war or essential production.

The Office of Price Administration on April 28 took another step to control the situation by issuing its General Maximum Price Regulation that established price ceilings. Semifabricated silver products and articles sold at retail were affected, and silver bullion henceforth was to have a maximum price of 35.375 cents within the country.

However, the civilian silver industry soon realized that this control did not extend to Mexico, and agents of the silverware, jewelry, and other nondefense concerns went to Mexico City to buy silver direct from the mining companies. At first they had to offer only a small premium above 35.375 cents to obtain the metal, but as competition became keener, bids up to sixty cents were reported for substantial amounts. So far as American regulations were concerned, there was nothing illegal about this acquisition or use of Mexican silver. However the practise decreased the amount of silver imported through the usual distributors; this shortage caused a stricter rationing to the nonessential user, and stimulated him to seek his own supplies more zealously in the outside market. By July the result was the end of voluntary rationing by the silver industry, since silver was available by allotment only to priority users of the metal.

The American silver industry furnishes an illuminating example of the struggles of a nonessential concern to survive in wartime. Most large manufacturers of silverware, because of the nature of their equipment and the capacity of their plants, had been able to adapt their operations at least partially to war work. The remaining nonessential users of silver operated chiefly in small plants where light machinery and hand labor performed most of the work. For various reasons these concerns were unable to convert to essential production.

These industries had had trouble obtaining enough silver for their expanding demands since early in the year. With the collapse of the rationing system, they were even prepared to buy domestic silver at the inflated price of seventy-one cents if the Treasury would withdraw from the buyer's market. On July 15 Secretary Morgenthau postponed delivery of contract silver from the producers, and several million ounces of new metal were released to industrial buyers. However, they were unable to obtain the total domestic output because some of the producers preferred to continue their business with the government.

OPA followed up the Treasury action by specifically authorizing the sale of newly mined domestic silver at 71.11 cents, and allowing an increase in the price of semifabricated articles containing this metal, but failing to increase the price of the finished articles. The ensuing rush of orders caused the demand to exceed the supply in September, and the industry attempted to ration the available domestic output. New rumors of favorable OPA action and of unfavorable

WPB moves on the use of domestic silver stimulated private buyers. All in all, the nonessential silver users spent a difficult year trying to keep in business from one month to the next.

Their worries were no greater than those of government officials in their attempt to assure a supply of silver to essential users. Faced with the emasculation of its program for channeling Mexican production into war uses, WPB in July confined the importation of silver to those with special authorization to import, sell, process, or ship. Its purpose was to prevent the bidding up of the price in Mexico by nonessential users. WPB followed this in a week with a conservation order that restricted the use of foreign silver after October 1 to the filling of orders with certain preference ratings. It went further and attempted after that date to distribute such foreign silver as was available for nonessential uses on the basis of preference ratings also. Those industries with little or no rating would be driven to a complete reliance on domestic silver.

During the summer, Mexico began to feel restrained by American regulations from realizing the maximum from her silver. Ramon Beteta, Under-Secretary of Finance, came to Washington to charge that imposition of price and import controls was unfair on a product that yielded substantial revenues to the Mexican government.[9] Mexico needed increased income for wartime expenditures, and wanted to restore the old export tax on silver to at least ten cents an ounce. OPA stood in the way of its restoration, for under prevailing American ceiling prices, the miners would get no more than twenty-five cents for their silver, and production would fall off.

The Mexican situation rested upon the anomaly of part of her silver being bid up to sixty cents in Mexico City, while the part that went into American war industries brought only thirty-five cents. Nevertheless, OPA next established a ceiling price of thirty-five and three-eighths cents on all imports of silver bullion. Its previous restrictions had cut down but not ended the bidding up in Mexico City by nonessential American users. Furthermore, OPA intended to facilitate imports of silver by abolishing any reason for speculative withholding in anticipation of higher prices. The ceiling brought the opposite result. Mexican sellers who had been receiving premiums from American buyers in the outside market were loathe to accept thirty-five cents, and they immediately restricted their sales.

Consequently, within a month OPA announced a new ceiling of forty-five cents for foreign silver. The price was satisfactory to the Mexicans and freed the metal that had been withheld in anticipation of such a rise. Mexico entered a "gentleman's agreement" to sell all her surplus silver only to the United States. Furthermore, the new price completely froze the nonessential user of silver out of the foreign market, thus re-directing supplies back into the channels of priority orders. This effect, together with the WPB conservation order that limited foreign silver to essential uses, revolutionized the situation in the war industries, where foreign silver became abundant by October.

Meanwhile it became known that the contract of the previous May for the loan of "free" silver had been executed slowly, and the press bombarded Washington for an explanation. The delay in delivery resulted from the fact that the plants in which the silver was to be used were only in the process of construction at the time the contract was made. However, by September daily deliveries were being made, and the Treasury announced that all the free silver would soon get into nonconsumptive war uses. It did not announce that it had just diverted 6,000 tons of this metal to the War Department as a substitute for copper on the highly secret Manhattan Project of atomic research. The fact later became known that silver wire, which conducts electricity better than copper, was used on the thousands of electromagnets required to concentrate U-235 and plutonium at Oak Ridge, Tennessee.[10]

The President himself was startled when he suddenly realized the system of control over silver that had been established in his name. He had always kept silver frames on hand with which to give distinguished visitors his picture. When Grace Tully sought Mr. Bernheim, the family silversmith in New York, she found he had gone out of business because he could get no metal without a priority. The President thought Bernheim must be crazy, because the country had more silver than it knew what to do with, enough to use for plumbing. He ordered Miss Tully to call Morgenthau. The Secretary of the Treasury explained that his hands were tied because the Silver Senators had the situation sewed up. Miss Tully decided that wooden frames would be fine.[11]

Several bills for repeal of the Silver Purchase Act were introduced into Congress in the late summer and early fall, but they caused hardly a ripple. Representative William S.

Hill, of Colorado, revealed the outlook for any such attempts by saying: "If they show any signs of life we'll present a united front against them. These boys from New York had enough to say about the country's finances. They've put us in a hole."[12] A more rewarding plan originated in the attempt of nonessential silver users to obtain supplies from the Treasury stocks. The first rumbles of the campaign came from Rhode Island, an important silver-fabricating state. In August, 133 jewelry and silverware concerns signed letters to their Senators and Representatives asking them to obtain Treasury silver for industry.

Senator Theodore F. Green early assumed the lead in the movement. He was aided in his campaign by the organization early in September of the Silver Users' Emergency Committee in Providence. Its chairman frankly announced that the Committee would "turn the torch of public opinion upon the silver situation and demand of Congress that the question of hoarding silver be faced."[13] Thus a counterpressure group was born that conducted an aggressive campaign to publicize its objectives.

The Committee considered itself engaged in the life-or-death struggle of the silver industry, which on October 1 was to be barred completely from foreign silver. Although the nonessential users could now acquire domestic silver at seventy-one cents, there was great dissatisfaction partly from the fear that there was not enough, partly from the failure of OPA to raise the ceiling price of finished articles made from expensive silver. The Committee regarded the Treasury stocks as the only guarantee, not only against a silver shortage in war industries, but also against the failure of many nonessential concerns. It declared that in wartime nonessential business should not complain of real scarcities, but denied that there was a shortage in view of the government's unused hoard. It asked that all silver not actually in the form of coins be made available to industry.

Senator Green introduced a bill summarizing this objective on September 14. It authorized the selling, leasing, or otherwise disposing of all government silver to the war effort, which was broadly defined to include civilian needs contributing to that effort. Specifically, it allowed the loan for nonconsumptive uses of silver pledged as backing for silver certificates, and the sale for consumptive purposes of unpledged silver at reasonable rates.[14]

The Green bill, together with proposals for repeal of the silver laws, aroused the fighting opposition of the Silver

Senators, fourteen of whom met in McCarran's office on
September 18 and agreed unanimously to oppose any change
in silver legislation, and the Green bill in particular. Since
the Treasury had not yet announced its position, McCarran
wrote Morgenthau to suggest that the Secretary's understanding with the Silver Committee included a promise to
oppose all legislation on silver, which Morgenthau immediately denied. The Senator insisted that there was no occasion for the bill, since the nonessential industry was not
really in need of Treasury silver.

McCarran made another attempt to enlist the opposition
of the Treasury in a conference at the Morgenthau home one
evening in October. Failing to persuade the Secretary to denounce the bill, he then pulled from his pocket an extortion-
ate substitute of his own that would limit the use of Treasury
silver to war industries, make it available at seventy-one
cents rather than at the proposed fifty cents, and require the
Treasury to push its purchase price of newly mined silver
to $1.29 an ounce. Morgenthau refused to consider these
proposals, and he told McCarran: "I don't think you can get
away with it."[15] Yet the fact that the Secretary did not take
the stump to promote the Green bill was interpreted as his
fear that the Silver Bloc would line up against the Treasury's impending war tax proposals.

The Green bill received a subcommittee hearing in mid-
October. Written testimony from Morgenthau and Donald
Nelson favored the law, as did oral arguments from labor,
WPB, the Navy's procurement office, and the silver industry. Under the impact of all this support, the subcommittee
reported it favorably with a recommendation for quick action.

The hearing before the Senate Banking and Currency Committee was finally held on December 1. There McCarran
petulantly expressed his grief and bewilderment at the violent press attacks on the Silver Bloc, being especially hurt
by two: the Saturday Evening Post's desire to see the
twelve Silver Senators gathered in one room and submitted
to a lead pipe, and Sylvia F. Porter's charge of treason in
the leading article of the Reader's Digest.[16] Indeed, a few
days later in Congress McCarran accused the two authors
of murder -- the murder of reputation, integrity, and sincerity. Yet theirs were but two of a swelling stream of articles and editorials, mostly under the heading of "The
Silver Scandal," and all excoriating a selfish group for ob-
structing the war effort.

McCarran refused to divulge his counterproposals before an unsympathetic Committee. Rather, he awaited a better opportunity, meanwhile vigorously opposing the bill as it stood. Consequently, it was considerably vitiated as the result of the hearing. The Committee reported it favorably to the Senate with a recommendation for quick action in the name of the war effort.

The time was now short. The session of Congress was nearly concluded, since Christmas adjournment was near. Delaying the bill in the Senate was a simple matter. McCarran instituted a one-man filibuster on December 4 to prevent its consideration. He produced his own substitute, substantially in the form he had shown Morgenthau in October except that he had dropped his project of pushing the Treasury's price for new silver to $1.29.

Congressional adjournment killed the Green bill on December 16. Even if it had passed, one of its amendments would have barred it from helping the nonessential users of silver. They were now completely cut off from foreign silver, for even when there was an excess of imports over current priorities, the Metals Reserve Corporation stockpiled it against anticipated increases in war demands. Nonessential users finished the year by buying domestic silver at seventy-one cents in a market frequently insufficient for their needs.

The long and tedious job of committee hearings had to be repeated in the new Congress that convened in January, 1943. A flood of silver bills was introduced in the House of Representatives, most of them proposing outright repeal of the silver purchase program. In the Senate, three bills were submitted, two by the doughty friends of silver, Senators McCarran and Murdock, and one the reintroduction of the Green bill as amended in the previous session. The Senate bills were referred to the Banking and Currency Committee, where the same routine was undertaken, starting with hearings on all three before a subcommittee late in April.

Facing the necessity for even further retreat in favor of the silver interests, Senator Green announced that although the proposed fifty-cent price of Treasury silver had been recommended by the Department itself, he was willing to let it go to seventy-one cents, as demanded by the silverites. The higher price eventually won out by default since the Treasury did not protest; the representatives of the silver industry merely emphasized their great need for the metal, regardless of its cost; and WPB, while favoring the lower rate, promised not to object to committee action.

The bill then moved swiftly to the floor of the Senate. Green asked for unanimous consent to consider it immediately, thinking it was now a noncontroversial measure. But McCarran was still to be heard. He objected to Senate action until another matter pertaining to silver was decided. At that time Senate and House conferees were trying to compose their differences over a House amendment to the Treasury-Post Office Appropriation bill that would deny funds to the Treasury for the purchase of silver, or for the execution of any provisions of the Silver Purchase Act. At McCarran's insistence Green agreed to let his bill wait for what should have been a quick disposition of the appropriation measure. Unfortunately the dispute over the latter continued for more than a month.

This was the second time that Representative Emanuel Celler, of New York, had sought to invalidate the silver purchase program by denying it financial support. The House had approved his amendment, the Senate had rejected it, and the two branches had gone into a long, drawn-out huddle.

The Celler amendment was finally deleted in conference and the silverites allowed Senate consideration of the Green bill on June 18, when its sponsor obtained a final amendment allowing silver to be made available both to war and nonessential industries. Then the bill passed unanimously, with the support of the Silver Bloc, which had used it as a lever for getting a higher silver price and for helping to defeat the Celler amendment.

The measure quickly passed the House, but almost a year had been needed to unlock the Treasury vaults by legislation. The final measure freed more than a billion ounces of silver to industry. It might be sold for consumptive uses at seventy-one cents on the recommendation of WPB, or it might be leased for nonconsumptive uses until six months after the war. The only restriction on quantities was that the Treasury must retain sufficient silver, either in its vaults or in nonconsumptive uses, to back up its silver currency.

The passage of the Green Act came at a time when it was most needed to implement both the foreign and domestic supplies, which by July were diminishing. Part of the shortage of foreign silver in 1943 resulted from Mexico's retention for coinage of a large part of her production. She first made an effort to have her cake and eat it too. She seriously proposed to Washington a large loan of Treasury silver to cover the costs of her new coinage, so that she could continue the delivery of all her own metal to American war industry. Morgenthau thought the suggestion made no more sense than loaning copper or nitrates to Chile, and he discouraged the Mexican request in its infancy.[17]

The shortage also resulted from the diversion of Mexican silver to silversmiths. They obtained the metal in a variety of ways, including purchase from dealers who melted silver pesos for the bullion content. The Mexican silver industry was highly profitable because of enlarged American demands for fabricated articles, as well as for those crude forms of "jewelry" that were hastily fashioned and sold abroad for industrial purposes. In order to check this practise the government imposed a high export tax on these items.

Furthermore, in order to get the maximum of income from the metal, and to direct it into American industry, the Bank of Mexico was appointed sole buyer and seller in the country. The Bank's system of allotments to the silversmiths merely encouraged the creation of a black market that still denied to American industry a substantial portion of the silver production.

The Green Act was also opportune from the point of view of domestic metal. Silver at seventy-one cents was scarce, partly because of reduced output resulting from a shortage of labor and materials, partly because producers resumed delivery to the Treasury rather than to industry. This was their reaction to the threat of a complete termination of Treasury purchases if the Celler amendment passed.

On July 29 WPB came to grips with regulations covering the newly released silver. The Board's difficulty arose from the need to distribute the metal for essential needs at two price levels -- seventy-one cents for Treasury silver and forty-five cents for foreign importations. It chose three categories to accomplish its purpose.

A) It restricted the use of foreign silver to the manufacture of medicines and health supplies, the photographic and electrical contact industries, and to orders with a high preference rating. Regardless of the rating, this cheaper foreign silver might not be used at all on silverware, jewelry, compacts, cigarette cases, and a long list of nonessential civilian items.

B) WPB must approve all purchases of Treasury silver for consumptive uses, which were arbitrarily limited to the four industries of engine bearings, official military insignia, brazing alloys, and solders. Originally, WPB had considered a plan whereby each industry might buy part forty-five cent and part seventy-one cent silver, but had dropped the idea when it learned OPA would have months of difficult investigation to untangle price ceilings.

C) All domestically mined silver was to go to nonessential industry for restricted uses, on the basis of 50 percent of 1941 or 1942 consumption, whichever was larger. OPA on the same date allowed the manufacturers who must use the more expensive silver to pass along the difference in price to the consumer.

The shortage of silver and its vital place in the industrial winning of the war made such regulations necessary, and probably they were as equitable as possible under the circumstances. They reserved all the low-priced foreign supplies to the most important of the war industries. Higher silver was divided between the essential and nonessential users. The regulations were extremely detailed and called for several amendments during the rest of the war. Furthermore, the high price of domestic and Treasury silver created an element of risk in the inventory of business concerns. The Treasury solved this problem by agreeing to repurchase any unused silver from the four designated buyers of its stocks.[18]

The entire silver industry thus operated under strict regulation until 1945. The import price of forty-five cents was maintained, and the supplies were more than adequate to fulfill the requirements of the industries specified by WPB. In periods of surplus imports the Metals Reserve Corporation continued its practise of stockpiling silver against emergencies. With the exception of some millions of ounces released by this organization for coinage purposes, the entire supply of foreign silver went into war industries.

The four uses of Treasury silver were expanded during 1944 to include Navy neck-chains and desalination kits. During the two years and a half of the Green Act's operation, a total of 167,380,000 ounces of silver was sold.[19] All of it went into industry except 12,900,000 ounces sold to the Philippine government after its restoration by American invasion forces.

Treasury silver was loaned to the Defense Plant Corporation for war uses under the contract of May, 1942. In 1944 it reached a peak of more than 900,000,000 ounces.[20] The Treasury's "silver" nickel consumed some 48,900,000 ounces of silver.[21] Treasury metal lend-leased to foreign governments under the authority of the Green Act reached a total of 410,814,000 ounces.[22] Altogether the Treasury loaned at home and abroad at least 1,410,000,000 ounces returnable on an ounce-for-ounce basis after the war. In fact, so important had the release become at the end of 1944, when the Green Act was scheduled to terminate, that Senator Green and others experienced little difficulty in extending it through 1945.

The provisions on domestic silver in the Green Act were somewhat less beneficial. Although Treasury purchases of newly mined silver dwindled almost to nothing, so that the nonessential industries obtained most of it, still there was trouble. The permissible uses were prescribed by WPB, and quotas of 50 percent of prior consumption were established for each industry. The output at the mines decreased each year until in 1945 it was only about 40 percent of the 1941 production. The greatest single factor in this decline was the lack of labor, but the shortage of equipment was partly responsible. As the available supplies fell farther below requirements, WPB was beseiged with requests to release Treasury silver for use in nonessential industries. The Green Act authorized this use of the metal, but WPB, unable to guess how long war needs would continue to drain Treasury stocks, refused to release them for other purposes.

Consequently before the end of 1944, the ration to silver users was considerably reduced and the industry was faced with a serious curtailment of operations. Therefore, in January, 1945, WPB abolished its distinctions in use between Treasury and domestic silver, maintaining only the quota system. The change guaranteed the minimum allotment to nonessential users, but actually it had few beneficial results. By this time the industry was unable to get enough labor to maintain production, and thus could not take advantage of new supplies of metal.

Relaxation of control over industry followed shortly after V-E day. On May 25, 1945, WPB abolished all distinctions between Treasury and domestic silver, ended quotas on the use of each, and kept control only over foreign silver, which was now extended to the manufacture of engineering, chemical, and bearing products. The changes had little effect on essential users of silver, which had been getting their requirements anyway, and the nonessential users were still unable to benefit because of the continued labor shortage.

After V-J day, with the wholesale cancellation of war contracts, WPB withdrew its control over all the uses of silver, whether foreign, domestic, or Treasury. With the exception of price ceilings, the silver industry was suddenly thrown back on its own. A scramble was made to purchase cheaper foreign metal by that part of the industry which had previously been limited to high-priced silver. But little success resulted. Sellers of foreign silver had their fingers to the wind and held up their stocks in the expectation that with the removal of differentials between foreign and domestic silver OPA would raise the ceiling on imported supplies.

The silverites were agitating for this step. OPA had little choice in the matter, for with the end of WPB controls over inventories of foreign and domestic silver, a two-price level could not be enforced. Therefore, in September a ceiling price of 71.11 cents was established for foreign silver that thereby was valued at the same price as domestic and Treasury silver.

As a result of OPA action, foreign supplies, chiefly Mexican, were available for a time in considerable quantity. Mexico took the opportunity to impose an additional silver tax, which now totaled twenty-one cents an ounce. However, her producers shortly began to withhold their metal again, partly because of McCarran's new drive in Congress for $1.29 silver. Harassed domestic users went back to the Treasury as their most reliable and adequate source. Withdrawals were resumed under the authority of the Green Act, accelerating toward the end of the year because of the fear that the Act would be terminated.

Meanwhile Senator Green had not been idle. On two occasions during 1945 he tried to get the Act extended. His second attempt was a bill introduced in October that proposed to lease or sell Treasury silver at seventy-one cents for manufacturing uses incident to reconversion and the building up of employment in industry. The bill stipulated only that this metal should not be coined or pledged as monetary backing for silver certificates. [23]

An identical bill was introduced into the House by Minority Leader Martin. It was approved a few days before adjournment in December. It traveled a rougher road in the Senate, where it was slow in receiving consideration by the Banking and Currency Committee. A hearing was finally held on December 18 at which Secretary of the Treasury Vinson favored passage and to which Chester Bowles sent OPA's blessing. But under the impetus of silverite opposition, the Committee decided to postpone further consideration of the measure until the next session of Congress. By its action it allowed the Act to lapse.

Although a financial panic in India was averted in 1940, an acute silver shortage continued. The Indian people developed a preference for silver over paper money that mounted precipitously with the rapid Japanese victories early in 1942. The government had difficulty finding enough silver for its needs, particularly because of hoarding by her war-frightened peasants, and the price on the Bombay market started an upward spiral.

As a result of American entry into the China-Burma-India theater of war, and of the need for a stable currency preparatory to using India as a base for fighting the Japanese, the American Treasury early investigated the situation. It found that the normal supplies of the metal from Burma and Australia were no longer available to India, and that her stocks of silver were insufficient to satisfy the war-hoarding of her own people, to say nothing of the needs of the British Empire. India thus furnished a key to the growing shortage of silver for coinage in the Empire, as well as the complete lack of the metal for wartime industrial demands. Not only was Great Britain desperate for industrial silver, but the presence of large numbers of American and other troops in the British Isles, Australia, and India helped to create an unusual demand for small coins.

Under the circumstances these nations had no recourse except to the huge idle hoard of silver in the United States Treasury. As early as April, 1942, London sought American silver for coinage, while Australia and several other countries shortly followed suit. The British also asked for a large monthly allotment for their war industries, but the Treasury thought silver for coinage was more important, and believed that authority for industrial purposes would be more difficult to find. The Treasury's General Counsel believed that the President had a legal right to transfer "free" silver under the authority of the Lend-Lease Act.[24]

Since Morgenthau had promised to consult the Silver Committee on silver matters, he asked McCarran to call a meeting early in July. The silver interests were engaged in a persistent attempt to raise the price of silver during wartime shortages, asserting that the metal deserved as much consideration as agricultural produce that was now subsidized at 110 percent of parity. Morgenthau mourned that his tax expert, Randolph Paul, sat up nights trying to close a couple of hundred-million-dollar loopholes in the law, only to have the savings squandered overnight on subsidies. The Secretary, therefore, was under no illusions about the intentions of the Silver Bloc, which he termed a "squeeze play" to get silver up to at least a dollar.[25]

Morgenthau listed for the silverites four countries that had already submitted direct requests, and two others about to do so. He called their fulfillment an aid directly or indirectly to the war effort of the allied nations. He quoted the Department of State's opinion that such a use of the metal was essential. Not to be stampeded on a matter so close to their hearts, the Senators postponed all silver proposals while they toured their Western constituencies. Facing an indefinite delay, Morgenthau announced that the urgency of the needs abroad forced him to proceed.

The Treasury first turned to the Lend-Lease Administration, where it hoped to reach quick agreement on foreign loans. A decision was not immediately forthcoming, for Lend-Lease officials felt that loans for industrial purposes were possible, but not the loans for coinage in which the Treasury was most interested. They maintained that the Lend-Lease Act limited loans to defense articles, which could not be defined to include silver coins; that the loan of silver for coinage might be denounced by the public as a direct loan of money; that in any case the appropriations committees of the houses of Congress should be consulted. Harry White for the Treasury argued that adequate coinage was a basic factor in effective production of defense articles, that foreign industries would suffer if industrial silver had to be diverted to coinage, and that American troops stationed abroad had contributed to the critical shortage of small coins.

The British themselves helped to break this impasse by making it clear that they did not want to return the silver after the war, because it was to be consumed as a substitute for tin in solder. This qualified request interrupted Washington plans, since it was assumed that the Silver Senators would approve nothing less than an ounce-for-ounce replacement. Harry White pointed out to Lend-Lease officials that it was dangerous to ignore the Silver Committee's opinions because "their dissatisfaction with the silver program will be manifested in their attitude on every important measure."[26]

The Treasury continued its appeal to Lend-Lease for approval of coinage silver that could be made returnable. Eventually Administrator Edward R. Stettinius, Jr., came

to view coinage as closely identified with the war effort, and
in December consented to loan silver for this purpose. Early
in 1943 India and several other countries applied for the
metal. Mexico sought a silver loan for her new coinage so
that her exports to American industry might continue un-
checked. The Mexican request received scant attention, but
the others were sympathetically considered at Lend-Lease
headquarters and the Treasury. Yet it was not until May that
a first loan of 3,000,000 ounces was made to Great Britain.
The contract did not specify how the silver would be used,
but called for return on an ounce-for-ounce basis after the
war. Lend-Lease cleared the matter with the Silver
Committee. [27]

Stettinius was now ready to execute all Treasury recommendations. But Morgenthau felt that he needed the approval
of the Silver Committee before he embarked upon full-scale
operations. Hence he again appealed to the group, one year
after he had first sought out the same men for an identical
purpose. Before the Committee he divided the requests for
aid into two categories. In the first, he put those demands
for coinage silver from Great Britain, India, Australia, the
Fiji Islands, Surinam, and Curacao, of which the first two
wanted regular monthly allotments. These proposals raised
no serious dissent, although Senator McCarran was not enthusiastic.

But the Secretary ran into trouble when he added India's
additional demand for 100,000,000 ounces immediately. Mc-
Carran stubbornly maintained that the amount was too large,
that the metal would find its way to Britain instead of to
India, and that American reserves would be endangered.
Morgenthau argued that the silver would be used to protect
Indian coinage and combat inflation, which was threatening
the country. Prices were already abnormal, and rising silver threatened to cause hoarding, the melting of coins and
an even more stringent shortage of circulating metal. The
Indian government would sell silver bullion to limit the inflationary rise in all prices and to encourage the continued
production of agricultural and industrial goods. Morgenthau
pointed out that far from impairing the world position of silver, the loan would really bolster it and guarantee at least
one country tied to the metal after the war.

The majority of the Committee viewed the loan as an aid
to the war effort in a place where plans for the whole future
of the Pacific war came to a focus. Only McCarran dis-
sented, but by the end of the conference even he appeared to

give tacit approval.[28] Yet on the same day he wrote a letter
of vigorous dissent. Far from being alarmed at one-dollar
silver in India, he feared that the American loan would be
used to depress rather than stabilize silver, and that the
United States would build her own guillotine by cooperating.

Morgenthau was worried by this single opposition, which
all too often in the past had been able to rally a solid front
on silver matters. Seeking to offset the responsibility he
would assume by pushing the Indian loan, he pressed the
British for a quick assent to the American proposal on reverse lend-lease. Since the signing of the original master
lend-lease agreements, the United States had received in
reciprocal aid only military equipment plus supplies and
services for American troops and bases on British, Indian,
Australian, and New Zealand soil. [29] As the war progressed,
reverse lend-lease from the British Empire, although
large, fell further and further behind American aid.

A movement consequently started in Washington in 1943
to make reciprocal operations include strategic raw materials which the United States was currently having to buy
with cash in lend-lease countries. Morgenthau linked the
proposal to India's demand for silver, and intimated to Lord
Halifax that the alternative to British agreement was a cut-
ting down of purchases in the United States.[30] Before the
summer was over Great Britain had agreed generally to
broaden reverse lend-lease. Negotiations for specific arrangements went forward during the fall, not only with the
United Kingdom, but also with other governments of the
British Commonwealth, including India.

Meanwhile Sir Cecil Kisch of the India Supply Mission in
Washington continued to urge immediate action on both the
coinage and the anti-inflation loans. He produced evidence
that the need of new coins was urgent and could not even
wait for the previously requested small monthly allotments
of American silver. Morgenthau pushed through a loan of
20,000,000 ounces for coinage purposes. The Indians desired that the loan be unpublicized so as not to alarm their
people about the weakness of their finances.[31]

But Sir Cecil was not as fortunate in his importunities for
the loan of 100,000,000 ounces. Washington officials were
not sure that the silver could perform all the functions that
India expected, or that the Indian government possessed
clear methods and objectives for handling it. Furthermore,
the British Empire had not yet made specific agreements
for reciprocal aid to the United States.

During November these agreements began to be reached.
The one with the United Kingdom and India provided that
mica, burlap, jute, and other strategic commodities were to
be supplied on reverse lend-lease from India. Convinced
that Silver was badly needed, and that it could not fail to
help even if it did not fulfill all Indian hopes, Morgenthau
recommended the loan early in January, 1944, to Leo T.
Crowley, Administrator of the Foreign Economic Administration, which now handled lend-lease.

The loan already had been under consideration for some
time in FEA, but the negotiations continued to drag on.
Therefore, India asked for an emergency advance of 65,000-
000 ounces. She was put off at the Treasury in the confidence
that the larger anti-inflation loan was about to be arranged.

It was not finally made until June, 1944. The delay resulted
from prolonged discussions over whether Great Britain
should guarantee the loan. India was eager to enter into the
arrangement without British participation as a recognition
of her sound financial position and as a matter of prestige,
while Great Britain hesitated to participate, partly because
of the additional responsibility it entailed, chiefly because
of her sensitivity to Indian charges of meddling. Her wartime relations with India left much to be desired, and she
wanted to avoid further aggravation.[32]

Crowley urged the State Department to let the British temporarily underwrite the Indian program, allowing Britain
and India to come to terms later. State rejected the suggestion on the ground that the risk of an agreement with India
alone was too great. Although the Treasury had been prepared to do business with India directly, it could not ignore
the State Department's desire for British endorsement.
Hence a decision was reached in Washington that lend-lease
should be arranged with both India and Great Britain.

But the deadlock remained. The British were still reluctant to enter the agreement, while the State Department
would not change its conditions. Furthermore, the American
attitude deeply angered the representatives of a new nationalistic India. One of them complained to Harry White that no
one in the State Department had the slightest understanding
of what was going on and that nothing was more destructive
of Indian-American relations than to assume that neither
India's word nor her future could be trusted. He ended with
a bitter burst of wonder that any foreign office could be so
stupid.[33]

When the Indians in desperation asked a second time for

an advance on the larger loan, the Treasury was sympathetic, while Lord Halifax personally gained the acquiescence
of both the State Department and FEA. The request for
10,000,000 ounces was filled immediately in an arrangement
with India.

During April the State Department reached a limited understanding with the British on the guarantees of Indian
loans. The terms were kept secret to minimize British fears
of public opinion in India. On June 8, 1944, the United States
and India signed a final agreement and the additional 90,000-
000 ounces of the loan were sent, a year after they were
first requested.

This silver was kept in bars in Bombay, where it was sold
as needed to combat inflation of the metal. The Indians felt
the whole quantity was necessary for such a precautionary
reserve. Thus by summer they were looking for more coinage silver, the demand for which, they pointed out, was increased by the presence of large armies and by the great
allied expenditures in their country. Sir Jeremy Raisman,
Finance Minister of India, who headed his country's delegation to the Bretton Woods Conference, in July asked Morgan-
thau for an additional 100,000,000 ounces for coinage purposes. A month later Mr. K. C. Mahindra, of the India Supply
Mission, repeated the request, lowering it to 65,000,000
ounces. The Treasury persuaded the Indians to accept this
amount in installments, the first to consist of 20,000,000
ounces and the rest presumably to follow at regular inter-
vals. The first installment became available in December,
1944.

Meanwhile during 1943 several other countries applied
for silver. Both Ethiopia and Iraq needed it for coinage. In
each case the Treasury was reluctant because neither country appeared to be a good risk. But in each case the State
Department favored the loans for political reasons. Morgan-
thau finally announced that he would honor written recommendations to that effect from State. Further, the Dutch
Government-in-Exile asked for 47,000,000 ounces in order
to have coins ready at the time of the invasion. Since the
Army favored the loan to help Dutch morale during its European operations, the request was eventually filled.

In 1943 the Treasury loaned some 40,800,000 ounces of
silver to five countries, and agreements were pending at the
end of the year with Ethiopia, the Netherlands, Saudi-Arabia,
and Australia.[34] During the winter the Ethiopian need for
new coinage became urgent. To start with, she asked for

only 5,430,000 ounces. When both the State Department and WPB urged the loan, Morgenthau joined in recommending it.

The Treasury hesitated to loan silver to Saudi Arabia. The Middle Eastern representative of the State Department was recommending as much help as possible to Arabia, even to the extent of an annual subsidy up to $20,000,000, if it would bring the assurance of an oil supply for the war. The Treasury saw no justification for a coinage loan, and opposed it as a subsidy unless State demanded it for political reasons. Eventually the Treasury was persuaded, and large loans went to the Near East.

Late in 1944 the Financial Counselor of the Polish Embassy sought a loan of silver for coins in anticipation of Poland's complete liberation from German occupation, and he also asked the Treasury to mint the coins. The request was not granted. Poland passed from occupation by Germany to occupation by Russia, and stopped looking to the West for assistance of this nature.

Lend-leasing of silver reached a peak during 1944. The recipients of loans were Australia, Ethiopia, Great Britain, India, the Netherlands, and Saudi-Arabia, totaling over 200,000,000 ounces, of which more than half went to India.[35]

In February, 1945, India petitioned Crowley for an additional 208,000,000 ounces, half for coinage and half for sale to combat inflation. Sir Jeremy Raisman recalled assurances of the previous winter that her requirements would be met by periodic installments, and complained of delays with each new application, complicated by an American demand for fresh statistics to support it. Pointing out that India's coinage needs had been so great that she had already coined more than one-third of the anti-inflationary silver, in addition to having sold another third, he pressed for a minimum of 45,000,000 ounces immediately.

To some extent these charges were true. Lend-Lease requests had to go through State, Treasury, and FEA, where disagreement or deliberations often consumed many weeks. On occasion the Indians exaggerated their needs and asked too much, causing a wariness in Washington. The Americans made several attempts to cut down on Lend-Lease items, other than military goods, to countries that were not lending in reverse an amount commensurate with the aid they were receiving.

However, this latest request received attention, and in May, 1945, a loan of 45,000,000 ounces was authorized. This was increased during the year to a total of 106,000,000 ounces. In 1945 some 163,700,000 ounces were made available to all countries, including India, Great Britain, the Netherlands, Saudi Arabia, and Belgium.[36]

For the two and one-half years during which the lend-leasing of silver was in operation, total foreign releases from the Treasury reached 411,000,000 ounces. (See Appendix for a tabulation of lend-lease silver by country.) The agreements under which they were made were not subject to cancellation, and required a return on an ounce-for-ounce basis within five, and in some cases seven, years after the President declared an end to the emergency. To date no silver has been returned.

BRETTON WOODS

In 1940 silver's Little White Father, Key Pittman, had prophesied on the basis of his monetary experience in the first World War that silver during World War II would be in great demand as the only satisfactory medium for paying soldiers. He declared further that after the war the world's chaotic finances would make an international metallic base necessary. There would be insufficient gold for such a purpose, and silver would provide at least a part of it.[37]

The Senator would undoubtedly have become the leader, through his post at the head of the Foreign Relations Committee, and his experience at the London Conference of 1933, in a silver program at the council tables of the second war. But Pittman died late in 1940. His prophecy came true on the expanded use of silver for coinage. But his followers in the United States for some time chose the policy of trying to prevent the use of Treasury silver to bolster foreign currencies.

On the other hand, the Silver Bloc took an active interest in an international monetary base. Its members were horrified at the Treasury's plan for an international gold-backed currency stabilization fund, which was first revealed on April 6, 1943. On the next day the Silver Committee met to chart its campaign for promoting silver in postwar plans. Senator Thomas declared that the metal must be considered along with gold because "Mexico, Central and South America, India and China regard silver as of first importance."[38] An early step in the campaign was McCarran's unsuccessful attempt in July to create a Senate committee to survey proposals for a postwar currency.

Francis H. Brownell, chairman of the American Smelting and Refining Company, took up the cudgels. He advocated the adoption of international bimetallism by agreement of the leading commercial nations of the world, and listed eight advantages. Basically he was convinced that the world's supply of gold was too small and poorly distributed to form a base for international currency, and he reviewed the breakdown of the gold standard during the 1930's as proof.

Brownell, who was being paid $100,000 a year by American Smelting for this kind of activity, and who had once been one of the mentors of Senator Pittman, argued his convictions before the House Committee on Foreign Affairs. He wrote, and his company published, a thirty-five-page pamphlet advocating world bimetallism, by the United States alone if necessary. He believed that the "accident of history" should be corrected by which England chose the gold standard, thus committing the world to that standard until its collapse in the twentieth century. He asserted that the war experiences and the general distrust of paper money now made much of the world ready to return to hard money. [39]

The battle lines were clear well in advance of the Bretton Woods Conference of July, 1944. Neither the British nor the American plan allotted much importance to silver. Mexico was ready to insist on its use as a monetary medium, an attitude which was warmly supported by the Silver Bloc and the American mining companies, who were preparing to demand recognition at the conference.

On June 21 the President received a letter from Senator Thomas in which twenty-five Western Senators asked that parities for member countries' currencies in the international fund be fixed in silver as well as gold. The Administration, opposed to silver in the proposed fund, was reported to have enlisted Representative Sol Bloom and Senator Green to wage a countercampaign. Following Brownell's testimony before his committee, Bloom asked Herbert Bratter, expert on finance and economics, to make a reply. Bratter took the matter out of the stratosphere of international affairs and posited it squarely as the attempt of silver producers, led by American Smelting, to increase the price and broaden the market for silver. [40]

The American delegation to Bretton Woods was headed by Secretary Morgenthau and was made up of men hostile to silver. The Secretary had made it known in advance that the Treasury would resist all attempts to include the metal in the World Monetary Plan, despite the appeal from Eduardo

Suarez, Mexican Finance Minister, that he "just leave the door open for silver."[41]

A flurry was caused at the conference by the expulsion of a New York publicity man. The correspondent for the Baltimore Sun, speaking for several members of the press, electrified the meeting on July 8 by asking "under what authority Mr. David Hinshaw of the American Smelting and Refining Company is present at this conference and in this room." Hinshaw left the conference, and no attempt was made to prove his identity. However, he later admitted that he had talked to journalist and Congressional friends and that his public relations firm had had intercourse with the American Smelting Company. After his departure, professional agitators for bimetallism were forced to work covertly, largely by telephone.[42]

The Silver Bloc was still to be heard from. On July 13 every member of each delegation at Bretton Woods received from Senator Thomas, in a franked envelope, a copy of the letter sent to President Roosevelt in which a consideration of silver was requested.

The chief pleader for the metal was Mr. Suarez, who urged international application of the silver stabilization policies pursued over the past ten years by the United States. He praised the American program and its execution as a benefit to all silver-producing countries, even as its administrator, Secretary Morgenthau, refused to lift a finger to second the Mexican proposals.

Sufficient agitation ensued that a committee of ten nations was appointed to study the problem. The silver-producing countries of South America were interested in achieving a position for the metal, but not to the extent of Mexico. Consequently, after a period of wide disagreement, the committee agreed only that the "subject should merit further study by the interested nations."[43]

Thus the Bretton Woods Conference avoided the type of silver activity that transpired at the London Economic Conference in 1933. The result was a foregone conclusion from the nature of the American delegation, most of which Morgenthau recommended, and the rest of which the President supplied. Between them they prevented the naming of anyone comparable to Key Pittman, thereby depriving the Silver Bloc of representation. Without aggressive advocacy of silver by one of the major powers, the metal stood no chance in the stabilization plan that emerged from Bretton Woods, particularly since the American silver program had already forced the abandonment of the metal by many nations.

Nevertheless, the American silverites were not ready to admit defeat. Article V of the Bretton Woods Agreement contained a germ of hope for expanding the importance of silver in the international fund. It provided that "in the opinion of the fund" account might be taken of members' willingness to pledge as collateral security either gold, silver, or securities, when a member wanted to use the fund's resources in excess of the amount determined by its quota. In that case the nation would ask for a waiver and offer to deposit money as collateral.[44] Silverites felt this recognition of silver was too limited, particularly because it was made dependent upon the whims of the fund's managers.

When the plans for a World Bank and a Stabilization Fund were submitted for the consideration of member nations, the American silverites got busy. They demanded a more definite commitment for silver as a medium for settling international balances. They let the Administration know that they would be in a trading mood when the legislation came before the Senate, where the Silver Bloc held the balance of the vote. Meanwhile they embarked on a series of meetings with Treasury representatives, officials of the American Banking Association which opposed the world monetary plan, and a member of the British Parliament, also opposed, in a search for allies and deals.

The Treasury warned that changes were impossible, since an insertion in the Bretton Woods Agreement would require the reconvening of the entire conference. But McCarran stated that the Bloc "will stand together on this." It was generally recognized that if help for silver was unobtainable in the Bretton Woods legislation, the silverites were "ready to work for anything else which would serve their special interests."[45] Another storm of protest was heaped upon the Silver Bloc as a selfish group trying to sabotage the peace as it had the war.

Unperturbed, Senator Thomas prepared for a fight. When the Senate Banking and Currency Committee held hearings on the Bretton Woods Agreement Act, he offered two amendments of a monetary nature -- one to create a new gold coin known as the gold ounce, worth $35; the other to direct the use of unpledged silver to pay the American subscription to the new International Bank. This metal should be valued daily in terms of gold, and be regarded as the full equivalent of gold.[46]

The silver proposal was bimetallic in purpose, and both it and the gold amendment were rejected in committee. The undaunted Senator introduced them in the Senate, where he faced more friendly faces than in committee. His gold proposal was voted down, but the silver amendment helped to accomplish a useful purpose for the Bloc before Thomas finally withdrew it.

During Congressional consideration of the Bretton Woods Agreement, Senator Abe Murdock visited the new Secretary of the Treasury Vinson to reach an understanding. He asked for the issuance of silver certificates to the full monetary value of silver at $1.29 an ounce, instead of the cost price of the metal, as Morgenthau consistently had done. He argued that in a period of high governmental expenditures it was unwise to issue bonds that contributed to credit inflation as well as to government indebtedness, when additional silver certificates would be no more inflationary and would involve no indebtedness. His arguments were sound, and in addition he was advancing the silver cause. The Secretary agreed in principle to such a treatment of his 300,000,000 ounces of free silver as the need arose; he received President Truman's assent, and the Silver Bloc thus thought it had obtained one of its old objectives. [47]

The moment that Murdock finished telling the Senate what he had accomplished, Senator Thomas withdrew his amendment on silver in the World Bank. On the same day the Bretton Woods Agreement Act, which had now played a part in giving silverites something "that would serve their interests," was passed by the Senate in basically its original form. International bimetallism would have to wait.

However, the silverite rejoicing was premature, for Secretary Vinson was not so naive after all. In February, 1946, Murdock was still asking him to start paying government debts by monetizing all the Treasury's free silver. He based his argument on the fact that the employment of all this silver would terminate the public pressure on Congress to pass the new Green bill, since there would no longer be any silver that the Treasury could sell under its provisions. And yet Secretary Vinson was backing the Green bill!

IX. SILVER TODAY

The unrestrained liberty of political association has not hitherto produced in the United States the fatal results that might perhaps be expected from it elsewhere.... If it does not throw the nation into anarchy, it perpetually augments the chances of that calamity.

Tocqueville, I, 194 f.

The postwar career of silver can best be told by surveying the most recent silver campaign, which was just as vigorous and ambitious as any that went before and equally successful. As for the future of pressure politics on the issue, a few comments will suffice to indicate the doubtfulness of any change in direction or emphasis.

Two events in 1945 opened up new possibilities for "doing something for silver." The termination of the war demobilized all the scruples the Silver Bloc had ever had about interfering with the war effort. Furthermore, the sudden changes at the White House and the Treasury offered new hope. Gone were the two leaders who had learned after years of experience the futility of any dealings with the silverites, and who, especially in the Treasury, had consistently stood in the way of all new silver ventures.

In many ways the situation was analogous to that of the spring of 1933, with a set of new and untried leaders who must attack a great national problem. In 1933 the crisis was the depression, for which silver was offered as a cure. In 1945 it was the clamor for a quick if painful conversion to the ways of peace.

Silver provided one of the keys to this conversion, and the Silver Senators were not slow to see their advantage. Chiefly because of labor shortages, the silver mines of North America had cut their production from a peak of 175,000,000 ounces in 1940 to 112,000,000 ounces in 1944. Yet over the same period, the industrial consumption of the United States alone had risen from 44,000,000 to 125,000,000 ounces. The Green Act made Treasury silver available during 1944 and 1945 to fill the gap between supply and demand, but the Treasury's free silver was consequently reduced to about a two-year supply for industry. Thus despite a vast

hoard of pledged silver at West Point, the country faced a
statistical shortage that led one magazine to comment that
"The bloc now proposes to cure the patient by giving him an
additional dose of what laid him low."[1]

The additional dose was prescribed in a renewed campaign
on several fronts to get some favors for silver. One was the
agitation after V-J day for the removal of all ceilings over
foreign metals. Another was the decision to oppose extension of the Green Act after 1945, except under certain conditions.

One of these conditions was announced by McCarran in
September when he began to urge that the Treasury pay
$1.29 for domestic silver. He wrote to the President, Sec-
retary of the Treasury Vinson, Secretary of State Byrnes
and Price Administrator Chester Bowles to point out that
the higher price would stimulate American production.
"There would be no expense to the Federal Government,"
he explained, "as such silver would immediately be coined
and placed in circulation at its full value."[2]

In the most ambitious silver move of the decade, McCarran introduced a bill in October calling for $1.29 metal and
for the repeal of three sections of the Silver Purchase Act
of 1934. He was merely continuing his ten-year attempt to
abolish the Treasury's authority to regulate all silver transactions and to nationalize silver, as well as the speculator's
tax that the Senator derided for producing only $3,300,000
in revenues, and for making London pre-eminent over New
York as the world's silver center.[3]

Along with McCarran's bill, Congress also was considering the identical bills introduced by Senator Green and Representative Martin to continue the Green Act into 1946.
Their failure has already been recounted.

The termination of the Green Act brought near panic to
the industrial users of silver. They had fought a hard battle
against extinction during the war, and the peace seemed no
more promising. In 1945 North American silver production
was at a new low of 103,000,000 ounces, only 28,000,000
from the United States. But in the same period American
industry alone consumed a record 140,000,000 ounces.[4] This
demand was met from hoarded foreign supplies that were
freed after the September price rise, from South American
production, and from Treasury sales. But the lapse of the
Green Act closed the Treasury as a source of supply; quick
sale at seventy-one cents helped to exhaust the hoarded
foreign stocks, while the Senate campaign for $1.29 silver

caused a new wave of hoarding until the summer of 1946. In addition, both the Mexican and American output was further reduced by strikes and a continued shortage of mine materials.

Consequently, the silver shortage in 1946 presaged a shut down of many American concerns, which were already forced to curtail activities. In June the industry appealed to President Truman for emergency action. Automotive concerns faced a slowdown because of the complete halt in deliveries of electrical contact points which were made of silver. The General Electric Company used 5,000,000 ounces of the metal annually on electrical production, but by June was near the end of its supply. The Photo-Engravers' Board of Trade of New York even melted silver dollars to obtain metal.

Against this background of distress to an entire industry, and of painful reconversion generally, the Silver Bloc waged one of the longest and most disastrous campaigns of its career. From January to July serious hardship resulted from the stubborn efforts of a small group of Senators, who eventually got most of what they wanted. They referred to their compromise on the final price of silver as a "generous gesture."

Western mining areas were faced with a different problem of reconversion. Long before the war the mines of some states, especially Nevada, had skimmed the top from the richest silver deposits, so that in some places ghost towns resulted, in others a declining production from marginal mines. Between 1941 and 1944 three-fourths of the 4,542 American silver mines were closed, partly because they could not meet their advanced operating costs, partly because they lacked men and materials.[5] Western states with small populations and miniscule incomes begged for silver prices adequate to revitalize their marginal mines.

Yet the creation of ghost towns in Wisconsin from the exhaustion of the timber resources or in New England from poor farm land has never led to a drive for subsidies in Washington. Furthermore, if the fact is recalled that at least three-fourths of American production is a by-product, it will be realized that a silver subsidy goes only in small part to silver mines, and mostly to mines of copper, lead, and zinc.

When Congress reconvened in 1946, the Green bill was still in Senate committee, having passed the House in the previous session as the Martin bill. It was bitterly opposed by all silverites because it made silver too cheap and there-

fore discouraged production. The Sunshine Mining Company
of Idaho, whose 1945 production was 7,000,000 ounces, wrote
its stockholders to try to defeat the measure. The concern
feared it would establish a permanent ceiling on silver, so
that the rapidly rising cost of production could not be met in
the future by price adjustments.

The House sought to break the deadlock by attaching to the
big Treasury-Post Office Supply bill a rider allowing Treasury sale of its silver at seventy-one cents. The proposal
reached the Senate subcommittee on Appropriations in mid-
February, where the ubiquitous McCarran was a member. It
was held up for more than two months, until McCarran got
his way. He obtained the adoption of an amendment to the
House rider which directed the Treasury to pay 90.3 cents
an ounce to domestic producers of silver for one year, during which time it might sell at the same price. Subsequently,
the Treasury must pay $1.29, and might sell at the same
price. Crowed McCarran, "This does not end the long fight
which began with the 'Crime of 1873,' when silver was demonetized, but it brings the end of that fight in sight."[6]

To insure his position, McCarran introduced in the Senate
a bill with similar requirements. The lines were drawn up
for a fight to the finish, with the Silver Bloc prepared to
hold out indefinitely, threatening to prevent action at the current session of Congress, and to let a prolonged silver shortage soften up its opponents.

In May sixty-six of the leading economists of the country
signed an appeal to Congress to reject the new proposal as
"inexcusable." It noted that "The attitude of the silver bloc
in respect to the public welfare...appears to be no better today than it was during the late war, especially in 1942."[7]

Not to be outdone, the Colorado Mining Association ran
large newspaper advertisements that urged letters to Congress in support of the new price of silver. Asserting that
the silver producers "cheerfully cooperated in the enact-
ment of special silver legislation" during the war, it suggested that a failure to reciprocate now would place the onus
squarely on the silver users.[8]

The supply bill with its silver rider passed the Senate
unanimously early in June. It went to a Senate-House conference, where it was fought over for a month. The House conferees stood by seventy-one cents for silver, and were
repeatedly supported by votes on their side of the capitol.
The Senate conferees were as stubborn until July 10, when
the Senate approved a compromise that kept the ninety-cent

price but removed McCarran's proposals for a later rise as
well as some of his other silver projects. The House refused
even this concession, while the Senate for a third time rejected House proposals by a vote of fifty-four to twenty-five.
Southern and Western Senators abandoned party lines: thirty-
five Democrats and eighteen Republicans voted for ninety-
cent silver, while eleven Democrats and fourteen Republicans
wanted seventy-one cents. Senator Taft called the higher
rate "a fair price in view of supply and demand" and "increased cost of production."[9]

The first of July ushered in a new fiscal year with neither
Treasury nor Post Office funds. The pay of 552,000 Federal
employees was threatened, and checks to postal employees
were not forthcoming at the mid-July period; still the deadlock remained.

July first marked another event that eventually helped convince some legislators that ninety-cent silver was better
than none. The price control law expired, automatically removing all ceilings. For the first few days, little silver trading was done at any price in view of the uncertainty of
Congressional action. But by July 11 accumulated stocks of
the metal created a pressure on the market, and trading occurred in considerable quantities at 90.375 cents, approximately the proposed Senate price. Industrial buyers seemed
willing to pay this price, and business was brisk for two
weeks. On July 26 OPA was revived, and with it the ceiling
price of seventy-one cents for silver. Immediately the market shut down. By this time it had been demonstrated that
silver would move at the higher price. Meanwhile, Congress
had finally come to terms on a rise, and the measure was in
the hands of the President.

The maneuvers between House and Senate need not be detailed here. Eventually new conferees from each body were
named, and they reached agreement in part by divorcing the
price of silver from the supply bill, which the silverites
allowed to proceed independently. The silver measure that
was finally adopted by both houses on July 19 required
Treasury purchase of the entire domestic production at
90.5 cents an ounce, and allowed Treasury sale to industry
of all free metal at the same price.

On August 1 OPA dutifully raised the ceiling to 90.5 cents.
It kept silver under control to assure that the price of foreign metal did not exceed the Treasury's rate. The silver
industry almost immediately was able to get the metal it
wanted from foreign sources. Yet in August the American

National Jewelers Association was warned at its convention
to gird for a real fight with the silver producers, whose
next move would be to skip $1.29 and push for $2.19 silver.

During the rest of 1946 the Treasury purchased the entire
domestic production at the mandatory price. However, it
sold only 4,889 ounces to industry at ninety-one cents.[10] By
December, domestic industry was consuming 10,000,000
ounces a month. It obtained 7,000,000 ounces of the new production of Latin America and Canada. The deficit came
chiefly from the stocks that were hoarded during the Congressional debate. With adequate supplies thus assured, industry did not find it necessary either to pay slightly more
at the Treasury or to compete for American production.

During the year an attempt was made to resuscitate the
racket in commemorative coins. When he approved silver
coins to commemorate Iowa statehood and Booker T.
Washington, President Truman warned that he would frown
on future measures. He agreed with the Treasury that such
issues led to confusion, counterfeit, private profit, and a
detraction from the fundamental purpose of coinage.

The year also brought a curious stir over the disposition
of surplus property. During the war hundreds of thousands
of kits were fabricated for making ocean water usable. Each
kit contained about five ounces of pure silver. After the war
this fact was overlooked, and the War Assets Administration
sold many for prices ranging from four to forty cents. No
particular attention was paid when the American Smelting
and Refining Company paid $2.80 each for 13,000 kits in
December 1945, nor to other large purchases. But as the
demands grew, the WAA had the kits analysed and discovered their value. The bags cost the government $20, and
WAA expected now to realize about four dollars. After a
brief suspension of sales, they were once more put on the
market for sealed bids.[11]

As in the months following the passage of the Silver Purchase Act, the American silver program of 1945-46 wrought
its worst havoc abroad. Although the Silver Senators continued to pay lip service to the enhancement of silver in the
world's monetary systems, their actions went far to complete the demoralization of several currencies that their
earlier activities had started. For example, Spain, Hong
Kong, and China continued to dispose of their demonetized
silver after the war.

Shortly after OPA raised the ceiling price of foreign silver to seventy-one cents in 1945, the Mexican government,

with its silver coins again facing the melting pot, halted the sale of pesos to the populace and forbade the export of coins and bars. Mexico and the United States canceled their "gentlemen's agreement" of August, 1942, whereby the latter was given priority on all the surplus Mexican silver production. Instead, the Bank of Mexico set out to retire its old coins preparatory to minting new ones of smaller silver content. Yet they were turned in very slowly, even at the high premium offered by the Bank, for people preferred them to the paper currency offered in exchange. Thus Mexican devaluation was not an accomplished fact at the end of 1946, although it was still the government's goal.

Meanwhile, after she had nailed down her financial cellar doors, Mexico was glad to be swept up by the cyclone of high prices. During the prolonged Congressional debate on silver, she let it be known that her stocks were growing, and that a substantial rise would unfreeze them. The American advance to ninety cents released much of the hoard. In December, 1945, Columbia announced a reduction of silver in her coins. The larger coins were to contain much less silver, while the small ones would now be made of copper and nickel. At one time the shortage of fractional coins because of hoarding led the government to cut the paper peso in half and overprint it with "provisional half peso." [12]

Indeed the American price "unfroze" great quantities of the world's silver. The imports of July, 1946, were seven times those of May, and by October, sixteen countries were shipping their metal to American industry. It came at slightly lower rates than the Treasury price and in such volume that for once the industrial demand was filled.

The end of the war made necessary the settlement of Lend-Lease accounts. Great Britain and India were both tremendous recipients of aid, of which silver was an important item. Both countries were dismayed at the advance in its price, for every rise added to the burden of repayment. Since neither was a silver producer, they must obtain supplies elsewhere to ship to the United States.

In May, 1946, India signed an agreement with the State Department canceling Lend-Lease between the two countries as nearly equal. Nothing could wipe out her debt of silver, the full 226,000,000 ounces of which must be repaid.

Meantime the wartime scarcity of the metal continued in India, speculation was rife, and the price on the Bombay market rose to $1.56 in May. The Indian government took the inevitable step of demonetizing when it withdrew from circulation all subsidiary silver coins and started replacing them with nickel. One of the purposes was to build up a stock of silver with which to repay the United States. The result was the termination of silver currency by one of its few remaining users.

The American rise in price in the summer increased the burden of Indian debt, and made her acquisition of silver extremely difficult during the last half of the year. Sellers wanted gold or dollar exchange, neither of which she was able to offer.

Great Britain had the same situation and adopted a similar course. She owed 88,000,000 ounces of Lend-Lease silver to the United States. She had no production of her own. Furthermore, her arts and industries during the war had become attuned to the use of quantities of the metal. Therefore, the British by autumn were spending $1,000,000 of their fast-dissipating dollar exchange monthly to buy silver for industry, while jewelry makers were sacrificed in large part on the altar of import controls.

Nevertheless, the Congressional steamroller complicated the problem by a new price advance. The British, seeking to repay the American silver loan, looked upon demonetization as the only solution. In September the announcement of this action was made. The British planned to replace the silver six-pence, shilling, florin and half-crown with cupro-nickel coins. Hugh Dalton, Chancellor of the Exchequer, told the House of Commons that silver was now too expensive for coins, and that the new type of coinage would stockpile 50,000,000 ounces annually for several years, a total after complete replacement of about $200,000,000.[13]

Meanwhile, China's inflation had gotten out of hand. With a civil war to fight against the Communists and the rehabilitation of the country following its long war with Japan, China needed above all a currency that would command confidence. Instead, by 1947 the Chinese dollar was exchangeable for the American at the rate of 55,000 to one.

Consequently, government and commercial interests, both in the United States and abroad, began to explore the possibility of bringing about a stable currency in China by the reintroduction of silver into her monetary system. There appeared to be only two means by which she could obtain the metal. One was by the slow price-raising method of buying on the open market. The other was by a large loan from the United States Treasury. China could either repay in kind or make deferred payment in dollars. But repayment in

silver would present the same difficulties to China that India
and Great Britain now face. On the other hand, American
silverites were not likely to demand less than complete repayment.

The United States, by embarking upon the European aid
program, in effect left China to meet her own problems by
herself. The deteriorating military situation has merely ac-
centuated her financial needs, but today no large scale aid
in the form of silver is likely.

And so the incredible tale continues to unfold year after
year, with no foreseeable end in view. Every aspect of the
story presents a paradox except that of pressure politics by
and for a small industry. In considering the future, there
are a number of factors that tend to discourage any prospect of a change either in tactics or achievements of the
Silver Bloc.

A) Although the Congressional Reorganization Act of 1946
abolished the Senate Special Silver Committee, it did not and
could not disband the Silver Bloc, which can still meet when
and where it pleases. John Gunther found in 1946 that "the
silver bloc is one of the most efficient, sophisticated, and
ruthless in the nation," approached only by the sugar bloc,
which includes many of the same states.[14]

B) The Senate still seats fourteen Senators from Idaho,
Utah, Montana, Colorado, Arizona, Nevada, and New Mexico,
who represent 3,600,000 people, while 51,900,000 easterners
have the same representation.

C) Outside support for the Silver Bloc continues to include
ready and willing groups. The currency expansionists are
always to be counted on. The Farm Bloc usually loans at
least part of its strength, chiefly because it traditionally
leans toward more and cheaper currency. Outside of Congress lobbyists of the mining industry and other small
groups assert themselves out of proportion to the size of
the interests they represent.

D) Any attempt to repeal statutes such as the silver purchase laws of 1934 and 1946 faces extreme difficulty. The
attack could be expected during a time of crisis, by the co-
operation of determined opponents, backed by the Administration. Yet even under these circumstances in the crises
of 1942 and 1946, the silver purchase program was not at
any time seriously threatened.

E) Nothing tends to indicate that changes of party control
in Congress make any difference. In the Senate vote on silver

in 1946, eighteen Republicans voted for the ninety-cent
price, while only fourteen voted for seventy-one cents.
Westerners, whether Democrats or Republicans, feel their
duty to their silver-conscious constituents. In this the late
Senator Borah of Idaho set the example.

F) The Senate's rules of debate cannot cope with filibus-
ters of the type that McCarran instituted in December, 1942,
to defeat the Green bill, and which recur periodically on one
subject or another.

G) As long as the United States subsidizes sugar, agricultural products, and several kinds of minerals, the Silver
Bloc will have an excuse for claiming its share. The Bloc
maintains that the silver industry is not receiving a subsidy,
because silver purchases are a self-financing proposition
by which the Treasury makes a profit on the coining of its
metal. Yet over a period of thirteen years the Treasury has
paid an average of twenty-four cents above the market price
for some 507,180,700 ounces of domestic silver alone, to a
total of $121,723,370. According to the Economists' National
Committee on Monetary Policy, that expenditure represents
an outlay from the pockets of the taxpayer.[15]

H) The longer the stockpiling of silver continues in the
American Treasury, and the more thoroughly the rest of
the world is denuded of all its supplies, the more completely
committed the United States will be to the maintenance of
the status quo as a protection to its investment.

I) Because silver is small relative to the national economy, it can continue its scandalous role without arousing
great outcries. To be sure, American newspapers and magazines are overwhelmingly in favor of repealing all the
silver legislation. Only the papers of some of the silver-
producing states continue to defend the policy. In the East a
few prosilver opinions appear in the press from silverite
Congressmen or Western mining companies.

In 1935 the Wall Street Journal wrote that "Silver is and
always will be the private and pernicious racket of Congress
members and their constituents in silver-mining states and
of speculators."[16] During the subsequent decade the paper
has written frequently in the same vein. In 1939 the Journal
of Commerce of New York decided: "The whole silver buying program was conceived in folly, and carried out with
primary attention to the political considerations involved."[17]
The New York Times and the New York Herald Tribune began their blistering attacks early in the 1930's and to date
have not called off their heavy guns. In 1934 Business Week

described its impotent rage over the fact that a small group, by sticking together and making loud protests, could win a subsidy for the tiny silver industry and a profit for silver speculators. By 1936 the same magazine reported that the silver program was completely discredited in its current form. [18]

No reputable organs of opinion in the business and financial world can be found with a good word to say about the modern silver program. Magazines present the same preponderance of opinion. For example, in the first eight months of 1946, nine articles condemning the silver policy appeared in such magazines as Fortune, Forum, Nation, Time, Business Week, and Colliers. During that period only one prosilver article appeared, and that was a reply by Senator McCarran to an earlier attack on his group.

Several organizations have labored to abolish the silver laws. Mention may be made of the Chamber of Commerce of New York which, beginning in 1939, advocated prompt repeal. It kept up a severe attack on the wartime policy of keeping silver out of use. The most persistent and noteworthy campaign against silver has appeared in the articles and appeals over a period of a decade from the Economists' National Committee on Monetary Policy, a large group of the country's leading economists. It has frequently tried to explode the myth of the need for silver currency.

Yet this antisilver publicity is not reaching or creating a great informed audience. The technical nature of the subject and the focusing of the citizen's attention on more startling political events nullify the efforts of editors and journalists. Furthermore, the Congressmen at the base of the policy are not affected by Eastern editorials, and Congressional votes continue to be swayed by a purposeful minority despite public opinion.

Indeed it can only be deeply regretted that such a self-perpetuating lobby should ever have become a leech on the body politic. Analysis of each silver campaign has only revealed the necessity of Administration compromise for the sake of more enlightened objectives, and in no way makes the grab more palatable.

The sole apology that can be made for the silver program over the last fourteen years is that it has been administered as well as possible in the interests of the public, despite its inevitably disastrous effects. Former Secretary Morgenthau consistently refused to allow speculation on government activity. At the expense of American export industries, he sought to create jobs by insisting that all foreign silver be refined in the country, and that it be imported on American ships. After a brief honeymoon, he steadily worked the world price of silver downward, not up. As rapidly as he could, he sought to make amends for the damage his policy had done to several countries by buying their demonetized silver and helping them stabilize their new currencies. Incidentally, he labored valiantly to assure a close understanding with those nations whose friendship was so valuable after 1941.

Morgenthau's successors in the Treasury have shown a similar reluctance to exercise the many inflationary and unstabilizing devices that the silver laws allow. Reasonable men shudder to contemplate the results of the administration of these laws by less responsible and conscientious heads of the Treasury Department.

APPENDIX

Table 1

Treasury Purchases of Mexican Silver, 1934 through 1941 [1]

	Ounces	Cost
1934	11,649,000	$ 6,175,000
1935	66,035,000	42,616,000
1936	55,571,000	24,893,000
1937	88,152,000	39,514,000
1938	43,933,000	19,144,000
1939	25,395,000	10,707,000
1940	13,420,000	4,698,000
1941	500,000	175,000
Total	304,655,000	148,012,000

Table 2

Treasury Purchases of Peruvian Silver, 1935 through 1941 [1]

	Ounces	Cost
1935	100,000	$ 62,000
1936	8,423,000	3,791,000
1937	8,216,000	3,697,000
1938	12,655,000	5,492,000
1939	9,192,000	3,719,000
1940	13,426,000	4,699,000
1941	7,080,000	2,478,000
Total	59,092,000	23,938,000

Table 3

Treasury Purchases of Canadian Silver, 1935 through 1941 [1]

	Ounces	Cost
1935	2,152,000	$ 1,213,600
1936	16,692,000	7,511,400
1937	18,642,000	8,388,900
1938	29,496,000	12,830,760

Table 3 (Continued)

	Ounces	Cost
1939	24,018,000	$ 9,343,000
1940	20,550,000	7,192,500
1941	18,844,000	6,595,400
Total	130,394,000	53,075,560

Table 4

Treasury Purchases of Other Latin American Silver,
1934 through 1941[1]

Country	Ounces	Cost
Honduras	16,941,000	$6,683,000
Argentina	3,494,000	1,359,000
Bolivia	2,671,000	1,235,000
Dominican Republic	190,000	82,000
Ecuador	157,000	70,000
Nicaragua	120,000	54,000
El Salvador	65,000	22,000
Cuba	57,000	23,000
Chile	12,000	5,000
Unidentified	1,212,000	457,000

Table 5

Treasury Purchases of Chinese Silver, 1934 through 1941

	Ounces	Cost
1934	19,506,000	$ 10,427,997
1935	50,115,000	32,166,303
1936	66,975,000	30,157,000
1937	130,026,000	58,512,000
1938	265,892,000	115,530,000
1939	33,341,000	13,787,000
1940	5,142,000	1,800,000
1941	805,000	282,000
Total	571,802,000	262,662,300

Source: Figures are based on summaries in Diary, February
15, 1940, CCXLI, 47 ff., and Diary, January 13, 1942,
CDLXXXV, 311.

Table 6

American Lend-Lease of Silver, 1943 through 1945

Country	Ounces
India	225,999,904
Great Britain	88,073,878
The Netherlands	56,737,341
Saudi Arabia	22,347,431
Australia	11,773,093
Ethiopia	5,425,000
Belgium	261,333
Fiji Islands	196,364
Total	410,814,344

Source: Annual Report of the Secretary of the Treasury...
1946, p. 87.

NOTES

I. THE GOOD OLD DAYS

1. Market prices, unless otherwise stated, are from Handy and Harman, Annual Review of the Silver Market, for appropriate years.

2. Figures of Under-Secretary of the Treasury Gilbert as quoted in Westerfield, Our Silver Debacle, p. 24.

II. HARD TIMES FOR SILVER

1. "Silver, Just Silver," Fortune, VII, No. 1 (July, 1933), 58.

2. Bratter, The Silver Market, p. 7.

3. Bratter, Use of Silver in 1933, p. 6.

4. Figures for 1925 from U. S. Bureau of Mines, Minera. Resources of the United States, Vol. I, 1925; for 1931 from the corresponding volume of that year.

5. Bratter, The Silver Market, p. 27.

6. Production figures come from the following sources: Memorandum on the American Smelting and Refining Company by the firm of Gilbert Elliott and Company, December 7, 1935; Thirtieth Annual Report...of the United States Smelting, Refining and Mining Company...December 31, 1935, p. 10; Memorandum on Cerro de Pasco Copper Corporation by the firm of Bryan, Penington, and Colket, August 16, 1934; Report of the Anaconda Copper Mining Company for...1929, p. 5; ...for...1932, p. 8.

7. New York Times, May 14, 1932.

8. Charles A. and Mary R. Beard, America in Midpassage, I, 112.

9. Economist (London), August 18, 1934.

10. Purchase of Silver: Hearings before a Subcommittee of the Committee on Banking and Currency, United States Senate, 72d Cong., 1st sess., on S. 3,606 and S. J. Res. 152, p. 9.

11. New York Times, September 21, 1932.

12. Ibid., November 8, 1932.

13. Silver and the Foreign Debt Payments, Senate Document No. 8, 73d Cong., 1st sess.

14. Purchase of Silver, Hearings...72d Cong...., p. 4.

15. New York Times, May 9, 1932.

III. NEW EFFORTS IN OLD DIRECTIONS

1. The Public Papers and Addresses of Franklin D. Roosevelt, 1928-32, p. 756.

2. Ibid., 1933, p. 14.

3. Lippmann, Interpretations, 1933-1935, p. 52.

4. For a full exposition of the theory, see Gold and Prices by Warren and Pearson; for a shorter account, see two articles by Warren, both in Forum: "Is Our Gold Standard Too Rigid?" LXXXIX, No. 4 (April, 1933), pp. 194-201; and "The New Dollar" LXXXX, No. 2 (August, 1933), pp. 70-75.

5. Beard, America in Midpassage, I, 206.

6. Moley, After Seven Years, p. 157.

7. Annual Report of the Secretary of the Treasury for... 1933, p. 2.

8. Congressional Record, May 8, 1933, LXXVII, 2,967.

9. Memoirs of Cordell Hull, I, 254.

10. The Public Papers...Roosevelt, 1933, p. 264.

11. "The Compensated Dollar," New York Times, July 23, 1933.

12. Morgenthau, unnumbered set of diary notes for 1933, pp. 37, 47, 50.

13. New York Times, July 24, 1933.

14. League of Nations, Journal of the Monetary and Economic Conference, No. 11, pp. 77 ff.

15. Ibid., No. 34, p. 202.

16. New York Times, October 15, 1933.

17. The Public Papers...Roosevelt, 1933, p. 537.

18. New York Times, December 22, 1933.

19. U. S. Bureau of Mines, Gold and Silver, Statistical Appendix to Minerals Yearbook, p. 417.

20. Business Week (December 30, 1933), p. 6.

21. New York Herald Tribune, January 3, 1934.

22. Letter from Edward S. Greenbaum, October 10, 1947.

23. Pasvolsky, Current Monetary Issues, p. 124.

24. New York Herald Tribune, December 19, 1933.

25. U. S. Bureau of Labor Statistics, Wholesale Prices, November, 1933, p. 1.

26. The Public Papers...Roosevelt, 1934, p. 44.

27. Congressional Record, January 27, 1934, LXXVIII, 1.445-56. 1.463.

28. See the Radio League of the Little Flower publications of sixteen lectures between October, 1933, and March, 1934, entitled The New Deal in Money and Eight Lectures on Labor, Capital, and Justice.

29. Gold Reserve Act of 1934: Hearings before the Committee on Coinage, Weights and Measures, 73d Cong., 2d sess., on H. R. 6,976, p. 65.

30. Childs, "Father Coughlin," New Republic, LXXVIII, No. 1,013 (May 2, 1934), 326-27.

31. Congressional Record, May 22, 1934, LXXVIII, 9,213.

32. Diary, April 29, 1942, DXXII, 18.

33. Congressional Record, March 19, 1934, LXXVIII, 4,814.

34. U. S. Treasury Department, Press Conferences, March 15, 1934, I, 237.

35. For a detailed analysis of the speculative market, see Bratter, The Silver Episode, pp. 819 ff.

36. Chicago Tribune, October 18, 1934.

37. Diary, April 23, 1934, I, 46.

38. Hoarders of Silver, Senate Document No. 173, 73d Cong., 2d sess., Parts I, II, III.

39. Detroit Times, April 29, 1934.

40. Diary, April 27, 1934, I, 49.

41. For the first index, see U. S. Bureau of Labor Statistics, Wholesale Prices, April, 1933, p. 2; for the second, see the publication for May, 1934, p. 2.

42. Lippmann, "A Silver Policy," New York Herald Tribune, May 15, 1934.

43. The Public Papers...Roosevelt, 1934, p. 254.

44. Congressional Record, May 22, 1934, LXXVIII, 9,218.

45. Ibid., April 11, 1935, LXXIX, 5,405.

46. Handy and Harman, Annual Review of the Silver Market, 1934, p. 5.

47. Congressional Record, April 11, 1935, LXXIX, 5,403; also Diary, January 6, 1935, IV, 53.

48. Treasury, Press Conferences, June 21, 1934, II, 176 f.

49. Diary, August 1, 1934, II, 3.

50. Diary, May 29, 1935, V, 185.

51. Report of the Secretary of the Treasury for...1935, p. 42.

52. New York Times, August 2, 1934.

53. Treasury, Press Conferences, August 2, 1934, II, 218 ff.

54. Report of the Secretary of the Treasury for...1934, p. 39;...1935, p. 422;...1936, p. 464.

55. Diary, June 28, 1935, VII, 183.

IV. DISILLUSIONMENT AT HOME

1. Report of the Secretary of the Treasury for...1935, p. 260.

2. Treasury, Press Conferences, April 25, 1935, III, 409.

3. Diary, April 26, 1935, V, 28.

4. Diary, April 26, 1935, pp. 29 ff.

5. Diary, May 14, 1935, V, 89.

6. New York Times, August 14, 1934.

7. Anaconda Copper Mining Company, A Brief Description of the Anaconda Reduction Works, pp. 5 f.

8. For the years 1932 and 1934, see Memorandum issued by Gilbert Elliott and Company, December 7, 1935; for 1937, see the Forty-eighth Annual Report of American Smelting and Refining Company, 1936, p. 13.

9. Anaconda Copper Mining Company Report for...1932, p. 8; ...for...1937, pp. 6 f.

10. Cerro de Pasco Copper Corporation -- Annual Report, 1937, p. 2.

11. Twenty-ninth Annual Report...of the United States Smelting, Refining, and Mining Company...1934, p. 12.

12. Diary, March 10, 1941, CCCLXXX, 275.

13. Congressional Record, March 26, 1935, LXXIX, 4,474.

14. Diary, April 11, 1935, IV, 196 ff.

15. From a study in the New York Times, May 5, 1935.

16. Diary, June 11, 1935, VI, 54 ff.

17. Diary, June 19, 1935, VII, 8A f.

18. Diary, May 15, 1935, V, 90.

19. Congressional Record, May 9, 1935, LXXIX, 7,239.

20. Spahr, "Silver Scandal," Saturday Evening Post, CCXV, No. 18 (October 31, 1942), pp. 19 ff.

21. Diary, November 7, 1935, XI, 35.

22. New York Times, May 25, 1936.

23. The Public Papers...Roosevelt, 1936, p. 448.

24. New York Times, June 26, 1936.

25. Diary, February 23, 1937, LVI, 80 ff.

26. Diary, September 20, 1937, LXXXIX, 49.

27. Congressional Record, December 6, 1937, LXXXII, 922-25.

28. Baltimore Sun (editorial), December 15, 1937.

29. New York Times, April 8, 1938.

30. Ibid., July 6 and 7, 1938.

31. Ibid., September 29, 1938.

32. Diary, December 19, 1938, CLVII, 60 ff.

33. Congressional Record, January 4, 1939, LXXXIV, 69.

34. Diary, February 7, 1939, CLXIII, 228 ff.
35. McConnell, Mexico at the Bar of Public Opinion.
36. Congressional Record, February 28, 1938, LXXXIV, 2,857.
37. Diary, July 6, 1939, CCII, 32 ff.
38. Diary, June 23, 1939, CXCVIII, 353.
39. Morgenthau, "The Morgenthau Diaries," Collier's, CXX, No. 15 (October 11, 1947), 79.
40. Diary, June 23, 1939, CXCVIII, 272 f, 358.
41. Treasury, Press Conferences, June 29, 1939, XII, 302.
42. Diary, July 6, 1939, CCI, 336.
43. Diary, February 13, 1940, CCXL, 415 ff.
44. Diary, February 23, 1940, CCXLII, 199 f.
45. Diary, February 15, 1940, CCXLI, 44 ff.
46. Diary, February 23, 1940, CCXLII, 188 ff.
47. Diary, March 21, 1940, CCXLVIII, 340.
48. New York Times, June 27, 1940.
49. Ibid., July 18, 1940.
50. Wall Street Journal, August 31, 1940.

V. CONFUSION IN LATIN AMERICA

1. Bratter, The Silver Market, p. 36.
2. New York Times, March 21, 1935.
3. Diary, April 16, 1935, IV, 225.
4. U. S. Bureau of Foreign and Domestic Commerce, Latin American Financial Notes, No. 171, May 14, 1935, p. 14.
5. Diary, April 29, 1935, V, 39.
6. Diary, December 11, 1935, XIII, 199 ff.
7. Commerce, Latin American Financial Notes, No. 203, September 14, 1936, pp. 10 f.
8. U. S. Department of State, Press Releases, XIX, No. 460, July 23, 1938, 51 f.
9. Diary, December 13, 1937, CI, 298.
10. Diary, October 6, 1941, CDXLVIII, 98.
11. Diary, October 6, 1941, CDXLVIII, 99.
12. Diary, December 16, 1937, CII, 178 f.
13. Commerce, Latin American Financial Notes, No. 177, August 14, 1935, p. 14.
14. U. S. Bureau of Foreign and Domestic Commerce, Foreign Commerce Yearbook, 1937, p. 252.
15. New York Times, December 19, 1937.
16. Diary, December 31, 1937, CIV, 285 f.
17. Diary, March 24, 1938, CXVI, 406.

18. State, Press Releases, XVIII, No. 444, April 2, 1938, 425.

19. Diary, March 28, 1938, CXVII, 267.

20. Daniels, Shirt-Sleeve Diplomat, pp. 248 f.

21. State, Press Releases, XVIII, No. 444, April 2, 1938, 435.

22. Ibid., No. 448, April 30, 1938, pp. 509 f.

23. Diary, April 1, 1938, CXVIII, 27 ff.

24. Diary, May 12, 1938, CXXIV, 346 f.

25. Diary, May 18, 1938, CXXV, 263.

26. Diary, July 13, 1938, CXXXIV, 164 f.

27. Welles, The Time for Decision, p. 200.

28. McConnell, Mexico at the Bar of Public Opinion.

29. Bernard, "The Lies about Mexico," Mexican Art and Life, No. 5 (January, 1939).

30. Diary, May 8, 1939, CLXXXVIII, 393.

31. Quotations from Washington Post, Portland Oregonian and Nashville Tennessean, of March 22, 1940, and Washington Star of March 24, 1940, respectively.

32. U. S. Department of State, Bulletin, II, No. 45 (May 4, 1940), 465 ff.

33. Diary, June 13, 1940, CCLXXIII, 291; June 21, 1940, CCLXXV, 420; June 19, 1940, CCLXVI, 227 f; July 25, 1940, CCLXXXVIII, 315 f.

34. U. S. Department of State, Treaties 1939-42, Treaty Series 980, November 19, 1941.

35. Report of the Secretary of the Treasury...1942, p. 291.

36. New York Times, May 4, 1935.

37. Diary, October 21, 1935, CXLVII, 139.

38. Diary, October 21, 1935, CXLVII, 139 f.

39. Hamilton, American Treasure and the Price Revolution in Spain, 1501-1650, pp. 42, passim.

40. Leavens, Silver Money, p. 285.

41. Diary, June 1, 1940, CCLXVIII, 186.

VI. CONFUSION IN CHINA

1. New York Herald Tribune, October 3, 1930.

2. New York Times, February 15, 1931.

3. Commercial Relations with China: Hearings before a Subcommittee of the Committee on Foreign Relations, Senate, 71st Cong., 2d sess., pursuant to S. Res. 256, p. 5.

4. Bratter, The Silver Market, p. 56.

5. Ibid., p. 57.

6. For a thorough study, see Lin, China under Depreci-ated Silver, pp. 97 ff.

7. Warburg, The Money Muddle, p. 268.

8. Lewis, and Lu-luan, Silver and the Chinese Price Level, p. 15.

9. "China's Foreign Trade," A Picture of World Economic Conditions at the Beginning of 1932, National Industrial Conference Board, pp. 285 f.

10. The Effect of Low Silver: Hearings...72d Cong...., p. 437.

11. For example, see the fluctuations of cotton imports in Commerce, China Monthly Trade Report (December 1, 1931), p. 29.

12. Kemmerer, Project of Law for the Gradual Introduc-tion of a Gold-Standard Currency System in China, p. 57.

13. The Public Papers...Roosevelt, 1933, p. 537.

14. U. S. Department of State, Executive Agreement Series, No. 63, insert following p. 12 of publication 613.

15. Finance & Commerce (Shanghai weekly), XXVII (April 8, 1936), 392.

16. State, Press Releases, XI, No. 264, October 20, 1934, 259 ff.

17. Welles, The Time for Decision, p. 285.

18. Diary, December 16, 1934, II, 294 ff.

19. Diary, February 17, 1935, III, 305.

20. Diary, February 18, 1935, III, 305, 328.

21. Memoirs of Cordell Hull, I, 207.

22. Diary, June 18, 1935, VII, 69 f.

23. Diary, July 26, 1935, VIII, 192.

24. Diary, November 2, 1935, XI, 25.

25. National Government of China, Ministry of Finance, Report for the 23rd Fiscal Year...., p. 22.

26. Diary, November 9, 1935, XI, 63 ff.

27. Diary, November 18, 1935, XII, 13 ff.

28. Diary, January 8, 1936, XV, 91 ff.

29. Diary, February 10, 1936, XVII, 174.

30. Diary, April 1, 1936, XX, 18 f.

31. Diary, April 14, 1936, XXI, 146.

32. Diary, May 12, 1936, XXIV, 114 ff.

33. Financial News, May 19, 1936.

34. New York Herald Tribune, May 20, 1936; New York Times, May 20, 1936; and Washington Herald, June 12, 1936, respectively.

35. Diary, June 30, 1937, LXXV, 48.

36. Diary, July 7, 1937, LXXVII, 285 ff.

37. Diary, July 8, 1937, LXXVIII, 19.
38. Diary, June 21, 1938, CXXX, 172.
39. New York Times, July 10, 1937.
40. Ibid., July 30, 1937, and August 24, 1937.
41. State, Press Releases, XVII, No. 413, August 28, 1937, 166 f.
42. Diary, September 4, 1937, LXXXVII, 178.
43. Diary, December 6, 1937, C, 394 f.
44. Diary, June 6, 1938, CXXVII, 300 ff.
45. Diary, November 29, 1938, CLIII, 303.
46. State, Press Releases, XIX, No. 474, October 29, 1938; No. 483, December 31, 1938.
47. Diary, June 28, 1939, CXCIX, 262.
48. White and Jacoby, Thunder out of China, p. 115.
49. Ibid., p. 239.

VII. OTHER FOREIGN RESULTS OF THE AMERICAN PROGRAM

1. Leavens, "Silver Coins to the Melting Pot," Annalist, XLVI (July 5, 1935), 3 f.
2. Diary, March 29, 1938, CXVII, 404.
3. Diary, June 7, 1938, CXXVIII, 18.
4. Diary, November 9, 1942, DLXXXII, 356.
5. Diary, February 24, 1939, CLXV, 290.
6. Diary, July 10, 1939, CCII, 153.
7. Banco de Espana v. Federal Reserve Bank of New York, 28 F. Supp. 958 (1939).
8. Diary, November 14, 1942, DLXXXIV, 94 f.
9. Diary, January 2, 1943, DCI, 93.
10. Diary, January 20, 1936, XVI, 14.
11. Diary, January 25, 1936, XVI, 45.
12. Diary, December 2, 1942, DXCII, 215.
13. Bratter, Use of Silver in 1933, p. 29.
14. Handy and Harman, Annual Review of the Silver Market, 1933, p. 29.
15. Diary, July 5, 1940, CCLXXIX, 353.

VIII. SILVER IN WARTIME

1. Handy and Harman, Annual Review of the Silver Market, 1941, pp. 11 f.
2. Ibid., 1942, p. 36.
3. Annual Report of the Secretary of the Treasury...1943, p. 263.
4. See Herbert Bratter in the New York Herald Tribune of March 29, 1942; T. H. Carmical in the New York Times

of March 29, 1942; Ernest K. Lindley in the Washington
Post of March 30, 1942, and an editorial in the New York
Times of August 4, 1942.

5. Diary, April 14, 1942, DXVI, 121.

6. Diary, May 6, 1942, DXXIV, 219 ff.

7. Diary, April 29, 1942, DXXII, 14 ff.

8. New York Herald Tribune, June 19, 1942.

9. Diary, July 17, 1942, DL, 196.

10. New York Times, August 26, 1945.

11. Diary, August 26, 1942, DLXII, 205 ff.

12. Worcester (Mass.) Telegram, September 22, 1942.

13. New York Times, September 8, 1942.

14. Congressional Record, September 14, 1942, LXXXVIII,
7,117.

15. Diary, October 10, 1942, DLXXVIII, 24 ff.

16. "Silver Is a State of Mind," Saturday Evening Post,
CCXV, No. 18 (October 31, 1942), p. 100; Porter, "Twelve
Men against the Nation," Reader's Digest, XLI, No. 247
(November, 1942), pp. 1-4.

17. Treasury, Press Conferences, July 8, 1943, XXIV,
108 ff.

18. Diary, July 21, 1943, DCL, 99.

19. Annual Report of the Secretary of the Treasury for...
1944, p. 245; ...1945, p. 231; ...1946, p. 217.

20. Annual Report...1944, p. 245.

21. Annual Report...1943, p. 263; ...1944, p. 245; ...1945,
p. 231; ...1946, p. 217.

22. Annual Report...1946, p. 87.

23. Congressional Record, October 24, 1945, XCI, 9,938.

24. Diary, July 3, 1942, DXLVI, 159 ff.

25. Diary, July 3, 1942, DXLVI, 3 ff.

26. Diary, July 25, 1942, DLIII, 144 f.

27. Diary, May 4, 1943, DCXXXI, 148 ff.

28. Diary, July 7, 1943, DCXLVII, 5 ff.

29. Stettinius, Lend Lease, Weapon for Victory, pp. 275 ff.

30. Diary, July 13, 1943, DCXLVIII, 73 ff.

31. Diary, August 30, 1943, DCLX, 76.

32. Diary, March 3, 1944, DCCVI, 81.

33. Diary, March 6, 1944, DCCVI, 245.

34. Diary, December 17, 1943, DCLXXXV, 88.

35. Handy and Harman, Annual Review of the Silver
Market, 1944, p. 12.

36. Ibid., 1945, p. 17.

37. New York Herald Tribune, June 1, 1940.

38. Ibid., April 8, 1943.

39. Brownell, Hard Money.

40. Reconstruction Fund in Joint Account with Foreign Governments for Rehabilitation, Stabilization of Currencies, and Reconstruction: Hearings before the Committee on Foreign Affairs, House of Representatives, 78th Cong., 2d sess., on H. J. Res. 226, April 28, 1944, pp. 94 ff.

41. Treasury, Press Conferences, June 29, 1944, XXV, 274 f.

42. New York Times, July 9, 1944.

43. Diary, May 28, 1945, 202.

44. New York Times, July 23, 1944.

45. Ibid., April 6, 1945.

46. Bretton Woods Agreement Act: Hearings before the Committee on Banking and Currency, Senate, 79th Cong., 1st sess., on H. R. 3,314, June 25, 1945, pp. 500 ff.

47. Congressional Record, July 19, 1945, XCI, 7,748.

48. Ibid., June 21, 1946, XCII, 7,287.

IX. SILVER TODAY

1. "Hi-Yo Silver," Fortune, XXXII, No. 6 (December, 1945), p. 272.

2. New York Times, September 21, 1945.

3. Congressional Record, October 15, 1945, XCI, 9,650 ff.

4. Handy and Harman, Annual Review of the Silver Market, 1946, pp. 28, 31.

5. "Silver: Ceiling Up," Newsweek (August 12, 1946), pp. 80 ff.

6. New York Times, April 26, 1946.

7. Ibid., May 20, 1946.

8. Ibid., May 31, 1946.

9. Congressional Record, July 12, 1946, XCII, 8, 751.

10. Handy and Harman, Annual Review of the Silver Market, 1946, p. 26.

11. New York Times, October 11 and 31, 1946.

12. Ibid., December 3 and 28, 1945.

13. Ibid., September 27 and October 16, 1946.

14. Gunther, Inside U.S.A., pp. 183, 221.

15. PM, July 25, 1946.

16. Wall Street Journal, April 13, 1935.

17. McConnell, Mexico at the Bar of Public Opinion, p. 199.

18. "Silver and Money," May 19, 1934, and "Silver Strategy," January 4, 1936, in Business Week.

BIBLIOGRAPHY

Allen, Robert S. "The Man Roosevelt," American Mercury, XXVIII, No. 109 (January, 1933), 18-25.

Alsop, Joseph, and Kintner, Robert. Men around the President. Garden City, N.Y., Doubleday, Doran, 1939. 212 pp.

American Smelting and Refining Company, Annual Reports, New York.

Anaconda Copper Mining Company. A Brief Description of the Anaconda Reduction Works. Privately printed. 30 pp.

Anaconda Copper Mining Company, Annual Reports, New York.

Anonymous. "Silver, Just Silver," Fortune, VII, No. 1 (July, 1933), 56-63, 98, 101-06.

_____ "What's to Become of Us?" Fortune, VIII, No. 6 (December, 1933), 24-30, 112, 114, 117-20.

_____ "Mr. Roosevelt's Men," Fortune, IX, No. 4 (April, 1934), 90-99, 141-50.

_____ "One of Two of a Kind," Fortune, IX, No. 5 (May, 1934), 60-64, 131-38.

_____ "Silver is a State of Mind" (ed.), Saturday Evening Post, CCXV, No. 18 (October 31, 1942), 100.

_____ "Hi-Yo Silver," Fortune, XXXII, No. 6 (December, 1945), 272-74.

_____ "Silver: Ceiling Up," Newsweek, XXVIII, No. 7 (August 12, 1946), 80-82.

Beale, Louis. Report on Economic and Commercial Conditions in China, 1935-37. London, Department of Overseas Trade, H. M. Stationery Office, 1937. 73 pp.

Beale, Louis and Pelham, G. C. Trade and Economic Conditions in China, 1931-33. London, Department of Overseas Trade, H. M. Stationery Office, 1933. 173 pp.

Beard, Charles A. and Mary R. America in Midpassage. 2 vols. New York, Macmillan, 1939.

Bernard, Allen. "The Lies about Mexico," Mexican Art and Life, No. 5 (January, 1939), D A P P, Mexico City. Unnumbered pages.

Bisson, T. A. American Policy in the Far East, 1931-1940. New York, Institute of Pacific Relations, 1940. 162 pp.

_____ America's Far Eastern Policy. New York, Institute of Pacific Relations. and Macmillan, 1945. 235 pp.

Blanchard, Paul. "The Roosevelt Leadership," Saturday Review of Literature, X, No. 14 (October 21, 1933), 197-98.

Bratter, Herbert M. The Silver Market. Bureau of Foreign and Domestic Commerce, Trade Promotion Series No. 139. Washington, 1932. 95 pp.

———— The Monetary Use of Silver in 1933. Bureau of Foreign and Domestic Commerce, Trade Promotion Series No. 149. Washington, 1933. 142 pp.

———— "Silver," Encyclopedia of the Social Sciences, XIV, 59. New York, Macmillan, 1934.

———— "The Silver Episode," Journal of Political Economy, XLVI (October and December, 1938), 609-52, 802-37.

Brownell, Francis H. Hard Money. Privately printed, 1944. 35 pp.

Bryan, Penington, and Colket. Memorandum on Cerro de Pasco Copper Corporation. New York, August 16, 1934, 2 pp.

Carothers, Neil. "Silver--A Senate Racket," North American Review, CCXXXIII (January, 1932), 4-15.

Carter, John F. The New Dealers. New York, Simon & Schuster, 1934. 414 pp.

Cerro de Pasco Copper Corporation, Annual Reports. New York.

Childs, Marquis W. "Father Coughlin," New Republic, LXXVIII, No. 1,013 (May 2, 1934), 326-27.

China, National Government of the Republic of China. Commission of Financial Experts. Project of Law for the Gradual Introduction of a Gold-Standard Currency System in China, together with a Report in Support Thereof. Shanghai, Bureau of Industrial and Commercial Information, Ministry of Industry, Commerce, and Labor, 1930. 182 pp.

———— Ministry of Finance. Annual Reports.

Chinese Economic Journal. Shanghai monthly.

Coughlin, Charles E. The New Deal in Money. Royal Oak, Mich., Radio League of the Little Flower, 1933. 128 pp.

———— Eight Lectures on Labor, Capital and Justice. Royal Oak, Mich., Radio League of the Little Flower, 1934. 132 pp.

Crawford, A. W. Monetary Management under the New Deal. Washington, American Council on Public Affairs, 1940. 382 pp.

Daniels, Josephus. Shirt-Sleeve Diplomat. Chapel Hill, University of North Carolina Press, 1947. 547 pp.

Economist, The. London daily.

Elliott, Gilbert and Company. Memorandum on the American Smelting and Refining Company, New York, December 7, 1935. 2 pp.

Finance and Commerce. Shanghai weekly.

Gayer, Arthur D. Monetary Policy and Economic Stabilization; a study of the Gold Standard. 2d ed., rev. New York, Macmillan, 1937. 288 pp.

Gordon, Wendell C. The Expropriation of Foreign-Owned Property in Mexico. Washington, American Council on Public Affairs, 1941. 180 pp.

Gunther, John. Inside U.S.A. New York, Harper, 1947. 979 pp.

Hacker, Louis M. A Short History of the New Deal. New York, Crofts, 1934. 151 pp.

Hamilton, Earl J. American Treasure and the Price Revolution in Spain, 1501-1650. Cambridge, Harvard University Press, 1934. 428 pp.

Handy and Harman. Annual Review of the Silver Market. New York, privately printed, annually.

Hsu, Leonard Shih-Lien, and others. Silver and Prices in China. Report of the Committee for the Study of Silver Values and Commodity Prices, Ministry of Industries. Shanghai, Commercial Press, 1935. 245 pp.

Hinton, Harold B. Cordell Hull. Garden City, New York, Doubleday Doran, 1942. 377 pp.

Hull, Cordell. The Memoirs of Cordell Hull. 2 vols. New York, Macmillan, 1948.

Investor's Guide Stock Reports, Vol. III, No. 191, Sec. 5, August 15, 1936.

Journal of the Monetary and Economic Conference. London, 1933, daily.

Kelly, Eugene A. "Morgenthau's Rise to Glory," American Mercury, XXXIV, No. 133 (January, 1935), 12-21.

Leavens, Dickson H. Silver Money. Bloomington, Ind., Principia Press, 1939, 439 pp.

———— "Silver Coins to the Melting Pot: the Known Supply Awaiting Higher Prices," Annalist, XLVI (July 5, 1935), 3-4.

Lend-Lease Administration. Report to the Seventy-eighth Congress on Lend-Lease Operations from the Passage of the Act, March 11, 1941, to December 31, 1942. Washington, 1943. 91 pp.

———— Twelfth Report to Congress on Lend-Lease Operations. Washington, 1943. 10 pp.

Lend-Lease Administration. Sixteenth Report to Congress on Lend-Lease Operations for the Period Ended June 30, 1944. Washington, 1944. 88 pp.

Leong, Y. S. Silver: An Analysis of Factors Affecting Its Price. Washington, Brookings Institution, 1933. 168 pp.

Lewis, Ardron B., and Chang Lu-luan. Silver and the Chinese Price Level. Nanking, University of Nanking, December, 1933. 39 pp.

Li Ming. "China's Foreign Trade," A Picture of World Economic Conditions at the Beginning of 1932. New York, National Industrial Conference Board, 1932. 14 pp.

Lin Wei-ying. China under Depreciated Silver, 1926-1931. The Foreign Trade Association of China, Monograph No. 1. Shanghai, Commercial Press, 1935. 230 pp.

Lindley, Ernest K. The Roosevelt Revolution, First Phase. New York, Viking Press, 1933. 328 pp.

_____ Half Way with Roosevelt. New York, Viking Press, 1936. 426 pp.

Lippmann, Walter. Interpretations, 1933-1935. New York, Macmillan, 1936. 399 pp.

McConnell, Burt M. Mexico at the Bar of Public Opinion. New York, Mail & Express Publishing Co., 1939. 325 pp.

Mexico's Oil. Government of Mexico. Mexico City, 1940. 881 pp.

Moley, Raymond. After Seven Years. New York, Harper, 1939. 446 pp.

Morgenthau, Henry, Jr. Diary, 1933-1945. 864 vols. Privately bound.

_____ Newspaper Clippings, 1933-1945. 80 vols. Privately bound.

_____ "The Morgenthau Diaries," Collier's, CXX, No. 12, 13, 14, 15, 16, 17 (September 20 and 27, October 4, 11, 18 and 25, 1947).

Morison, S. E., and Commager, H. S. The Growth of the American Republic. 2 vols. New York, Oxford University Press, 1942.

Murad, Anatol. The Paradox of a Metal Standard. New York, Graphic Arts Press, 1939. 212 pp.

New York Herald Tribune. New York daily.

New York Times. New York daily.

Paris, James D. Monetary Policies of the United States, 1932-1938. New York, Columbia University Press, 1938. 128 pp.

Parkes, Henry B. A History of Mexico. Boston, Houghton Mifflin, 1938. 432 pp.

Pasvolsky, Leo. Current Monetary Issues. Washington, The
    Brookings Institution, 1933. 192 pp.
Perkins, Frances. The Roosevelt I Knew. New York, Viking
    Press, 1946. 408 pp.
Pinnick, A. W. Silver and China: an Investigation of the
    Monetary Principles Governing China's Trade and Pros-
    perity. Shanghai, Kelly & Walsh, 1930. 90 pp.
Porter, Sylvia F. "Twelve Men against the Nation,"
    Reader's Digest, XLI, No. 247 (November, 1942), 1-4.
Richberg, Donald R. The Mexican Oil Seizure. New York,
    Arrow Press, 1939. 195 pp.
Rogers, James H. America Weighs Her Gold. New Haven,
    Yale University Press, 1931. 245 pp.
_____ "Gold, International Trade Balances, and Prosperity,"
    Economic Series Lecture No. 11. Chicago, University of
    Chicago Press, 1932. 9 pp.
Roosevelt, Franklin D. The Public Papers and Addresses
    of Franklin D. Roosevelt. 5 vols., New York, Random
    House, 1938; 4 vols., New York, Macmillan, 1941.
Salter, Sir Arther. China and Silver. New York, Economic
    Forum, 1934. 117 pp.
Spahr, Walter E. "Silver Scandal," Saturday Evening Post,
    CCXV, No. 18 (October 31, 1942), 19, 79-82.
Stettinius, Edward R., Jr. Lend Lease, Weapon for Victory.
    New York, Macmillan, 1944. 358 pp.
Stewart, Maxwell S. Silver--Its International Aspects. Vol.
    VII, No. 13, September 2, 1931. New York, Foreign Policy
    Association. 18 pp.
Tocqueville, Alexis de. Democracy in America. 2 vols.
    The Phillips Bradley Edition. New York, Knopf, 1946.
U. S. Bureau of Foreign and Domestic Commerce. China
    Monthly Trade Report, 1927-1934. Washington, Depart-
    ment of Commerce.
_____ Commerce Reports. Washington, Department of Com-
    merce, weekly.
_____ Commerce Yearbook, 1922-1932. Washington, Depart-
    ment of Commerce.
_____ Foreign Commerce Yearbook, 1933-1939. Washington,
    Department of Commerce.
_____ Latin American Financial Notes. Washington, Depart-
    ment of Commerce, semimonthly.
U. S. Bureau of Labor Statistics. Wholesale Prices. Wash-
    ington, Department of Labor, Monthly.
U. S. Bureau of Mines. Mineral Resources of the United
    States. Washington, Department of the Interior, annual.

U. S. Bureau of Mines. Minerals Yearbook. Washington, Department of the Interior, annual.

U. S. Congress. Congressional Record. Washington, daily during sessions.

_____ Commercial Relations with China. Hearings before a Subcommittee of the Committee on Foreign Relations, United States Senate, Seventy-first Congress, Second Session, Washington, 1930, 1931. 4 parts, 552 pp.

_____ The Effect of Low Silver. Hearings before the Committee on Coinage, Weights, and Measures, House of Representatives, Seventy-second Congress, First Session, on H. Res. 72, a Resolution to Investigate the Cause and Effect of the Present Depressed Value of Silver. Washington, 1932. 4 parts, 530 pp.

_____ Purchase of Silver Produced in the United States with Silver Certificates. Hearings before a Subcommittee of the Committee on Banking and Currency, United States Senate, Seventy-second Congress, First Session, May 9, 1932. Washington, 1932. 46 pp.

_____ International Monetary and Economic Conference, London, England. Hearings before the Committee on Foreign Affairs, House of Representatives, Seventy-second Congress, Second Session, on H. J. Res. 536, January 10-11, 1933. Washington, 1933. 32 pp.

_____ Silver Currency. Hearings before the Committee on Coinage, Weights, and Measures, House of Representatives. Seventy-second Congress, Second Session, February 1-10, 1933. Washington, 1933. 241 pp.

_____ Silver and the Foreign Debt Payments. Seventy-third Congress, First Session, Senate Document, No. 8. Washington, 1933. 29 pp.

_____ Gold Reserve Act of 1934. Hearings before the Committee on Coinage, Weights, and Measures, House of Representatives, Seventy-third Congress, Second Session, on H. R. 6,976. Washington, 1934. 218 pp.

_____ To Establish the Federal Monetary Authority. Hearings before the Subcommittee of the Committee on Banking and Currency, House of Representatives, Seventy-third Congress, Second Session, on H. R. 7,157 as amended and Reintroduced as H. R. 8,780, January to March, 1934. Washington, 1934. 514 pp.

_____ Hoarders of Silver. Seventy-third Congress, Second Session, Senate Document, No. 173. Washington, 1934. 3 parts, 41 pp.

_____ Silver Purchase Act of 1934. Hearings before the Committee on Ways and Means, House of Representatives, Seventy-third Congress, Second Session, on H. R. 9,745. Washington, 1934. 200 pp.

U. S. Congress. Silver. Hearings before a Special Committee on the Investigation of Silver, United States Senate, Seventy-sixth Congress, First Session, and Seventy-seventh Congress, Second Session, Pursuant to S. Res. 187 (Seventy-fourth Congress), 1939-42. Washington. 9 parts, 10 vols.

_____ To Authorize the Use for War Purposes of Silver Held or Owned by the United States. Hearings before the Committee on Banking and Currency, United States Senate, Seventy-seventh Congress, Second Session, on S. 2,768, October 14 and December 1, 1942. Washington, 1942. 2 parts, 152 pp.

_____ Treasury Department Appropriation Bill for 1943. Hearings before the Subcommittee of the Committee on Appropriations, House of Representatives, Seventy-seventh Congress, Second Session. Washington, 1942. 433 pp.

_____ Reconstruction Fund in Joint Account with Foreign Governments for Rehabilitation, Stabilization of Currencies, and Reconstruction. Hearings before the Committee on Foreign Affairs, House of Representatives, Seventy-eighth Congress, Second Session, on H. J. Res. 226, April 25-28 and May 16-17, 1944. Washington, 1944. 188 pp.

_____ Bretton Woods Agreement Act. Hearings before the Committee on Banking and Currency, United States Senate, Seventy-ninth Congress, First Session, on H. R. 3,314, June 1945. Washington, 1945. 670 pp.

U. S. Department of State. Press Releases, 1930-39. Washington.

_____ Bulletin, 1939-48. Washington.

_____ Treaties, 1939-42. Washington.

U. S. Executive Agreement Series, No. 63. Silver; Memorandum of Agreement between the United States of America, Australia, Canada, China, India, Mexico, Peru, and Spain with Supplementary Undertakings; Signed at London July 22, 24, and 26; Effective April 24, 1934. Washington, 1934. 12 pp.

U. S. Treasury Department. Annual Report of the Secretary of the Treasury on the State of the Finances. Washington.

_____ Press Conferences, 1933-45. 27 vols. Privately bound.

United States Smelting, Refining and Mining Company. Annual Reports. New York.

Warburg, James P. The Money Muddle. New York, Knopf, 1934. 272 pp.

_____ Hell Bent for Election. Garden City, N. Y., Doubleday, Doran, 1935. 78 pp.

Warren, G. F. "Is Our Gold Standard Too Rigid?" Forum, LXXXIX, No. 4 (April, 1933), 194-201.

_____ "The New Dollar," Forum, LXL, No. 2 (August, 1933), 70-75.

_____ and Pearson, F. A Gold and Prices. New York, Wiley, 1935. 475 pp.

Welles, Sumner. The Time for Decision. New York, Harper, 1944. 431 pp.

Westerfield, Ray B. Our Silver Debacle. New York, Ronald Press, 1936. 214 pp.

White, T. H., and Jacoby, A. Thunder out of China. New York, William Sloane Associates, 1946. 331 pp.

Willis, H. Parker. "Silver," New Republic, LXVI, No. 849 (March 11, 1931), 92-94.

Woolf, S. J. "Morgenthau: Handler of Billions," Literary Digest, CXVII, No. 7 (February 17, 1934), 7, 43.

INDEX

Acheson, Dean G., as Treasury Under-Secretary, 22, 32, 33; resigns, 33; acts in Hull-Morgenthau disagreement, 131

Adams, Sen. Alva B., consulted by Morgenthau, 52; traces benefits from silver laws, 65

Agricultural Adjustment Act, decreases inflationary pressures, 56

American Banking Association, opposes Bretton Woods Agreement, 162

American Economic Association, opposes increased use of silver, 41

American Metal Company, works for repeal of silver tax, 76; production of silver, 79, 97

American Smelting and Refining Company, silver production of, 9, 10, 54, 79; chairman of, promotes silver, 10, 160; promotes postwar use of silver, 160-161

Anaconda Copper Mining Company, silver production of, 9, 10, 54, 79; behavior of stocks of, 71

Arbitrage, 2

Ashurst, Sen. Henry F., discusses silver with Morgenthau, 39

Australia, and London Silver Agreement, 29; fears for silver coinage, 125; silver needs of, in World War II, 152; seeks loan of silver, 154, 155, 157, 158, 179

Bankhead, Sen. John H., sees high cotton from high silver, 58

Bank of Mexico, obtains gold from U.S., 80-81; speculates in silver, 81; controls Mexican silver in wartime, 148

Barkley, Sen. Alben W., advises silver compromise, 72-73; postpones Senate vote, 74; postpones committee vote, 75

Barnes, Julius H., quoted, 13

Barton, Rep. Bruce, labors against silver program, 66

Belgium, demonetizes, 8; obtains silver loan, 159, 179

Beteta, Ramon, protests silver price, 142

Biffle, Leslie L., works for Administration on silver, 74

Bimetallism, eighteenth century, 1; nineteenth century, 1-2, 3-4, 5; Congressional agitation for, 15, 24, 27, 30, 162-163; under Thomas Amendment, 26; urged in postwar world, 160, 161, 162-163

Bland-Allison Act of 1873, 3, 5, 31

Bloom, Rep. Sol, works against postwar silver, 160

"Bombshell" message, 27, 28

Borah, Sen. William E., works for silver legislation, 43, 44; consulted by Morgenthau, 52

Bowles, Chester, favors extension of Green Act, 151

"Brains Trust," 18, 20

Bratter, Herbert, testifies against silver, 160

Bretton Woods, controversy over silver at, 160-163

Bretton Woods Agreement Act, Congressional fight over, 162-163

Brookings Institution, appraises gold buying, 35

Brownell, Francis H., as company spokesman for silver, 10; advocates bimetallism, 160

Bryan, William Jennings, in campaign of 1896, 4

Buck, Prof. J. Lossing, represents Treasury in China, 110; to be